Y0-CBG-824

ROADS NOT TAKEN

PITT SERIES IN RUSSIAN AND EAST EUROPEAN STUDIES

JONATHAN HARRIS, *Editor*

ROADS NOT TAKEN

AN INTELLECTUAL BIOGRAPHY OF WILLIAM C. BULLITT

ALEXANDER ETKIND

University of Pittsburgh Press

Published by the University of Pittsburgh Press, Pittsburgh, Pa., 15260

Copyright © 2017, University of Pittsburgh Press

All rights reserved

Manufactured in the United States of America

Printed on acid-free paper

10 9 8 7 6 5 4 3 2 1

ISBN 13: 978-0-8229-6503-9

ISBN 10: 0-8229-6503-8

Cover art: William C. Bullitt leaving the White House after a conference with President Roosevelt, January 13, 1939, Harris & Ewing (photographer), Library of Congress Prints and Photographs Division; Moscow General Plan, 1935. Cover design by Alex Wolfe

Yet knowing how way leads on to way,
I doubted if I should ever come back.

ROBERT FROST

CONTENTS

ACKNOWLEDGMENTS

Many years ago, my conversations with Paul Roazen contributed to my interest in William C. Bullitt. More recently, Dmitry Bykov's initiative helped to launch this book project. Jay Winter's generous guidance at many stages of this work is very much appreciated. Eli Zaretsky and Federico Romero directed me to important sources. Librarians at Yale's Sterling Memorial Library helped me to work with Bullitt's archive; I am particularly grateful to Dika Goloweiko-Nussberg. In the Freud Museum in Vienna, Daniela Finzi provided the right information at the right time. Vladimir Alexandrov and Laura Downs organized helpful discussions of this project at Yale University and the European University at Florence. Isaac Webb and Linda Kinstler helped me to edit the text. Jay Winter, Julia Fedor, Masha Bratishcheva, Ivan Kurilla, and Tatiana Zaharchenko read the manuscript and gave me invaluable advice, comments, and corrections: I followed many but, sadly, not all of them. Over a memorable dinner, Derk Moses rejected several titles of this book. Eventually Elizabeth R. Moore helped me choose the right title. I am grateful to the European University at Florence for supporting my work on this book.

INTRODUCTION

This is a book about a man who knew how the world worked and how it was changing throughout the twentieth century. He wished to save it and shared his insights with the most powerful people of his time. But they preferred his company to his advice. Usually, his foresights proved to be true when it was already too late to follow them. Time and again, he was on the right side of history.

A journalist, diplomat, and writer, William Christian Bullitt was a member of the American delegation to the Paris Peace Conference (1919), the ambassador to the Soviet Union (1933–1936) and France (1936–1940), and the Special Representative of the President of the United States in the Middle East (1940). His political role was significant; it was also controversial. In *The Wise Men*, a collective biography of several American statesmen who shaped the world of the late twentieth century, Walter Isaacson and Evan Thomas wrote about two men whose careers, as diplomats and political figures, were launched by Bullitt—George Kennan and Charles Bohlen, two world-shapers out of six.[1] David Fromkin, in his magisterial account of the interwar period in Europe, described Bullitt as a witness rather than an actor: "when important things were happening, he so often was there" but, according to Fromkin, played supporting roles and did not have an "intrinsic historical importance."[2] In contrast, John Lukacs compared Bullitt to Henry Kissinger, who was in many ways his opposite: one was an idealist, the other a realist;

one became famous, another all but forgotten. Still, it was Bullitt rather than Kissinger, Lukacs wrote, who carried "both the vision and the force of the age, of the Pax Americana of the twentieth century."[3] Written by experts in international relations, several biographies of Bullitt criticize his political turns and twists but largely ignore his intellectual contributions—his novels, plays, essays, and unrealized projects.[4] Yet, Bullitt spent most of his life as an intellectual rather than as an official. Taking seriously Bullitt's words, foresights, and laments, this book addresses Bullitt as an original thinker and elucidates his role as a political actor.

The most cosmopolitan of American politicians of the era, Bullitt spoke several languages, lived in Europe for many years, and eagerly traveled through Asia. A Wilsonian Liberal who gradually became a Cold War Conservative, he was always engaged with the ideas of the Left. He was also a sincere patriot, who believed in the superiority of American values and had no doubt they should proliferate throughout the world. Bullitt adored France, disliked Britain, presciently understood the importance of China, and was deeply compassionate toward Poland. Throughout his life, he was professionally involved in Russian affairs. Always engaged with high politics but rarely invited to contribute to it, he regularly wrote about the missed opportunities that he believed could have made the world a better place. Often arrogant and always impatient he was, surprisingly often, right when so many others were wrong.

Part of the secret to Bullitt's foresight was his network. He established personal relationships with some of the twentieth century's most important people, including Vladimir Lenin, Franklin Roosevelt, Chiang Kai-shek, Charles de Gaulle, Sigmund Freud, and Mikhail Bulgakov. Particularly important was his short friendship and long rivalry with John Reed. In his photos, he is bald, assiduously dressed, and smiling: a personification of American success. But this conventional appearance belied a complex character. Vice-President Henry Wallace described him as "an unusually attractive personality" and a master of witty conversation; Wallace admired Bullitt's knowledge of European "sophisticated pleasures" and the "anecdotal stories . . . of the many famous people abroad."[5] In similar fashion, Charles Bohlen, a leading diplomat of the Cold War who was once Bullitt's protégé, wrote that Bullitt was a person who radiated light but was able to control it, turning his glow on or off at will.[6] George Kennan, whose career Bullitt also launched from Moscow, attributed to him a "dangerous freedom—the freedom of a man who . . . had never subordinated his life to the needs of any other human being."[7] Rather undiplomatically, Kennan described Bullitt as a cold egoist but also an impatient enthusiast. In Kennan's characterization, Bullitt was a man "full of charm and vivacity; also brilliant; but deeply unhappy, a species of Midas of the spirit, in whom all the golden qualities turned to stone because he never loved anyone as much as himself"; it was a startling but also cruel portrait. Still, Bullitt deserved more from his country than he received, Kennan said.[8]

During and after the First World War, Bullitt made a name for himself as the pioneering American expert in Russian and European socialism. The leading specialists on the Soviet Union of the next, post–Second World War generation developed under him. Yet, although he did study Russian he never mastered the language, and his knowledge of Russian history and literature, though substantial, always remained amateurish. At the same time, Bullitt had "a distinct bias against the British," his brother wrote; Orville Bullitt traced this attitude to impressions made on the brothers in childhood by revelations about British imperialism in Africa and stories of the American Revolution.[9] British-Russian philosopher Isaiah Berlin, who knew Bullitt and befriended his disciples, wrote with surprise that in the United States, "the Anglophile and Russophile feelings move in inverse ratio. Up with the Russians, down with the British, in almost exact proportion."[10] Bullitt exemplified this proportion, but he was hardly a Russophile. Socialist theories, Soviet practices, and the huge distances between them captured his imagination. In this respect, Bullitt's changing attitudes foreshadowed the general disenchantment with communism that came to characterize Western intellectuals much later. A political thinker, Bullitt was puzzled by his tragic century, had original and valuable insights, and tested many ways to implement his ideas.

Early in the twentieth century, Bullitt realized that the collapse of the old regimes in Europe was inevitable, and he became an intense though ambivalent observer of socialist movements. It was a popular sentiment; Leon Trotsky called such people "fellow travelers," a moniker that has endured even the collapse of the Soviet Union. It took Bullitt years of personal experience with Russia—an experience that few American fellow travelers had—to become disenchanted with the Soviet "God that failed." Ultimately, Bullitt's encounter with communism would turn him into a political conservative and a Cold War hawk. A witness to Wilson's "idealism" and Roosevelt's "gamble" in two world wars, Bullitt wrote that, in politics, wishful thinking was the worst vice.[11] But he did not accept isolationism. In fact, he saw American liberalism and European cosmopolitanism, two great Western legacies, as being deeply connected.

Brilliant and bitter, Bullitt was also mysterious. He did not like compromises: though he had a knack for making and keeping friends, he was at times intolerant, pernicious, and eager to quarrel even with those upon whom he depended. He was always the subject of gossip, and the conjectures about him were vicious; Dean Acheson, for example, wrote that Bullitt's middle name, Christian, was "singularly ironic."[12] Even according to his brother, Bill was "a controversial person": some believed that he was a Bolshevik, others that he was a fascist; some thought he was a warmonger, while others saw him as an appeaser. In fact, Orville Bullitt saw his brother as a good American liberal: Bill had "deep feelings for the rights of man and an intense dislike for the rigidity of the ruling classes."[13]

Bullitt was controversial and inconsistent; the future demonstrated that sometimes he was right and sometimes wrong. It was his focus on the future that was invariable. He read history books and respected historians, but in his own writings and political advice he was interested in the future and not the past. He loved Homer's line "After the event even the fool is wise." There is no truer saying, he wrote, than the old French aphorism: "To govern is to foresee."[14] Carefully choosing his own words, Bullitt wrote about "a terrible obligation to be right before the event": terrible indeed, because the risks of the arguments about the future in democratic politics are tremendous.[15] But, he argued forcefully, "in world affairs, charm is not a substitute for foresight. The epitaphs of nations can often be written in the words: 'Too late.'"[16] His eagerness to talk about the future was a part of his peculiar gift, which at times betrayed him. But, untypically for a politician, he was eager to take these risks.

Soldiers fight wars, but civilians start and end them. An intellectual and a diplomat, Bullitt respected the military but hated war. He took part in the negotiations that ended the First World War and those that failed to prevent the Second World War, and he was involved in discussions that determined the course of the Cold War and the building of the European Union. Much of his advice was ignored, but Bullitt did influence some key positions taken by the American administration between the two world wars. He fashioned a loose but identifiable school of thought, represented by "the Russian experts" of the State Department. His disciples and appointees played a crucial role at the beginning of the Cold War, which Bullitt anticipated and helped shape. He died in his beloved Paris but was buried in his native Philadelphia. Thus, even in death he revealed his particular ability to fuse cosmopolitanism with patriotism.

ROADS NOT TAKEN

1

THE WORLD BEFORE THE WAR

William Christian Bullitt was born in 1891 to an aristocratic family in Philadelphia. His ancestors were French Huguenots on the paternal side and Prussian Jews on the maternal; both sides could trace their roots to some of the first settlers on the East Coast. His French ancestor, Joseph Boulet, came to Maryland in 1685; there he changed his name to Bullitt. Several generations later, one of his descendants, Bill's grandfather, wrote the first city charter of Philadelphia. On his mother's side, Jonathan Horwitz arrived in America around 1710. Baptized in the Episcopal Church, he graduated from the University of Pennsylvania and became a doctor.

Bill's father, William Christian Bullitt Sr., ran in Philadelphia's most elite circles: he managed the supply of coal from Pennsylvania mines to the US Navy and transatlantic steamship companies. His wife and Bill's mother, Louisa Gross Horwitz, spoke French with her two sons, giving Bill a faculty with languages that benefited him tremendously over the course of his career. During the summer, the family sailed to Europe; young Bullitt learned on these journeys, he would write much later, to appreciate people from all over the world—their various looks, sounds, and even smells. He liked them all but considered the European states to be somehow inferior to the United States. The more he traveled abroad, the more patriotic he became. At home, he enjoyed decidedly American pastimes, including duck hunting with his father. Later, he took an interest in other aristocratic arts such as boxing and riding. There were good horses on his family's estate, and Bill loved horses.

His father died young, but Bill maintained a strong relationship with his mother for decades. When he was in America, she often stayed with him for weeks. She did not want to be anything other than a good wife and mother, he wrote, always subscribing to the era's traditional gender roles. In his old age Bullitt wrote that he could not imagine having had better parents or a happier childhood. The family was religious and he shared their faith; he also shared his family's patriotism, which was characteristic of an aristocracy that had good reasons to be grateful to their country. In his unfinished memoirs, Bullitt wrote that, while walking in Philadelphia, his father used to take off his hat in front of the Liberty Bell. His father made him feel that "my country is my country in the same sense as my hand is my hand. I was a part of it, and it was a part of me. I was responsible for its safety and for what it did. The United States owned me and I owned the United States." Forty years later Bullitt said something to this effect to Roosevelt. The president replied: "But this country is mine too," and the two men shared a hearty laugh.[1]

A student at Yale, Bullitt was mostly interested in European languages; he spent the summer of 1909 in Munich studying German. Bullitt did not become a member of the famous "Skull and Bones" secret society but was the president of the Yale Dramatic Association. On June 4, 1910, the *New York Times* reported that the Yale Dramatic Association performed in the ballroom of the Waldorf-Astoria in New York; Bullitt, who played a female role, was seen as having been a particular success. In his memoirs Bullitt mentioned a pioneering sociology course taught at Yale by Albert G. Keller and a psychology course taught by Roswell Angier. From the latter, Bullitt first learned about psychoanalysis, which became one of his main intellectual influences; these classes had such an effect on him that for a time Bullitt considered a career in psychology. Charles Seymour taught European history to Bullitt; later the two would participate in the Paris Peace Conference together.

After graduating from Yale in 1913, Bill went to Harvard Law School, where he studied for a year but did not graduate. He considered the atmosphere there "cynical": when students brought up justice, they were advised to go next door to the School of Theology. Like his hero in those years, Woodrow Wilson, a professor of history who became the president of Princeton and later of the United States, Bullitt did not trust lawyers. During his student years, Bullitt fell ill and was wrongly diagnosed with appendicitis. The surgery to remove his appendix caused adhesions, which had to be removed later. Because of these adhesions, he escaped conscription into the military.

Bill's father died in March 1914. To cope with her grief, his mother went on a tour of Europe. The doctor had advised to go to places that she had not visited with her husband, and she traveled with Bill to Russia. They were in Moscow on July 28, 1914, when Austria-Hungary declared war on Serbia and the First World War began. Staying at the "National" hotel in the center of the city, they heard a crowd chanting on Tverskaya Street: "Down with Austria! Hurrah for Serbia!" They decided to go home, catching the last train to Berlin.[2]

Following their father's death, William and Orville inherited modest funds that supported them to the tune of six thousand dollars per year. This was not a large sum, but it was considerable compared with the starting salary of a journalist in Philadelphia, for example, which was one hundred dollars per month. "Father's conviction that it was bad for American boys to have much money was absolute.... He brought us up—as he, his father, and his grandfather had been brought up—to understand that, while he would give us any education we might want, we would have to earn our livelihood from the days our studies were completed."[3] Still, Bill loved to spend money. Orville sometimes tried to restrain him, but he was rarely successful. Spending money lavishly, Bill threw parties, flaunted his wealth, and ignored warnings from his friends about his fiduciary recklessness. Bill's friends never understood where he got his money and frequently discussed his financial situation behind his back. In reality, Bill depended on wages earned from his job as a journalist and diplomat, and his purported wealth was largely fictional.

Bullitt's first job was at a well-respected Philadelphia newspaper, the *Public Ledger*. After only one year on the job, he became the paper's deputy editor. Later, Bullitt satirically depicted these years in his novel, *It's Not Done*: the rich owner of a newspaper arranges a job for a young journalist—a relative—but dismisses him years later when the relative, now the editor, stops listening to his benefactor. As a journalist, Bullitt developed a fluent and powerful style of writing, using rich details about the past and sharp judgments about the present, which he combined with his unusual interest in the future.

As a reporter for the *Public Ledger*, Bullitt took part in Henry Ford's famous voyage to Europe in December 1915. An eccentric millionaire with ambition to change the world, Ford chartered an ocean liner, filled it with intellectuals and activists, and sailed this "Peace Ship" to Europe with the intention of mediating talks between the warring countries. From the ship, Ford sent a telegram to soldiers on both sides of the conflict, calling them to join a general strike on Christmas Day, 1915.[4] Almost daily, Bullitt cabled satirical reports from the ocean about his journey and the war, which top American newspapers published, often on the front page. He reported that, before leaving New

Jersey, Ford had offered one million dollars to Thomas Edison to take part in the mission; Edison refused. Aboard the Peace Ship, Bullitt met Inez Milholland, a famous beauty who later became a feminist activist; Bullitt courted her then, and he remembered her many decades later. Bullitt wrote chidingly that Ford hoped that the sobs and kisses of the "pilgrims" from his ship would convince the Germans to leave Belgium. Arriving in Oslo, the Peace Ship, also known in the press as the "Ship of Fools," ended its mission. Bullitt returned to the United States to marry.

His bride was Ernesta Drinker, who, like Bullitt, came from an old and wealthy Philadelphia family: her ancestors, Quakers, were among the first families in William Penn's colony. The daughter of the president of Lehigh University, Ernesta was beautiful and well educated. She studied sociology and economics at the Sorbonne and then at Radcliffe, though she did not graduate from either. Before accepting Bullitt's marriage offer, she had turned down fifty other proposals.[5]

For their honeymoon, the newlyweds chose to sail back to Europe. They brought their recently acquired passports and eighty-nine letters of introduction to European celebrities. In May 1916 they arrived in Berlin, where Bullitt interviewed diplomats and military leaders; from there they went to occupied Belgium and then to Austria-Hungary. Officials in Berlin willingly granted interviews to Bullitt. The United States was still neutral, but an American correspondent in Germany was something of a rarity at the time.

Despite traveling frequently, Bullitt did not keep a diary, but both his wives did. Ernesta Drinker wrote a lively book about her adventures with Bill in wartime Central Europe. Keeping a diary was something of a family tradition for Ernesta: her great-grandmother kept one during the American Revolution, and the whole family loved to read and re-read her notes. Ernesta chose to publish her diary "for our own great-granddaughters"; she was mostly interested in women's issues and wrote for a female audience. Her book documented the increasingly difficult situations in Germany and Austro-Hungary in the lead-up to their military defeat.

During the war female employment in Germany, as elsewhere, grew rapidly. Women worked in factories and mines, places from which they had been excluded before the war. Interviewing the leaders of the women's movement in Berlin, Ernesta tried to figure out how employment changed their position in the family. Doing the same work, women earned less than men, she noted; however, most of the female workers were new to their jobs, so this was probably fair, she suggested. Germany had recently introduced maternity leave, but women still did not have voting rights. The schools were separated by gender as in America, but during the war the German women were given the right to teach in the male gymnasiums.

The German government subsidized hospitals, nurseries, and canteens for the poor. To Americans, these forms of welfare were unprecedented; they represented the kind of modernity that Ernesta and Bill were seeking in Europe. Socially progressive but culturally conservative, they were pleased to see that the German Empire offered welfare without revolution, and the Prussian aristocracy was able to maintain its manners and privileges. Later, Bullitt compared his German experience to the devastation he saw in France and revolutionary Russia. These comparisons were indeed important for the future enthusiast of the New Deal.

In 1916 and 1917, the *Philadelphia Ledger* regularly published Bullitt's extended dispatches from Germany, but not before they had passed through German censorship; there were visible markings on the text where the censor had crossed out words or entire passages. The essays addressed the atmosphere in Berlin; attitudes toward America; Holland's role in the war, the state of its army, and the possibility of using its canals and dykes for defense; the Kaiser's intention to sail to America for a peace conference in December 1917; and the German economy, banks, food stamps, and social support. In September 1916, Bullitt traveled to the Eastern Front to see the war from the German side. In the ruins of Jewish settlements, he walked the trenches that had been locked in stalemate for months; it was Bill's first military experience. He interviewed the German officers, heard shells explode, saw a parade of Prussian hussars, and flew over the Russian trenches with a German plane. Russian machine gunners shot at their plane, and Bill had "a great time," according to Ernesta's diary.

In Berlin Bullitt spent long hours with Walter Rathenau, a German-Jewish industrialist who would later become the minister of foreign affairs. He was murdered by right-wing fanatics in 1922. In their conversations, Rathenau correctly predicted that the war would be over by 1918, but he did not foresee a revolution in Russia. He did not expect that Germany would take control of new lands in Europe, but he wished to gain some African colonies. In the wartime government, Rathenau was responsible for procuring natural resources—mainly coal, ore, and oil, as the British naval blockade had cut Germany off from its suppliers. Bullitt asked him whether Germany was ready to give Constantinople to Russia in exchange for a separate peace.

"We might," Rathenau replied.

"Would it not be rather hard to throw over the Turks?" Bullitt asked reasonably.

"No," said Rathenau. "We would only have to publish full accounts of the Armenian massacres, and German public opinion would become so incensed against the Turks that we could drop them as allies."

Despite certain hardships, Ernesta concluded that her life with Bill in wartime Germany was not altogether bad: "War corresponding to-day must be a pleasant life. You go *de luxe* as the guests of the government; you are dined and wined by Generals. . . . Dress parades and cavalry maneuvers are given for your benefit, and you have automobiles and wagons at your disposal. The only drawback is that, if you happen to say anything either uncommon or interesting in your story to the newspapers, it is cut out by the censor." Ernesta proudly called her book *The Uncensored Diary*. As the title suggests, it contained some rather unflattering passages about Germany: "Billy says the Germans are the most moral people in the world when it comes to dealing with Germans, and the most immoral in their dealings with the rest of the world."[6]

The manners of European aristocracy excited the young Americans as much as their wealth thrilled the Europeans; both sides were fascinated by each other. Their trip to wartime Germany and Austria-Hungary gave Bullitt a three-dimensional vision of Europe, which surprised his friends and readers who were dependent on their British and French contacts for news from the Old World. There, in the capitals of belligerent and potentially hostile empires, Bullitt first felt like a member of the European elite—not just an outsider but a welcome adviser, a mediator between its conflicting parts, a prophet of its misfortunes.

Indeed, there was much for Bullitt to digest in Berlin. The First World War was not a war of ideologies; rather, it was a fight for natural resources, the most important being coal, iron ore, grain, and rubber. Desperate for commodities, European powers sought colonies from the Congo to Ukraine. However, two key allies—Russia and America—already had an abundance of most of these natural resources, and their aims were different. Fighting for access to the Mediterranean, Russia wanted Constantinople; America insisted on its right to control the Western Hemisphere.

In America the liberals in power detested European-style imperialism: keenly aware of their country's own experience as a European colony, they believed that colonialism could only bring war and destruction. For the first time since the American Civil War, southerners came to power in the United States: Woodrow Wilson and his closest adviser, Edward House, were both from the South. They saw the Civil War as having been caused by the imperialist ambitions of the North, which needed the South for its resources, and they viewed the European conflict in similar terms. They did not blame Germany for the war; it was no guiltier of unleashing an imperialist war than Britain was. Exporting the American Revolution to the European continent, this circle of liberal, post-imperial politicians conceived the idea of "self-determination of nations" as the solution to European problems. The United States would oversee the collapse of the antiquated empires and the emancipation of oppressed minorities—at least, in Europe. With this in mind, America entered the war after Germany sank American ships and in February 1917 openly refused to stop such attacks. In addition, Germany tried to engage Mexico in the war, which the American leadership saw as an attempt to spread European imperialism in the New World.

The United States' entry into the First World War in April 1917 came shortly after the February revolution in Russia. The American public came to understand the war as a decisive battle between modern democracies and obsolete monarchies. The awkward alliance between Western European powers and tsarist Russia undermined this reading of the war. Written in 1926, Bullitt's novel *It's Not Done* describes the 1916 American debates on war in Europe. The protagonist becomes embroiled in an argument with his sister:

> "Wilson's written another note. . . . It starts this way: 'Words. Words, words! We have had enough of this!"
>
> "Why do you add any more? But you don't really mean it, do you? You don't really want us go to war."
>
> "I certainly do. . . . If we don't the Allies will be licked! Then it will be our turn. . . . They are fighting our fight and they are fighting for our kind of a civilization."
>
> "Including that ardent republican, the Czar."[7]

2

COLONEL HOUSE
AND PUBLIC RELATIONS

In February 1917 Bullitt interviewed Edward House, President Wilson's adviser and trusted strategist. A southerner, he was known as Colonel House, though he had never served in the military. A graduate of Cornell, House owned a plantation in Texas. He was also a writer. He shared with Bullitt his fear that the war would lead to an aggressive pact between Germany, Japan, and Russia. The specter of this tripartite alliance was "no more evanescent nightmare; it is the subject of constant speculation in every Foreign Office in Europe," House said. This century, he predicted, would be the bloodiest in human history because of an alliance between Russia, Germany, and Japan—the "league of the discontent." This coalition would be directed against Britain, France, and the United States.[1]

The encounter would define Bullitt's career. His mentor in politics and diplomacy, House continued to support him over the long term; fifteen years later, House introduced Bullitt to Franklin Delano Roosevelt who had just started his first presidential campaign. A major player in American foreign policy during the First World War, House was a secretive man and a mysterious thinker. His novel, *Philip Dru, Administrator: A Story of Tomorrow*, reveals his ideals and objectives better than his diplomatic correspondence. Written in 1912, the utopian fiction imagined a second civil war in America in 1920. The protagonist, Philip Dru, is a military academy graduate. Endowed with superhuman abilities, Dru uses them to lead a national revolt against a corrupt American president whose policies have impoverished the middle class. Interestingly, it is the new technology that triggers the revolution—"a dictagraph to record what was intended to be confidential conversations," which is used by the president's banker to blackmail opponents. It was a very modern device: "The character of the instrument was carefully concealed. It was a part of a massive piece of office furniture," which answered for the negotiation table as well. The administration uses this "dictagraph" to consolidate its power. But when the records of their negotiations are leaked to the newspapers, these records push the people over the edge, igniting rebellion. Led by Dru, the rebels win a decisive victory over the presidential troops in a major battle. Dru takes Washington by force, suspends the American Constitution, and declares himself the "Administrator" in charge of the country.[2]

Dru's methods of governance enact socialist ideas using dictatorial methods. In an attempt to eliminate unemployment, he introduces a progressive tax for the rich (up to 70 percent) and redistributes funds for the benefit of the poor. He gives workers shares of company profits and seats on corporate boards, but he deprives them of the right to strike. He replaces the constitutional separation of powers with an "Emergency Committee" that appoints managers according to their "efficiency," and he undermines the sovereignty of states. At the same time, the new Administrator introduces universal suffrage and institutes federal pensions for the elderly, farm subsidies, and mandatory health insurance. Dru protects freedom of trade and eliminates customs tariffs. In foreign policy, he starts a new war in Mexico to extend his rule over Central America. But he invites European powers, including Germany, to take part in a trade coalition, giving them all equal access to colonial resources and thereby eliminating reasons for war.[3]

House reached the pinnacle of his career at the end of the First World War, lived through the Depression and the New Deal, and died on the eve of the Second World War. He had many chances to re-think his old novel. Still, the political program of his protagonist was extraordinary. Combining the incompatible, it surprises the reader of the twenty-first century by its bold socialist initiatives combined with cynical authoritarianism. Drawing upon European dreams to overcome human nature and specifically American disappointment with democracy, House's utopia resembles an earlier and more successful novel by Edward Bellamy, *Looking Backward* (1887). But in contrast to Nietzsche or Bellamy, House practiced real politics.

Dru sounds a bit like Lenin, but on the whole he is closer to Mussolini. He

does not aim to eliminate capitalism but wishes to subordinate it to his imperial aims. The author does not condemn or ridicule his hero—in general, the
novel lacks irony. It expresses a sincere dissatisfaction with democracy, admiration for technical progress and a naive hope for a superhuman politician.
In this novel House combined two European utopias: the Nietzschean dream
of the Übermensch and the Marxist dream of socialism. An American
Zarathustra, Administrator Dru shifts the area of super-humanhood from
aesthetics to politics, and even to practical policy.

Anticipating a major war, Colonel House imagined that it would resemble
the Civil War in America; shrewdly, he argued for the moral and strategic
necessity of fair treatment for the enemy. After the Union army's victory, the
North turned the South into the impoverished and uneducated part of the
country, and there had been no southerner in the presidential office, House
argued.[4] Woodrow Wilson, the first southern president in half a century, was
the governor of New Jersey when *Philip Dru* was published, and pondering
his presidential chances. House's arguments helped him decide to run. Advising President Wilson, House also headed his second campaign in 1916. Until
the very end of the Paris conference in 1919, when the two experienced their
final conflict, House had unrivaled access to the president. Freud and Bullitt
wrote later that Wilson listened to House's arguments and appropriated them,
sincerely believing them to be his original thoughts; when he repeated them
back to House, the diplomat agreed eagerly. Wilson's economic innovations
realized those of House's dystopian novel, albeit in a weakened form. According to Freud and Bullitt, Wilson's "notable legislative programme of the years
1912 to 1914 was largely the programme of House's book *Philip Dru, Administrator*." As a result, Wilson's "domestic policies produced distinguished
results and by the spring of 1914 the domestic programme of *Philip Dru* had
been largely embodied in legislation." In contrast, Wilson's foreign politics
revealed his own "unconscious desires" of a messianic nature, and "the international programme of *Philip Dru* remained unrealized."[5]

In House's novel, when the heroic Administrator completes his political
agenda, he decides to leave office rather than remain dictator for life. Dru
plans his departure as precisely as he planned his ascendance to power:
together with his faithful girlfriend, he heads for the California coast, where
a yacht is waiting to take them across the ocean. Their destination is left
unmentioned, but readers learn that during his last year in America, Administrator Dru learned "one Slavic language" and taught that language to his
girlfriend. Thus in the end of the novel we learn that Dru is determined to

repeat his exploits in Russia. Five years later Colonel House oversaw the formulation of the Fourteen Points, Wilson's program for peace. The program considered relations with Russia an "acid test of good will" for the international community.

The intensity of House's dream was unusual, but he foreshadowed the search of those professors and gentlemen who served as American diplomats in the early twentieth century and were also, like House, infatuated with Russia. In the mid-1930s George Kennan (a protégé of Bullitt, who was in turn a protégé of House), wrote in his diaries how he would amend the Constitution in order to give special rights to selected members of the American elite so that they would be able to enact their own executive orders. Kennan, a rank-and-file American diplomat, did not dare make that idea known to the public but was eager to share his ideas with his former boss, Bullitt. In 1936 Kennan wrote Bullitt that after years in Moscow, he returned to the United States "almost a complete convert to the horrors of capitalism." But what he found in America worried him. He sounds like Dru when he writes, "It seems to me that this country does not want government. . . . I know that our geographical position is wonderfully favorable, . . . but no oceans can spare us the internal consequences [of our anarchism]. The only alternative to strong central power (far stronger than the present constitution would allow) is the increased power and willfulness of private groups."[6] Later, this discontent with democracy enabled Kennan to construe the emerging Cold War as an implacable yet fruitful challenge: in America, this challenge would produce a new form of state power. As he wrote in 1947, "the thoughtful observer of Russian-American relations will find no cause for complaint in the Kremlin's challenge [but] will rather experience a certain gratitude to a Providence," which confronted the American people with "the responsibilities of moral and political leadership." To counter the threat, Kennan wrote, democratic states had to become "no less steady in their purpose" than the Soviet Union. The totalitarian challenge could not be countered by a politics based on "the momentary whims of democratic opinion"; American society needed "self-confidence, discipline, morale and community spirit." In defense of democracy, America had to become less democratic.[7]

Adjusting inherited truths to political realities, Wilson and his entourage believed in the superiority of Western civilization and universality of its values. In the twentieth century, they thought, global progress would follow the democratic, though uneven, development of post–Civil War America. They celebrated their success in peaceful rebalancing the political power of the

American South and the overindustrialized, imperialist North.[8] Righting the mistakes of the past wars, their "progressive" and "idealistic" agenda meant self-determination for the oppressed nations of Europe, decolonizing Asia and Africa, and including all democratic states, old and new, in a global organization that would comply with international law.

Wilsonian idealists were not competing with Germany, Britain, or France for colonies and their resources. Instead, they rejected "imperialism" as something foreign and archaic. In contrast to this "idealism," political realism recognized the variety of national interests, which could not be resolved by rational arguments. Created by these idealists, the League of Nations failed to prevent the Second World War. Decades of military confrontation between superpowers defined the triumph of their opponents, the political realists. But American politicians and diplomats have not forgotten their idealistic heritage. The liberal universalism of American policy during the Cold War and the neoconservatism of the twenty-first century sprang from Wilson and House's particular breed of idealism. Richard Nixon hung Wilson's portrait over his White House desk.

Despite his idealism Colonel House was also concerned about mundane affairs. He was inclined to promote his relatives and friends, a traditional practice that shocked the unusually honest Wilson. When House selected the Inquiry, a group of 150 American professors who formulated the Fourteen Points program, he appointed Sidney Edward Mezes, a professor of philosophy from Texas and House's brother-in-law, to be the group's chair. He also appointed his son-in-law, Gordon Auchincloss, to serve as his secretary. When the US delegation sailed to France in 1919, President Wilson forbade members of the delegation from bringing their wives. However, on board of the luxurious steamer, the SS *George Washington*, Wilson met House's sister and daughter, who were married to Mezes and Auchincloss respectively.[9] Secretary of State Robert Lansing, his permanent opponent, accused House of creating a "secret society" within the Wilson administration, which turned the US delegation to the Paris Peace Conference into a closed club.

The principle of national self-determination belonged to Wilson, but its implementation required a detailed knowledge of Europe, which only professors had. Many of them came to Paris as members of the Inquiry, and Wilson, a professor himself, told his colleagues, "Tell me what is right, and I will fight for it."[10] However, the pace of events made all these experts rather helpless; in fact, very few people could tell Wilson what was right, and by the end of the conference, there were no such people around.

The executive director of the Inquiry, Walter Lippmann, was a young left-wing journalist and a lifelong opponent of Bullitt. Graduating from Harvard together with John Reed and T. S. Eliot in 1909, he was a founder of the Harvard Socialist Club and later, of the *New Republic*. Lippmann argued that the power of the press and other institutions such as schools, universities, churches, and trade unions shape the "common sense" that defines democratic politics. In his books *A Preface to Politics* (1913), *The Stakes of Diplomacy* (1915), and *Public Opinion* (1922), he turned the focus of political criticism from the "common man" to the intellectual elite and its creation, public opinion. He rejected the classic idea that the sense of the common man defines public good, and that political institutions should respond to the diversity of these common voices. Influenced by these ideas, Wilson created his Committee for Public Information, but he went with a safer choice than Lippmann. The journalist George Creel formed a huge organization with thirty-seven departments, hundreds of employees, and thousands of volunteers. At the beginning of 1917 Bullitt worked in this structure, and Lippmann took part in military preparations: with young Franklin D. Roosevelt, he organized training camps for the Navy. His former classmate John Reed, the rising star of the American Left, publicly accused Lippmann of betraying the radical ideals of their common youth. Reed was then in Mexico, where he wrote enthusiastic reports about the revolutionary troops of Pancho Villa, who fought with the US imperialists.[11] Lippmann outlived Reed for decades. A liberal journalist with a particular interest in socialism and Russian affairs, Lippmann coined the term "Cold War" and became a public advocate for the Soviet Union in the 1950s. He opposed the idea of containment, and a fierce controversy broke out between him and Bullitt on the subject. One of the last successes of Lippmann's career was his 1961 interview with Nikita Khrushchev.

The era of Wilsonian idealism promoted disenchantment with democracy among those who supported the history professor turned wartime president. The disenchantment took many forms. Some were irritated by the opacity of social reforms. Others were critical of government interventions into the public sphere and the market, which in the twentieth century became a mandatory aspect of executive policies. Others lacked faith that democracy—not only in sinful Europe but also in a fresh, mighty America—could confront the new kinds of despotism that were developing in Russia and Germany. These opinions led to disappointment with the moral meaning of political action. Human nature itself, with its limited faculties of autonomy and solidarity, seemed inadequate for the "idealist" democratic politics.

This new, particularly American sentiment differed from both the Russian nihilism that sprang from inescapable alienation from power and the German resentment that responded to weakness in the face of the enemy. American thinkers were looking for practical ways of maintaining political life in conditions where democracy was failing, ways that would hopefully remain within the framework of the American constitution but could go beyond it as well. House's *Philip Dru* demonstrates how far those American dreams could go.

Lippmann understood this situation as a springboard for a new social science. In democratic politics, he argued, people do not react to the facts—they react to the news. Journalists, editors, and experts play a decisive role in the political process. But in contrast to the political machine with its parties, laws, and separation of powers, the information work is not organized from the top down. In 1920 Lippmann ran a major study of how the *New York Times* reported the revolutionary events in Russia. Having analyzed almost four thousand articles on the topic, Lippmann and his coauthors traced the cycles of unjustified optimism about the Russian Revolution, which were later displaced by waves of frustration and calls for intervention. The paper's reports did not match the few facts firmly known about the events in Russia, such as the stabilization of the Bolshevik regime. In general, Lippmann characterized the coverage of the Russian Revolution by the leading American newspaper as "nothing short of disaster." Misleading news was worse than none at all, he said.[12]

Lippmann proposed a bureaucratic solution to the problem. He suggested creating Expert Councils, which would organize the flow of information in every department of the administration. Individually, people cannot reach beyond their casual experiences, wrote this disciple of William James; but human limits could be transcended by the organized construction of bureaucratic "knowledge machines." Lippmann's speculations coincided with the first formal studies of public opinion, popularity ratings, and polls. Since public opinion is so important to democratic politics, and since experts comprehend this opinion better than the voters and journalists, these experts should play special roles in forming public opinion.

Edward Bernays—Sigmund Freud's nephew and an Austrian immigrant to America—brought this vision to business. A graduate of Cornell, he became a staff member of the Committee for Public Information and took part in the Paris Peace Conference. Influenced by Lippmann's ideas about public opinion, Bernays invented his own term, "public relations," and in 1919 opened the first

PR consultancy. He devised advertisements for soap and clothing, women's cigarettes, and anti-smoking campaigns. All his life he promoted Freud, turning him into "the mentor of Madison Avenue."[13] Bernays visited his uncle during his visits to Europe, maintained a constant correspondence with him, and often referred to Freud in his work. It was probably Bernays who introduced Bullitt to Freud in the mid-1920s, and it seems likely that Bernays was Freud's source for what he knew about Wilson.

Having left the war in November 1917, the Bolsheviks published the "Secret Treaties"—documents signed by the leaders of the Entente powers that would give Constantinople to Russia and some other parts of the world to other members of the Entente. Wilson had long ignored these agreements, acting as though they never existed. But in a partial response to the publication of the "Secret Treaties," the Committee on Public Information (CPI) published documents indicating that the Bolsheviks' revolution had been supported by German money. A member of the CPI, Edgar Sisson, traveled to Russia in the winter of 1917–1918. There, he distributed one million copies of Wilson's Fourteen Points and brought back documents testifying that the Bolshevik leaders, Lenin and Trotsky, were German agents. The sensational documents reached President Wilson in May 1918, and in September the *New York Times* made them public. In the pro-communist *Liberator*, John Reed published an extensive analysis of Sisson's documents, highlighting many unaccountable mistakes and accusing Sisson of forgery. Bullitt did not trust these papers, either; following in Bullitt's footsteps, George Kennan later argued at length that they were fabricated. But Wilson seemed to believe in their authenticity, and his partners in the Paris Conference trusted them too; the Russian-German treaty of Brest-Litovsk, which was very generous to the Germans, gave credence to these suspicions. Publicizing these documents was a major success for Sisson; after returning from Russia with the discovery in his hands, Sisson was promoted to head of the Foreign Section of CPI.

In contrast, Colonel House believed then that the Bolsheviks had come to power not because of German money but because they had satisfied the only real demand of the Russian peasants: the redistribution of land.[14] Using British intelligence officers in Moscow as mediators, House and Trotsky played with the idea that the Bolsheviks might reject the Brest-Litovsk Treaty in exchange for American aid. Wilson refused to make such a commitment, but House counted on "national revival of Russia, such as that which was seen in the time of Napoleon": this time, Russia's revival would be directed against the Germans. To some extent, Bullitt shared these hopes.[15] Trying to clarify the events, on November 18, 1918, Bullitt suggested that the Department of State send a query to the incoming German president, Friedrich Ebert, seeking to publish the names of those who had been hired by the German General Staff to spread Bolshevik propaganda in Russia. Coming from Ebert, "such [a] publication would reveal and discredit the leading Bolshevik propagandists throughout Europe."[16]

Much later, in 1936, Ambassador Bullitt wrote a diplomatic cable to the State Department about a former employee of the CPI, Kenneth Durant, who "witnessed" Sisson fabricating his documents. This Durant was "a curious fellow whom I have known from childhood," Bullitt wrote, from "an excellent Philadelphian family." Durant was another one of John Reed's classmates at Harvard who later became Edward House's aide at the Paris Peace Conference, and there his paths crossed with Bullitt's. As it happened, Durant was on the payroll of the Soviet government well before Bullitt opened diplomatic relations between the two countries. Starting in 1923, and for at least the following twenty years, Durant worked for the Soviets as the official representative of the Telegraph Agency of the Soviet Union (TASS) to the United States. In a December 1936 memo from Durant to the head of TASS, Durant criticized Bullitt's work in Moscow; he wrote that he knew Bullitt from childhood and understood his "peculiarities."[17] For his part, Bullitt explained Durant's dramatic transformation by the fact that "he became violently disgusted with the publication by the American government of the forged 'Sisson documents,' which purported to prove that Lenin and Trotsky were both in the pay of the German Government." These documents were "palpably false," Bullitt wrote, and their dissemination by the CPI had the adverse effect on "people who care for fair play": for one, "Durant became so incensed that he swung over completely to the revolutionary point of view."[18]

Kenneth Durant is all but forgotten now, but the choice he made in life demands explanation. Writing in 1936, when Durant became his political opponent, Bullitt seemed to believe that Durant had been incensed to witness Sisson's fabrication and that working for the Soviet Union had redeemed him in some way. This is a complex psychological hypothesis; what is certain is that the Soviet authorities did support Durant for decades.

The origin of Sisson's documents and Durant's connection to them remains obscure. What is clear, however, is the foundational role these papers, whether forged or partially true, played in the development of the most successful institutions at managing public opinion in the twentieth century—the CPI and TASS. Substituting America's democratic institutions, new methods of manipulating the public opinion aspired to return power to the educated, well-financed elite of experts and administrators. These new methods ceaselessly referred to their "scientific" origins but trafficked in obscure areas of emotion, innuendo, and deception.

Controlling information flows, the authorities acquired superhuman traits that were projected onto the leader. This was a third way between idealism and realism, and I venture to call it "political demonism." In Europe it led to dictatorships and new wars, but in America it remained in the background, beneath the fabric of democratic politics. Colonel House's novel about *Dru, Administrator*, Bullitt's disjointed words, and Kennan's forgotten drafts all reveal the covert popularity of these anti-democratic ideas even among those who helped define the Progressive agenda. Later, Franklin Delano Roosevelt, who also started his service in the Wilson administration, became the peerless master of manipulating the public. "In the invention of political mechanisms and expedients, President Roosevelt was in a class by himself," Bullitt wrote. "In ability to handle American public opinion he was unrivaled. At his best, he was a political genius. This was a great asset to our country when the policy the President wanted to follow was in our national interest. But his very ability enabled him to lead our country toward disaster when he was wrong."[19]

3

GLOBAL RESPONSIBILITY

From the start of the First World War, Russia had been an important ally of France and Britain. Having come to power largely as a result of the war in February 1917, the Provisional Government confirmed its commitment to the Triple Entente. In April, the United States entered the war, and the Wilson administration supplied weapons and gave loans to the Provisional Government. Both Wilson's adviser for foreign policy, Edward House, and Secretary of State Robert Lansing came to believe that Russia could become an American partner, a member of the belligerent "community of democratic nations."[1] Voicing support for the Provisional Government of Russia, in August 1917 Wilson called for a revolution in Germany, which he thought could be modeled on the Russian revolution.

Instead, the Bolshevik Revolution came in November. The Wilson administration saw in this event the strategic success of Germany. A separate peace between Germany and Russia could seriously weaken the coalition of democratic powers, so the Wilson administration continued to recognize the overthrown Provisional Government and refused to negotiate with the new regime. Wilson came to Paris disturbed about the new Russian revolution, a view shared by British prime minister David Lloyd George. The Reds and their civil war with the Whites were very much in the news and minds of the Allies. According to Kennan, the president pictured Russia "as a country of frustrated idealists," and it was in the focus of Wilson's "emotional-political complex."

Because Wilson treated the Bolsheviks as agents of the German government, their victory forced him to resort to a policy of unconditional surrender.[2]

On their part, the Bolsheviks immediately stopped fighting on the German front. One day after their revolution, they published the Decree on Peace, which proclaimed "an immediate peace without annexations and without indemnities." The decree eloquently defined annexation as "every incorporation of a small or weak nation into [a] large or powerful state without the ... wish of that nation, irrespective ... of the degree of development or backwardness of the nation ... and irrespective, finally, of whether this nation is in Europe or in distant, overseas countries." The decree's call for emancipation applied to every land and nation, whether it was "forcibly annexed" by a stronger nation or "forcibly retained within [its] borders." These definitions made the Decree on Peace a comprehensive call for the decolonization of the former Russian Empire and of the entire world. In December 1917 the Bolsheviks started negotiations with the Germans in Brest-Litovsk. It was in response to this situation that Wilson issued his program of peace, the famous Fourteen Points.

In his speech given to Congress on January 8, 1918, Wilson applauded Russian peace efforts, offered help to the Russian people, and called for friendly dialogue with Bolshevik leaders. "Whether their present leaders believe it or not, it is our heartfelt desire and hope that some way may be opened whereby we may be privileged to assist the people of Russia to attain their utmost hope of liberty and ordered peace," said Wilson. In the same speech, he rejected all secret treaties between the Allies, including the promise of Constantinople that had kept the former rulers of Russia at war. Praising the Russian people and hoping to stop their "present leaders" from signing the separate peace, Wilson appealed to the same ideas of national self-determination and peace without annexations and indemnities. Wilson's Fourteen Points developed these ideas in juridical terms, articulated by House and his team of university professors. A huge public success, the Fourteen Points program brought Wilson popularity in Europe and a Nobel Peace Prize.

Having stopped the war on their side of the front, the new government in Petrograd tried to balance Wilson's sublime words with the very real threat of a new German offensive. While holding negotiations with the Germans in Brest-Litovsk, the commissars also hoped to get American help. Lenin, who had just returned from his long emigration to Switzerland, was eager to cede territories to the Germans in exchange for armistice. Trotsky, who had returned from the United States, strove to drag out the Brest-Litovsk talks.

Like Wilson, these Russians were idealists who confronted grim realities on the ground; swelling with pride, they read what the eloquent American president said to Congress. There is a voice, Wilson said, "more compelling than any of the many moving voices with which the troubled air of the world is filled. It is the voice of the Russian people.... Their conception of what is right, of what is humane and honorable for them to accept, has been stated with ... human sympathy which must challenge the admiration of every friend of mankind."[3] No American president had talked about Russia with such enthusiasm.

Like the Bolshevik Decree on Peace, Wilson's Fourteen Points called for the general decolonization of the world on the principles of universal self-determination. One point declared Russia "the acid test of good will" and demanded that all belligerents (which at the moment meant primarily the German troops) evacuate Russian territory. Wilson advocated for freedom of navigation and equal opportunities for both the winners and the losers of the war. He did not blame the enemy for starting the war, nor did he demand retribution. The key to achieving global peace was the creation of a new international organization, the League of Nations.

A descendant of Philadelphian coal magnates, Bullitt looked to wartime Germany as a model for social justice. When the Bolshevik Revolution took place in Russia, his New York friends, social radicals such as John Reed and Lincoln Steffens, applauded the revolution. The Wilson administration continued to support the overthrown Provisional Government, but the American Left preferred the new rulers of Russia. Some of these people had known Leon Trotsky in New York, where he spent the spring of 1917 before sailing across the Atlantic to foment revolution in Russia; others were surprised by the unexpected victory of Russian Marxists in an agrarian empire. But American support for the new wave of Russian revolution extended far beyond Greenwich Village society; some of the City bankers, such as Jacob Schiff, gave money to the Bolsheviks and lobbied for their recognition.

An ambitious polyglot who knew and loved Europe, Bullitt strove to deal with Russia even though he did not speak Russian and did not understand its political turmoil. "I wish I could see Russia with as simple an eye as [John] Reed. I am unable to win through the welter of conflicting reports about the Bolsheviki to anything like a solid conviction," he wrote in his notes in February 1918.[4] A friend and rival of Reed, Bullitt hoped to find a role for himself in the reconstruction of Russian-American relations, which were rapidly changing with the revolution in Petrograd. Throughout 1918, Bullitt wrote several memos to President Wilson and Secretary of State Lansing, advising them on how to deal with Trotsky and the Russians.

Colonel House supported Bullitt and shared his interest in the Russian revolutionary movement. In February 1918, their mutual friend, the famous journalist and poet Lincoln Steffens, told House that the challenge for American diplomacy was the fact that the Bolsheviks did not trust Wilson's new initiatives. With House's approval, Steffens sent a telegram to John Reed in Moscow: "Trotsky making [an] epochal blunder doubting Wilson's literal sincerity. I am certain President Wilson will do whatever he asks other nations to do. If you can and will change Trotsky's and Lenin's attitudes you can render historical international service."[5] Another mutual friend, the New York journalist Max Eastman, later spent many years working for Trotsky as a translator and literary agent.[6] Liberal, broad-minded, and also secretive, House attracted journalists and activists who were far to the left of his politics.

The assurances Trotsky received from his American friends significantly influenced his position in Brest-Litovsk. While Lenin advocated a quick agreement with the Germans, Trotsky dragged out the talks: he was waiting for help from the Allies, for Germany's surrender, or for peace talks with the Entente. None of these materialized, and only Germany's threats were real. Finally, Trotsky approved the separate treaty of Brest-Litovsk. Signed on March 3, 1918, the German-Russian peace weakened the Entente. The Germans transferred their divisions from Russia and Poland to their Western Front. By signing this peace, Bolshevik Russia renounced not only its recent claims over Constantinople but also its colonial domains in Poland, Ukraine, and the Baltic. With Russia withdrawing from the war, only the intervention of American troops could stop the German offensive in France.

The Bolsheviks consoled themselves with hopes of world revolution that would level the playing field between the war's winners and losers, abolish covert diplomacy and eliminate governments, armies, and borders. But the cynical Europeans and the idealistic Americans understood the peace of Brest-Litovsk to be a regional victory for the enemy. The German Empire imposed a peace that was defined by annexations and indemnities that Lenin and Wilson equally feared. Signed by the new Muscovite leaders, the treaty turned Russia from an ally of the Entente into a traitor. Now led by the United States, the Allies refused to recognize the new authorities as the legitimate government of Russia.

Europe was still at war. The talks in Brest began a year before the Paris talks that ended the First World War. The anti-imperialist slogans of the Bolsheviks, advocating an end to annexations, national self-determination, and so on, chimed with Wilson's Fourteen Points, but they were incomprehensible to Germany and Austria-Hungary. The Paris Peace Conference demonstrated that Russian and American ideas of peace were also alien to the British and French leaders. With Brest-Litovsk, Germany extended its influence over Eastern Europe, forming a line of "buffer" states, from the Baltic to Poland, Ukraine, and Turkey. At this juncture, the European leaders of the Entente seemed to have forgotten Wilson's points and returned to their secret treaties. Suspecting the Bolsheviks of aiding the Germans, the Allies landed troops in Arkhangelsk, Murmansk, and Vladivostok in 1918. The Wilson administration supported the troops under Admiral Kolchak, who had spent a large part of 1917 in America, and expected him to defeat the Bolsheviks. The French and the British also had their favorites among the White anti-Bolshevik forces fighting the civil war in the former Russian Empire. In October 1918, the People's Commissariat of Foreign Affairs passed a note to President Wilson, via America's attaché in Norway. Using a similar tone to Wilson's manifesto, the Bolsheviks demanded the evacuation of Allied troops from Murmansk, Arkhangelsk, and Siberia. The Bolsheviks also reneged on all Russian debts—including the biggest one, to France.

In this difficult context, Bullitt acknowledged the responsibility of the Allies, especially the United States, for events in Russia and Europe. In November 1918 he prepared two detailed memoranda, one about the "Bolshevik movement in Europe" and the other about the situation in Germany. Both memos recognized the victory of the Bolsheviks in Russia, which Bullitt saw as a fait accompli. He predicted that the Bolsheviks would come to power in the Baltics, Poland, and Ukraine as soon as the Germans retreated. In Sofia, socialists had come to power, he pointed out, and the same was bound to happen soon in Budapest, followed by Tyrol, Croatia, and Bohemia. Strikes and demonstrations under the Red banner were occurring throughout Europe, from Sweden to Italy. Mass starvation was creating a breeding ground for pan-European Bolshevism, Bullitt wrote. Bolshevism now posed a threat not only in defeated Austria and Turkey but also in France and Wales, where powerful forces that Bullitt called "half-Bolshevik" were also on the rise. Social Democrats controlled many German lands, and Bullitt suggested that the Wilson administration should support them because only they could effectively resist the Bolsheviks. If America did not support moderate German politicians, Bullitt warned, "Germany will become Bolshevist. Austria and Hungary will follow Germany's example. And the remainder of Europe will not long escape infection."[7] Revolution was rising in Europe, and Bullitt hoped American aid would help moderate socialists and stop Bolshevism. He was probably right in this judgment, though he could not predict that, without "material and spiritual support" from America, German socialism would lose to a particularly virulent form of Nazism.

In February 1919 Bullitt attended the International Socialist and Labor Conference in Bern. The conference called for disarmament, free trade, democratic elections, and the opening up of the League of Nations to all democracies. From Bullitt's perspective, this program of the European Left was no different from Wilson's. In Bern Bullitt met the socialist leaders of Europe and developed a network that would be crucial to his diplomacy. He praised Victor Adler, leader of the Austrian Social Democrats, as a "thoroughly safe man" and "the chief hope" for quelling Bolshevism in Austria. Yet Adler's position in Vienna was precarious, Bullitt wrote. Young Social Democrats were more radical than Adler, and the miserable conditions of postwar Vienna fed their Bolshevik sympathies. In Berlin the Ebert government also deserved urgent support from America, Bullitt wrote in his memorandum. "The Bolshevik movement in Europe can be combated successfully only by cooperation with the moderate socialist and labor leaders of Europe." Bullitt proposed to dispatch Herbert Hoover, then head of the American Relief Administration (ARA), to Berlin, arguing that aid from the ARA would decrease the likelihood of a Bolshevik revolution in Germany. Though usually Bullitt's proposals drowned in piles of bureaucratic correspondence, the ARA did deliver food to Germany and then to Russia. "Economic disorganization and famine are the parents of Bolshevism," Bullitt wrote. If postwar Europe was going to remain in its miserable condition, nothing would protect it from the murders and robberies that come with the dictatorship of the proletariat, he warned.

In postwar Europe, Bullitt speculated, the struggle between capitalism and socialism had turned into a struggle between moderate Social Democrats and anti-democratic Bolsheviks. "In dealing with the Bolshevik movement in Europe it is necessary to distinguish with the utmost care between the Socialists who advocate the immediate establishment of a dictatorship of the proletariat created by force and maintained by murder and terror, and the Socialists who advocate the establishment of democratic movements by peaceful means. . . . The latter variety of moderate socialist is the bitterest opponent of the Bolshevik," Bullitt wrote. Bolshevism could only be defeated through cooperation with the socialists.

"The movement for social democracy is beginning to occupy much the same place in the political arena of the twentieth century that the movement for political democracy occupied during the nineteenth century," Bullitt wrote in the same memo. Referring to history, he suggested that revolutionary movements were usually victorious, and that social democracy throughout Europe was also "inevitable." Moderate European socialists needed support, and democratic America (also a product of revolution, he pointed out) ought to be their ally. With respect to revolutionary Russia, Bullitt had similar advice: the US government "objects strongly to the government by murder and mass terror," he wrote, but "has no objection to the establishment of a Socialist government in Russia."

In this 1918 memorandum, Bullitt formulated a strategy of support for the non-Communist Left that, decades later, would become a major element of the European policy of several American administrations. But Bullitt took this idea even further. Together with his patron Edward House, he proposed establishing new departments in American embassies, and later in the League of Nations, that would deal specifically with questions of labor and monitor socialist movements. This idea would grow into the International Labor Organization, an agency of the League of Nations.

It was a revolutionary moment, and Bullitt embraced it fully. From 1918 into the spring of 1919, he sent a stream of memos interpreting the impact of labor conflicts in Germany and elsewhere in Europe—strikes, manifestations, and confrontations between moderates and radicals within the socialist parties—for the American government. He consistently drew comparisons between the developing situations in Germany and Russia, arguing that the German radical socialists who threatened Friedrich Ebert's government resembled Russian Bolsheviks. "[Karl] Liebknecht represents anti-democratic dictatorship in Germany," Bullitt wrote. If he won power, the resulting terror and mass murder in Germany would be similar to the Bolshevik Revolution; that was why, in Bullitt's view, the American government had to support moderate socialists like Ebert.

Re-reading these dusty papers today, one senses the lively feeling of global responsibility that infused young Bullitt's writings. "Kerensky fell and Lenin succeeded him partly, to be sure, because of Kerensky's own mistakes, but partly because the Allies and the United States did not take his appeals for material and spiritual aid at their face value. So today there is a grave danger that Ebert will fall because the Allies and the United States will not take his appeals . . . at anything like their face value," he wrote. Bullitt proposed to support Ebert's social-democratic government "a little more strongly than the Russian Bolsheviki are supporting the Spartacus group" of Liebknecht. Otherwise, he warned, "Germany will become Bolshevist," and Austria and Hungary would follow.

Wilson and Lansing were not ready to respond to this entirely new genre of intelligence, but House liked it. Appreciating the young journalist, House included Bullitt in the American delegation to the Peace Conference in Paris and recommended that the State Department hire him in January 1918. Bullitt, then twenty-seven years old, started at the State Department with a salary of eighteen hundred dollars a year. His new position promised a successful career. Bullitt shared the liberal and internationalist ideas held by senior members of the US delegation, who were largely selected by Colonel House. He reported to Lansing, who was significantly more conservative than House; but his actual boss was House, and Bullitt could play on their long-standing rivalry. His new title was Chief of the Division of Current Intelligence, which required him to give daily briefings to Allied leaders. He conveyed news of events at the front, reports from intelligence services, scandals in the press, and word of strikes, demonstrations, and riots happening across Europe. Bullitt appreciated his chance to socialize with the world leaders, but he did not want to be one of them. He wanted more: to change the world.

4

BETWEEN VERSAILLES AND THE KREMLIN

In Paris in 1919 the victors wished to end the world war. However, their objectives were different, as happens among friends. Guided by secret treaties, the European allies were fighting the war to redivide the former colonial world. Most of them believed in an old, but still popular, idea that their natural resources were insufficient and that their national economies depended upon revenue from the colonies. For some those colonies were overseas, in Asia and Africa. For others they were in Europe—in Ukraine, Poland, and the Balkans. The war was fought over all of them. A young John Maynard Keynes, then economic adviser to the British delegation in Paris, believed that in contrast to other continents Europe was not self-sufficient—its agriculture could not feed its growing population and its mines could not supply its booming industries. This worldview inspired Keynes's understanding of the causes of the First World War. In his 1919 book, *Economic Consequences of the Peace*, Keynes wrote that the growth of the North American population diminished America's role as a supplier of grain to the Old World. Germany and Austria-Hungary depended on grain from Russia and Romania. But the war halted the supply, and a famine was threatening Europe, Keynes argued.[1]

In fact, the supply of natural resources such as grain, coal, and oil depends on scientific discoveries and technological progress. Some British, French, and German strategists were guided by theories of political economy that stemmed from eighteenth-century mercantilism, refreshed by the modern regulations governing passports and visas, border guards, and customs fees. In contrast, Keynes proposed to complement the new League of Nations with a "Union of Free Trade" that would cover the whole of Eurasia; he believed that relieving maritime and terrestrial trade from duties and tariffs would benefit everyone. Led by Wilson and House, the American Progressive movement shared this ideal. Decolonization and free trade would allow all the participants of the conflict, including Germany, equal access to the resources of former colonies, from Indonesian rubber to Ukrainian grain. During talks in Paris, the Americans unsuccessfully tried to impose their ideas onto the older, selfish European countries.

The Paris Peace Conference was a sumptuous event, the first European summit in which the Americans took part; in fact, they played a leading role, though they may not have realized it. The event involved an amazing collection of future celebrities: many prospective European and American leaders started their careers by serving in the Paris delegations, where they witnessed meetings and speeches, bluffs and conspiracies, friendships and conflicts. Paris marked one of the first international events in which technical espionage, bugging, and clandestine recording played a role. With his predilection toward undercover diplomacy, Colonel House was particularly interested in secrecy. As his old novel, *Philipp Dru*, demonstrates, House was much concerned with these unfortunate aspects of modernity; the plotline starts with the corrupted American president wiretapping his opponents. Bullitt shared these concerns, and some participants of the Paris Conference reminisced that he was "obsessed" with the dangers of dictograph and undercover wiring. He remained anxious about these issues throughout his diplomatic career, and usually for good reason. However, in 1919 his concern about secrecy and microphones seemed exaggerated; Arthur Schlesinger, a liberal historian of the younger generation, dismissed the "obsession" with wiring as Bullitt's idiosyncrasy.[2] In the twenty-first century we have seen, sadly, that these technologies and anxieties have become a routine part of modern politics; retrospectively, the concerns of House and Bullitt look prescient.

In Paris, negotiations dragged on, moving further and further away from Wilson's Fourteen Points. Subverting Wilson's vision, British and French leaders blamed Germany for starting the war, dismantled the Austro-Hungarian Empire, and focused on the annexations and indemnities. France claimed the disputed lands in Western Europe, Britain wanted the German possessions in Africa, and everyone was thinking about the former Austrian, Ottoman, and Russian colonies in Eastern Europe.

President Wilson understood—but was not able to defend—the argument that House, Bullitt, and Keynes were making: if Germany turned into a failed state, a new war would emerge. Bullitt would later dramatize Wilson's dilemma in a play, "Tragedy of Wilson." A young secretary advises the president how to talk to the Allies: "Say to them: I came here on a signed contract with Germany to make peace on the Fourteen Points upon which Germany asked for an armistice. If you gentlemen have no intention of keeping that promise, I shall return to Washington." In the play Wilson objects: it would be a defeat, he says, one that would waste America's war efforts, as well as his own speeches. "That's better than making all ideals and idealists a joke," responds his secretary.[3]

Bullitt wrote this tragic play in three acts around 1925, but he never attempted to publish or stage it. Lively, with fast dialogues and realistic scenery, the play depicts Wilson and his entourage at the Paris Peace Conference. Some characters bear the real names of their historical antecedents; other characters had their names changed but remained recognizable. The same goes for their words: Bullitt took some quotes from historical sources, some he quoted from memory, and others he made up. The play depicts negotiations in the Council of Four and in Wilson's Paris residence in detail, including the tricks that British and French leaders played on the president, his capricious changes of mind, and his lofty but flirtatious attitude toward male secretaries. "We fight in order to establish the peace that will put an end to all wars," Wilson says. His fictional young secretary gives a touching twist to the story. Wilson loves him like a son; patriotic and dignified, the secretary leaves for the war. In the next act, he returns wounded and blind. "It is not so bad if I can think it will never happen to anybody again and that I helped a little," he says. He does help: looking at him, Wilson realizes the injustice he has brought upon this boy and the world. He stops the negotiations and orders the presidential steamer to bring him back to the States. But Allied leaders threaten the president: if he leaves the conference he would see "Bolshevism all over Europe," they warn. According to the play, Wilson mourned the huge difference between the Versailles treaty and the Fourteen Points. Mixing flattery with deception, the European leaders persuade him to continue the negotiations. The play ends back in America, where a semi-paralyzed, delusional Wilson gives a long oratory to a random flock of sheep. Bullitt invested complex ideas in this text, such as Wilson's obsessive self-identification with Christ, the analogy between the Paris Peace Conference and the Congress of Vienna (1814–1815), and the belief in the structural incapacity of the League of Nations—or of any international organ in which great powers have the power of veto—to confront one of these powers. Mostly lively, sometimes moving, and deprived of romantic plot, the play buckles under the weight of its message.[4]

Wilson's failure to act according to his own principles, which he offered to the world so convincingly, struck many observers. Lenin wrote that Wilson "turned out to be a perfect fool, whom Clemenceau and Lloyd George twirled like a pawn."[5] In their psychobiography of Wilson, Freud and Bullitt argued much the same, though using more sophisticated language. They followed in detail, almost on a daily basis, how Wilson's inability to confront the pressure of his allies led him to moral collapse and physical paralysis. Rarely in human history, they wrote, did the fate of the world depend so much on a single individual, as it did in Paris in the spring of 1919.

During the war Freud's sons were fighting for Austria-Hungary and Bullitt interviewed the leaders of Germany. Their personal experiences were very different, but they were equally critical of the American involvement in the war. Indeed, their book all but mourned the defeat of Germany in the First World War. The coauthors argued that the war aims of Britain (to suppress the German competition and take its colonies in Africa), France (to return Alsace), and Russia (to capture Constantinople) were all at odds with the interests of the United States. Although coming from different starting points, Freud and Bullitt agreed in their strategic analysis, which foresaw the next world war and blamed the Paris Peace Conference for laying the groundwork for a new catastrophe in Europe.[6] Writing their book during the Nazis' rise to power, they saw the radicalization of Germany as a product of the Versailles treaty. They believed that, had America not gone to war, the countries of the Entente would all have had to sign something resembling the Brest-Litovsk Treaty.

Writing in the late 1920s Freud, then in his seventies, and Bullitt, in his thirties, were both convinced that history would have been different if only Wilson had held firm to his principles. His "fear was overwhelming," they wrote. "He had exaggerated the danger of fighting and minimized the chance of fighting successfully. One threat to leave France to face Germany alone might have brought Clemenceau to compromise; one crack of his financial whip might have brought Lloyd George to heel. But ... he feared that his withdrawal would result in an immediate renewal of war, . . . that starving French armies would in the end dictate a peace far worse than the peace he faced, . . . that the whole Europe would succumb to Bolshevism." Freud and Bullitt characterized Wilson's fears as childish, emphasizing his fear of Bolshevism foremost among all. "He hated and feared Communists far more deeply than he hated and feared militarists. There was no spark of radicalism in his body," they wrote.[7]

One of the many problems that members of the Paris talks tried unsuccessfully to ignore was the fate of the most troubled of the belligerent countries, Russia, still embroiled in a civil war involving international troops. Bloodshed had been continuing unabated there since the start of the First World War. Famine had set in more recently. Allied troops stationed there faced attack. In July 1918, protests against the Brest-Litovsk Treaty led to an armed uprising in the new Russian capital, Moscow, which the Bolsheviks brutally repressed. The victors of the war feared that due to the Brest-Litovsk Treaty, Germany had received undeserved and untold benefits from Russia. On January 16, 1919, Lloyd George raised this question: "It would be manifestly absurd," he said at a formal meeting, "to come to any agreement and leave Paris when one-half of Europe and one-half of Asia is still in flames. Those present must settle this question or make fools of themselves."[8] The British prime minister proposed to invite "the representatives" of all Russian forces, Red and White, to Paris. Some believed that if the Bolshevik delegates came to Paris, they "would convert everyone to Bolshevism"; this would not happen, Lloyd George promised. Meanwhile, the senseless British, American, and Japanese landings in the distant harbors of the Russian Arctic and Pacific continued for almost a year. The commanders leading those missions sent back conflicting messages: one dispatch requested permission to withdraw the troops and ships; in another, reinforcements were demanded.

Unlike the British government, which was actively developing intelligence in Russia, the Wilson administration had no agents there. The American ambassador and his staff had left Petrograd in 1917. Two American representatives of the Red Cross, Thomas Thacher and Raymond Robbins, forwarded Bullitt lengthy reports that were unusually sympathetic to the Bolsheviks. They believed that the Bolshevik regime was stable and popular, and they predicted a new conflict between Russia and Germany, which would turn the Bolsheviks into allies of the Entente. The pro-Bolshevik position of these Americans was distinctly different from that of British agents, who detested

Bolshevism and were determined to overthrow it by force.[9] However, Lloyd George was against a full-scale intervention in Russia. He proclaimed in Paris that the British working class would not support it; if he issued such an order, he said, he would face mutiny.[10]

Wilson proposed to invite "the representatives" of all sides of the Russian conflict to a separate conference to be held some place far away, perhaps on the Turkish island of Prinkipo. Clemenceau objected to the plan—he did not want to deal with Russia because the Bolsheviks were refusing to pay their debts to France. In February Clemenceau barely survived an assassination attempt; the assassin was an anarchist, not a Bolshevik, but the lesson to be drawn was clear. The French leader saw Bolshevism as a contagious, incurable disease that had to be quarantined.

Freud and Bullitt later wrote that whenever Wilson faced a problem, his response was to suggest setting up a discussion club like the one he chaired in his student years at the University of Virginia. Following his instructions, the American delegation sent invitations to a number of Russian leaders. When the responses came back, Wilson learned the difference between a debating club and a civil war: those who were killing each other in Russia had no interest in talking to their enemies abroad.

In the meantime, six thousand Americans were still in Arkhangelsk. In a memo Bullitt advised House to withdraw them. Failure to do so, Bullitt wrote on January 30, would entail a new catastrophe, a "northern Gallipoli."[11] The British objected to that plan, and troops were withdrawn only in the summer. Since the Russian conference failed to materialize, Bullitt proposed an alternative plan to House. He advised sending an Anglo-American fact-finding mission to Russia, geared toward assessing the situation on the ground and the intentions of the Bolsheviks. Given Clemenceau's hostility toward the Bolsheviks, he suggested, it would be better to keep this plan secret from France.

At that moment the Bolsheviks' future was not clear to anybody, not even to themselves. One of their enemies, the self-declared "supreme ruler of Russia," Alexander Kolchak, had American support. With British help, another White leader, Nikolai Yudenich, threatened Petrograd. In spring Yudenich met in Stockholm with the representatives of the Entente and requested further assistance. Czech troops controlled the Trans-Siberian Railway. Southern Russia was changing hands, and pogroms were incessant. When the Bolsheviks arrested the American consul in Tashkent, it became clear that they had power over parts of Central Asia. Watching this storm from Paris, some hoped that the Bolsheviks would soon vanish into thin air; some feared that the power vacuum in Russia would benefit Germany; others were afraid of the world revolution that Russians would bring to Europe. Nobody, not even the educated experts who worked for Wilson and House, could keep track of Russian events, let alone predict their outcome.

But as soon as the military defeat of Germany was official, the victorious countries lost interest in Russia's problems. During the war it had been strategically important to keep Russia as an ally, because doing so forced the Central Powers to fight on two fronts. But when Russian soldiers abandoned the German front, the Entente happily forgot its promise to give Constantinople to Russia; after all, the British had protected it from the Russian Empire for centuries. In Paris the Allies faced plenty of other problems, and many of them—dismantling the Austro-Hungarian Empire, creating a new Poland, mapping the Baltic and Balkan states—were easier to resolve without Russia at the negotiating table. Russia was irrelevant when it came to resolving the deepest causes of the war, such as the dispute about colonial possessions and the elimination of German submarines. In these disputes the United States was to be the arbiter, Wilson's favorite role. But when Britain insisted on annexing the German colonies in Africa and the Pacific, directly contradicting the Fourteen Points, all the American president could do was edit the treaty so that the detested words "annexation" and "colony" were erased. Distributed between Britain, France, and Belgium, the former German colonies were now to be ruled as "mandate territories."

The left-leaning British leader, Lloyd George, still made some efforts to include representatives of the Bolsheviks in the peace process, and Wilson supported his initiative. Wilson's friend and early biographer William Dodd produced a revealing account: "That would have meant that the Lenin government would become less eruptive . . . as all radical government have done in the past when they became 'legitimate.'" It would also have meant, Dodd wrote, that "Russia would have become another economic bonanza as the Rocky Mountain regions was to the North after the American Civil War." According to Dodd, Edward House promoted this project within the American delegation. If it were accomplished, "Wilson, Lloyd George and Lenin, strange as this comment may seem to some, would have rearranged the world and written the terms of peace. It was a great dream that came near the realization." Dodd blamed Clemenceau, who wanted Russia to repay its debts, and Japanese leaders, who wanted to control Siberia, for defeating the project. "Far-seeing Liberals thus lost a great chance," Dodd wrote in 1922.[12]

Wilson presented the charter of the League of Nations in Paris on February 14, 1919. Years later, Freud and Bullitt wrote ironically that Wilson had modeled himself after Christ, leading "the world to new peace and himself to immortality."[13] This sublime task, however, necessitated a new initiative toward Russia. Four days after Wilson's speech, Secretary of State Lansing asked Bullitt to lead a mission to Moscow. The official purpose of this mission would be to explore political and economic conditions in the country. However, both Lenin's revolution in Russia and Wilson's revolution in international relations invited more than fact-finding.

Together with Lloyd George's personal secretary, Philip Kerr, Bullitt formulated the task of this mission. According to the terms of the Russian truce drafted by the two young men, all existing authorities in Russia—Trotsky, Kolchak, Yudenich, Mannerheim, and others—would end their hostilities and remain in power in the territories they controlled on the hypothetical day of the armistice. In exchange, they would all receive international recognition. On February 21, Kerr enumerated the points he had informally discussed with Lloyd George in a letter to Bullitt: "1. Hostilities to cease on all fronts; 2. All de facto governments to remain in full control of the territories which they at present occupy." Kerr's other conditions included freedom of ports and trade and amnesty for all political prisoners and prisoners of war. Bullitt received a general approval of this plan from House. To make the plan more attractive to the Bolsheviks, Bullitt proposed deferring the discussion about the Russian debts, and House agreed.[14] The mission was supposed to be kept secret, though newspapers learned of it quickly.

On this trip to Russia, Bullitt was to be accompanied by journalist Lincoln Steffens and W. W. Pettit, a military intelligence officer. Both were sympathetic to the Bolsheviks. Steffens was a popular writer and poet who openly proclaimed his socialist views. Pettit spoke Russian and had previously visited Petrograd as an officer; on this trip, he was ordered to wear civilian clothes. Bullitt received five thousand dollars for their expenses. On February 22, 1919, the three men set out from Paris to London, then sailed from Newcastle to Bergen before finally reaching Stockholm. There, Bullitt met the Swedish Communist Charles Kilborn, who had spent several months in revolutionary Russia. Kilborn helped establish contacts with the Bolshevik leadership by telegraph. On March 5, the men made it to Helsinki, and from there it took three more days to reach Petrograd. "Journey easy," Bullitt telegraphed from the road. "Reports about frightful conditions here ridiculously exaggerated."[15] In Petrograd, Bullitt and his companions met the Bolshevik leader of the city,

Grigory Zinoviev, as well as the People's Commissar for Foreign Affairs, Georgy Chicherin, and his deputy Maxim Litvinov. Chicherin spoke French; Litvinov, who had spent years in London and was married to a British woman, spoke English. A little later, all except Zinoviev traveled to Moscow to meet with Lenin. Bullitt and his companions spent three days in Moscow, the new capital.

The Bolsheviks were under siege. For them, early spring 1919 was the worst part of the civil war that followed the socialist revolution. They desperately needed international recognition of their power, and welcomed their American guests. Lenin and his comrades perceived Bullitt to be an official representative of the American government; this was the first but certainly not the last time that Bullitt exercised his skill at bluffing. The negotiations were quick, direct, and unexpectedly constructive. The Bolsheviks fed them bread and caviar; no other food was available in the Kremlin. Caviar became Bullitt's favorite treat; everywhere he went, in America and Europe, he welcomed guests with caviar and champagne. As it happened, the self-proclaimed "people's commissars" accepted the Bullitt-Kerr project almost without alteration. Beating Bullitt's expectations, they even promised to pay off Russia's debt to France, provided that Kolchak and other White leaders would share this responsibility. However, the debt became a secondary concern in light of the enormous shift in the military and political situation on the ground that could result from these negotiations. The Bolsheviks in Moscow went further than anybody in Paris could have expected, and indeed further than the Kremlin would ever agree to fulfill in the future.

On March 14, Bullitt received an extraordinary document from the Kremlin that contained the Bolshevik consent to his proposal. The Central Executive Committee of the Bolshevik Party, chaired by Lenin, discussed and approved "The Projected Peace Proposal" offering to cease military activity across the territory of the former Russian Empire. They proposed that the Allies recognize all authorities operating on Russian territory as legitimate governments over the areas they actually controlled at the date of the armistice. In exchange for international legitimacy, the Bolsheviks agreed to recognize the jurisdictions of Kolchak, Yudenich, Denikin, and other White leaders. They also agreed to national self-rule for almost all colonies of the former Russian Empire, from the Baltic to the Caucasus and Central Asia. In addition, they agreed to a continuation of the occupation of Arkhangelsk, Murmansk, and Vladivostok by the Allies. The Bolsheviks would have been satisfied to control the territories that they actually ruled in the spring of 1919:

Moscow, Petrograd, and several surrounding provinces. Twenty-three parallel wars in the former Russian Empire would be stopped in a single moment, according to Bullitt's count. The Bolshevik draft also offered general amnesty and free movement of people across the former Russian Empire. According to the document, the commissars agreed to acknowledge the Russian debt, provided that the Bolsheviks shared this responsibility with the new states. Lenin's government wanted to get an answer to this offer before April 10, 1919, from the Paris Peace Conference. A week after the armistice, the Bolsheviks agreed to attend an international conference about Russia; they proposed to organize it in Oslo. The new independent states would be recognized at this conference.[16] The document was as much of an official decision that an unelected, unrecognized power could proffer.

Bullitt immediately sent Pettit to Helsinki, where he cabled the document to Paris. Bullitt and Steffens also hastened to leave. On March 17, Bullitt cabled House: "If you had seen the things that I have seen during the past week and talked with the men with whom I have talked, I know that you would not rest until you had put through this peace." House sent his congratulations.[17]

Bullitt returned to Paris on March 25. He left Pettit in Petrograd to liaison with Shklovsky, the local representative of the People's Commissariat for Foreign Affairs, who had recently returned from his emigration to the United States. From Petrograd, Pettit sent investigative reports that said many people he met in Russia supported the Bolsheviks. He was arrested on the Finnish border when returning from Petrograd; the Finns searched him, identified his rank, and released the gallant but credulous captain. Bullitt's reports from Russia closely mirrored Pettit's; both narrated the revolution with much optimism. "The destructive phase of the revolution is over," Bullitt wrote, "and all the energy of the government is turned to the constructive work. The terror has ceased. . . . Executions are extremely rare." Bullitt saw Lenin as a moderate politician like Wilson, almost a centrist. "Lenin, indeed, as a practical matter, stands well to the right in the existing political life of Russia."[18] To illustrate his point, Bullitt described how Lenin's government had abandoned its earlier plan to nationalize land, reestablished the banks, and intended to pay foreign debts. Bullitt was right: two years later, Lenin began implementing his New Economic Policy. He was more pragmatic than many of his comrades, which he probably made clear to Bullitt when they talked over bread and caviar. Unlike John Reed, who admired Trotsky, Bullitt preferred Lenin, writing of the Bolshevik leader as a direct and sincere man—high praise. Even later in life, when Bullitt became sharply critical about the Soviet regime, he still made an exception for Lenin.

In short, Bullitt believed that his three days in Moscow would change the world no less dramatically than the ten days in Petrograd depicted by John Reed in his book about the Russian Revolution. Those three days did change his life, but they failed to turn history around. In late 1919 Bullitt gave a detailed assessment of his Russian mission to the Committee on Foreign Relations of the American Senate and then published the proceedings at his own risk. About ten years later, Bullitt included a summary of his Russian mission in the book on Wilson he coauthored with Freud. The summary was a brief and effective presentation of the failed treaty: "Lenin had offered to make an immediate armistice on all fronts, and to accord de facto recognition to the Anti-communist governments, which had been set up in the following areas of the territory of the former Russian Empire: 1) Finland, 2) Murmansk and Arkhangelsk, 3) Estonia, 4) Latvia, 5) Lithuania, 6) Poland, 7) the western part of White Russia, 8) Rumania, including Bessarabia, 9) more than half the Ukraine, 10) the Crimea, 11) the Caucasus, 12) Georgia, 13) Armenia, 14) Azerbaijan, 15) the whole of the Urals, 16) all Siberia. Thus Lenin had offered to confine Communist rule to Moscow and a small adjacent area, plus the city now known as Leningrad." Bullitt realized, of course, that Lenin and his fellow Bolsheviks would violate the deal just as soon as they could afford to do so; still, such a treaty would be a huge breakthrough. "As a Communist, Lenin naturally expected to expand the area of Communist rule whenever he could safely, regardless of any promises he might have made. Yet by reducing the Communist state to an area not much larger than that ruled by . . . Ivan the Terrible, Lenin had offered the West a unique opportunity," Bullitt and Freud wrote.[19] George Kennan evaluated the proposed treaty in similar terms: it was, he wrote, "not an ideal" option, but it "did offer the most favorable opportunity yet extended, or ever to be extended, to the Western powers" in their dealing with Russia.[20]

Having consented to Bullitt's project for peace, the Bolsheviks prioritized their own survival, hoping to consolidate their power in Central Russia and continue their fight for world revolution from there. They also followed the logic of decolonization that inspired both their Decree on Peace and Wilson's Fourteen Points. In exchange for diplomatic recognition, the Bolshevik government was ready to cede control over the populated and industrialized areas of the former Russian Empire—the Urals, Siberia, Northern Russia, and the

Caucasus. Finland had declared its independence from Russia a year earlier; under the terms of the Brest-Litovsk Treaty, the Bolsheviks had already retreated from a major part of Ukraine and the Baltic lands.

Had the belligerent powers fighting the Russian Civil War signed on to the peace in Oslo after a more global treaty was signed in Versailles, the decolonization of the world would have gone much further than what even the Inquiry's most idealistic professors could have expected. The resulting losses of the territory and population of the former Russian Empire would have been much larger than those resulting from the Brest-Litovsk Treaty. If the hypothetical treaty were signed, in Oslo or another suitable place, in the presence of high international representatives, it would be the first accomplishment of the new League of Nations. Had this happened, the League would have earned much higher repute in the US Congress and around the world. The regional success would have had global consequences. The termination of the Russian Civil War would have saved many thousands from dying in combat, from famine or pogroms. Warfronts would have acquired the status of state borders, and about a dozen new states would have appeared on the world map. In conflict with each other, these newly independent states would have had to establish new relations with the outer world, each in its own way. Surrounded by a ring of large and small Russian and non-Russian states, Bolshevism would have become localized and isolated. Internationally recognized, Lenin's government would have had to compete for people, capital, and might with a panoply of liberal, nationalist, and monarchist neighbors. The Soviet Union would probably never have been formed had this version of history come to pass. The emancipation of Siberia and the fragmentation of European Russia would have changed the balance of power so much that the history of the twentieth century would have been different. And could it have been worse than what actually happened?

5

RESIGNATION

Bullitt and Steffens returned from Moscow along with Arthur Ransome, a British writer and agent who was working for the Secret Intelligence Service. They could not have found a better interlocutor. A biographer of Oscar Wilde, Ransome moved to Russia in 1913 to report for British newspapers. He was in Petrograd during the First World War and both Russian revolutions, befriended Karl Radek, the founder of the Communist International, and had a relationship with Trotsky's personal secretary. Officially, Ransome was interested in Russian fairy tales, which he was collecting for a book project, but he also sent reports about the Bolsheviks' plans and military developments to his contacts in London. A left-wing activist who lived in the world of fantasy, he would later become involved in smuggling Russian diamonds to Europe to finance the Comintern. Allegations arose that he was a double agent.[1] Politically, he differed from other British agents in Russia, who were vehemently anti-Bolshevik; with his leftist leanings and Russian sympathies he had more in common with Bullitt and Steffens. "Shakespeare looked different after Russia, and, unlike some other authors, still true," he told Steffens while they were heading to England in 1919. But they talked mostly about the Bolsheviks, whom Bullitt and Steffens also saw differently after their short trip to Russia.[2] Ransome eventually married Trotsky's former secretary, and he published many collections of fairy tales, most of them invented from scratch. Also a storyteller, Steffens depicted the new Bolshevik state in a famous formula: "I have been into the future, and it works."[3]

Bullitt's arrival back in Paris was less fortunate. Colonel House greeted him and reported to Wilson that Bullitt had arrived with "news of supreme importance": this news, he said, would bring peace where there still was war. Wilson asked Bullitt to brief him the next day. For his part, Lloyd George was pleased to have breakfast with Bullitt; he listened to the amazing details of the negotiations with the Bolsheviks and seemed to approve of them. Clemenceau, as planned, was kept in the dark. Then, however, events started to unfold brutally and inexplicably, just as if Bullitt was inside a Russian fairy tale. The president had a headache and canceled the meeting. He told House that he could not think about Russian affairs because he was so caught up with German issues: he had a "one-track mind," Wilson explained, as if he was proud of it. The president asked House to make decisions about Russia. Also tasked with mitigating France and Britain's demands on Germany at the time, House told Bullitt to prepare a draft of a political declaration, rehashing the provisions Bullitt and Lenin had agreed upon. The declaration was to be signed by the Allied Powers and would serve as the Paris Peace Conference's official response to the Bolshevik proposal.

In the meantime, the British secret service interviewed Steffens about his trip to Russia. The intelligence officers were more competent than Steffens had expected. When the conversation ended, Steffens praised their knowledge of Russia: "You have proved to me that my government is honest and yours is not." They were startled, and so he continued: "Well, your government, like mine, talks lies, but evidently your government knows the truth. Mine does not. My government believes its own damned lies." Despite his fondness for the Bolsheviks, Steffens was happy to get back to Paris. Surprised, Bullitt asked him why. Steffens thought deeply and responded: "because, though we had been to heaven, we were so accustomed to our own civilization that we preferred hell."[4]

On April 4, Wilson fell ill. Although the president's illness was concealed from the public, all negotiations stopped. His ailment may have been the first of several strokes or a flaring up of old neurological problems. He had a fever and severe coughing fits and could not move the left side of his body. Years later, Freud and Bullitt would try to prove that Wilson's symptoms were psychosomatic responses to his feelings of failure and guilt—a bodily reaction to his neurotic inability to make decisions at crucial moments. "He faced alternatives both of which were horrible to him," they argued. "He could break his promises and become the tool of the Allies, not the Prince of Peace, or he could hold to his promises, withdraw the financial support of the United States from Europe, denounce Clemenceau and Lloyd George, return to Washington and leave Europe to—what? and himself to—what?"[5]

The Bolsheviks' April 10 deadline for an agreement was fast approaching. Bullitt reminded House about this deadline daily, but House understood the risks of signing such a declaration or asking the Allies to do so. He clearly did not want to make the decision alone; it was also the moment when his relationship with Wilson deteriorated sharply. The president was only seeing his doctor at this time, so House was not able to confer with him. On April 6, Bullitt was able to convince the president's physician, Admiral Cary T. Grayson, to ask Wilson about the Russian proposal. The president did not respond. On the same day, Bullitt asked Moscow to extend the deadline to April 20. He also sent a personal letter to Wilson:

> You are face to face with a European revolution. . . . For the past year the peoples of Europe have been seeking a better way to live for the common good for all. They have found no guidance in Paris. They are turning towards Moscow. To dismiss this groping of the peoples for better lives—this European revolution—with the word "Bolshevism" is to misunderstand it as completely as Lord North misunderstood the American Revolution. The peoples turn towards Moscow; but the impulses which drive them are remote from theoretic communism. . . . Six months ago all the peoples of Europe expected you to fulfill their hopes. They believe now that you cannot. They turn, therefore, to Lenin, and in so doing they are as honorable and as deserving of sympathy as when they turned to you.

Responding to the revolution with military force and an economic blockade "would only spread famine, chaos, and bloody class war over the whole of Europe." Indeed, Bullitt wanted the American government to aid the Russian Revolution rather than suppress it. Challenging the president, Bullitt put his career on the line. "Today you may still guide the Revolution into peaceful and constructive channels," he wrote. In conclusion, Bullitt asked Wilson for an urgent meeting: he wanted fifteen minutes to explain to the president that no question was "heavier with possibilities of good and evil [than] the peace with the European revolution."[6] Again, Bullitt received no answer.

But on the same day, April 6, 1919, Wilson went to war one last time with Clemenceau and Lloyd George. First, he ordered that the transfer of credit to

America's allies be stopped, though the funds for the next six months had already been disbursed. Then, he ordered that his steamer, the *George Washington*, be readied to bring him back to Washington. "It is a bluff, isn't it?" Clemenceau asked Admiral Grayson. "He hasn't a bluffing corpuscle in his body," Wilson's physician replied earnestly.[7] A few days later, the president surrendered; his mood changed again, and he now accepted the French and British demands, which he had resisted for months. He had neither the time nor the energy for the new agenda that Bullitt's mission had proposed.

Harold Nicolson, an ambitious British diplomat, talked to Bullitt on the dramatic day of April 10, 1919, and found "a young man with beliefs." They talked about the Bolsheviks: "Bullitt says that the only danger for Lenin comes from the left extremists, not the Whites." Bullitt also predicted that the Russian question would become "one of the great problems of my middle age." Nicolson was "agnostic" about the Bolsheviks, but he liked the American delegation. "Had the Treaty of Paris been drafted solely by the American experts it would have been one of the wisest as well the most scientific documents ever devised," he wrote. But the British delegation was also very strong, featuring Arnold Toynbee and John Maynard Keynes. These brilliant intellectuals were smart enough to understand the failure of the Paris Conference. As for Wilson, Nicolson could only wish "that the final clouding of his brain spared him the horror of understanding what he had done for Europe."[8]

Bullitt was in a rush, but so was everyone in Paris. Wilson needed the League of Nations to come together to ensure his legacy. British and French leaders hastened because they knew that their annexations and indemnities depended on Wilson's survival. Still unknown to the public, Lenin's proposal expired on April 10, 1919. Four days later, the Allied Powers agreed on the Versailles treaty and sent it to the Germans. The German government declared that it could not accept the treaty. It had signed the armistice on the basis of Wilson's Fourteen Points, but the treaty left most of those points unrealized. However, Germany did eventually sign the treaty after French troops began a new offensive.

The Allies did little to change their policy toward Russia. After a massive anti-Bolshevik riot on the Volga, and Admiral Kolchak's US-backed spring offensive across the Urals, there was renewed hope among the Allies that the Bolsheviks would be defeated: indeed the Red Army was at its weakest in March and April 1919 when Bullitt brought the peace proposal to Wilson. This was no coincidence: the Bolsheviks had also agreed to make peace with the Germans in the Brest-Litovsk Treaty because they were negotiating from a position of weakness. For the same reason, the participants of the talks in Paris felt "very lukewarm," as Bullitt diplomatically put it, about negotiations with the Bolsheviks; they hoped that the Russian problem would take care of itself. Had they accepted or even considered Bullitt's plan in any meaningful way, the British and American governments would have had to revise their commitments to the White Army. Knowledgeable members of these governments understood that the preservation of the Russian Empire was a central aim of the Whites; though partially financed and supplied by the Allies, the anti-Bolshevik leaders—also "idealists" in their own way—would have rejected any proposal to dismember Russia. Bullitt had managed to get Lenin's consent, but nobody knew how long it would take to bring Denikin to negotiations in Oslo, or what would happen if Trotsky met Kolchak there.

Thus, Bullitt's mission failed, but there were some positive takeaways from this mission, including the release of Roger Calver Treadwell, the American consul in Tashkent, who had been arrested by local Bolsheviks; in Moscow, Bullitt had negotiated his discharge. After his release, Treadwell reported from Stockholm on May 2, 1919: "The dictatorship of the Bolsheviks has simply succeeded that of the Czar bureaucracy. . . . The loss of individuality, the absence of all moral force, and the present inertia of the intelligent class, are the greatest obstacles in the way of helping the Russian people."[9]

Bullitt first acknowledged his failure in a letter to his former companion Captain Pettit. On April 18, he wrote to Pettit that he was "rather ashamed" of the results of the mission. In this letter Bullitt's sentiments closely resembled later, more polished statements. He wrote that though Lloyd George was hesitant about the plan because he was afraid of backlash from the conservative press on the eve of parliamentary elections, it was Wilson who had refused to discuss the Russian peace project.[10] Bullitt also blamed House's son-in-law and secretary, Gordon Auchincloss, and David Hunter Miller—the commission's legal expert and a partner in the same law firm as Auchincloss—for blocking the proposal on legal grounds. Bullitt went so far as to call Miller "the blackest reactionary we have here." Auchincloss wanted to send a mission to supply food to Russia in exchange for certain concessions from the Bolsheviks; he wanted them to give control over ports and railroads to the Allies. Auchincloss wrote up the proposal for the mission and Bullitt rewrote it, but Clemenceau refused to sign that version. Later they agreed to a compromise that Bullitt found unrealistic; he was right, it did not work. As he wrote to Pettit, "the fact is that everyone in Paris, except the French, knows that we ought to make peace with the Soviet government, but the old gentlemen who are running the things simply have not the courage, nor the straightforwardness, to go at peace via a direct route."[11]

Unlike some of his counterparts, Wilson had a relatively sophisticated understanding of Bolshevism. Clemenceau compared it to a contagious disease and warned that an epidemic loomed, but Wilson saw Bolshevism as the wrong answer to the right questions, which his progressive agenda also raised. As he put it at the Paris Peace Conference, "capital and labor in the United States are not friends. Still they are not enemies. . . . But they are distrustful, each of the other. Society cannot go on that plane. . . . The whole world was disturbed by this question long before the Bolsheviks came into power. Seeds need soil, and the Bolsheviks seeds found the soil already prepared for them."[12] Although Wilson wanted the Reds to be defeated, he did not want the tsar's archaic regime to be reestablished. Most of all, Wilson was concerned that the Bolsheviks' violent revolution would spread into Europe, and this concern was the reason that he ultimately acceded to the French and British demands. Freud and Bullitt wrote later about the terrible "word pictures" that crossed Wilson's mind when he imagined what would happen if he withdrew from the Paris conference. "He described the French army marching into Germany, obliterating whole cities by chemical warfare, killing women and children, conquering all Europe and then being submerged by a Communist revolution."[13]

Robert Lansing, Wilson's conservative secretary of state, believed during the Paris Peace Conference that a proletarian revolution across the continent was imminent, and that Moscow was financing agents and plotters in Europe. In hindsight, he acknowledged that his fears were exaggerated: "the peoples of the Central Empires possessed a greater power of resistance to the temptations of lawlessness and disorder than was presumed in the winter of 1918–1919," Lansing wrote after his resignation.[14] The Allies thus overestimated the influence of the Reds in Europe and, having seen how easily Lenin's government had ceded territory to the Germans at Brest-Litovsk, underestimated their strength inside Russia. These misperceptions made the Allies' policy toward Russia singularly unsuccessful. Counting on the Whites, fearing a Red revolution in Europe, and declaring Russia irrelevant for the peace, the Allied leaders committed one grave mistake after another.

In Western Europe, hostilities ceased, but the situation in the East was changing with terrifying speed. Exhausted and suddenly very cautious, the great powers could not and did not want to keep up with these changes. Unhappy with Kolchak's monarchic ideas, they stopped giving him aid precisely at the moment when his victory was most likely. When Kolchak was defeated, the British sent a mission to support General Denikin—who was no less a monarchist than Kolchak—but he was also defeated. Nobody expected success from Trotsky and his inexperienced armies, but the sporadic interference and non-interference of the British and American governments certainly contributed to this success.

In their call for world revolution, the Bolsheviks did indeed give Western governments cause for concern. Trotsky's emissaries, including John Reed and Arthur Ransome, did smuggle diamonds and gold to finance the Bolshevik activities in Europe. Echoes of the socialist uprisings in Munich and Budapest could be heard in many European capitals, from London to Rome. By the end of 1919, Trotsky achieved a decisive breakthrough in the war. Bringing revolution to Europe with whips and bayonets, the Red Cavalry launched a victorious offensive in Poland in the summer of 1920. Only the "Miracle on the Vistula," the Polish victory in the Battle of Warsaw, stopped this advance. If Polish Lieutenant Jan Kowalewski had not cracked the Red Cossacks' radio code in late 1919, they would have seized Warsaw and advanced on Berlin, igniting the unrest there. The negotiators in Paris could not have known about these potentialities. Rushing to make peace because of the seeming inevitability of Bolshevik influence in Europe, the Allies missed an opportunity to isolate the revolution in Russia, where it had started.

Writing together in the mid-1920s, Bullitt and Freud reflected on these missed opportunities: Wilson's rejection of a deal with Russia may have been "the most important single decision that he made in Paris," they wrote.[15] Had Bolshevik Russia been reduced to a few provinces around Moscow but recognized as a legitimate state, the entire course of the twentieth century would have been different. Perhaps the USSR would not have emerged and the Stalinist terror would not have happened; perhaps there would have been no Nazi Germany, no Second World War, and no Holocaust. Of course, Moscow's rulers could have disregarded any agreement they signed; at will, they could have resumed the civil war or started a new war in Europe. In 1920, Lenin told a British reporter that when he "proposed a treaty to Bullitt, a treaty which left tremendous amounts of territory to Denikin and Kolchak," he did so only because of his "knowledge that if peace were signed, those Governments could never hold out."[16] But of course nobody then could have had such "knowledge." In 1919, even the Bolsheviks underestimated their own strength, organizational capacity, and the attractiveness of their ideology; so it should come as no surprise that Lloyd George, Clemenceau, and Wilson also underestimated them. The victors of the Great War could do nothing but let the massive, deeply troubled Russian Empire consolidate under the Bolsheviks' radical rule. This crucial mistake shaped the future of the century.

How might international relations have unfolded differently in the 1920s in light of the emergence of a dozen new states in northern Eurasia, all fiercely competing to find trading partners and political allies in Weimar Germany, Japan, France, the new Poland and Turkey, the British Empire, and the United States? This possible world seems far more attractive than what Europe and America actually found after the Versailles treaty. Imagine, for example, a Siberian state, with its huge resources and potential markets, and its prospects as a political ally and trading partner for both the United States and Japan, which were still allies at the time. The Great Depression and Pearl Harbor could have been avoided in this imaginary world. Much else besides would have occurred there, but this is where I stop this little experiment in counterfactual history.

Back in London, Lloyd George reported the results of the Paris talks to the British Parliament. Asked about the secret negotiations with Russia, the prime minister denied he was aware of Bullitt's mission. In response, a few months later on the floor of the American Senate, Bullitt said that Lloyd George was guilty of "the most egregious case of misleading the public."[17] Clemenceau was scared of the Bolshevik "contagion," Lloyd George was afraid of the British conservative press on the eve of elections. But at that moment, in the spring of 1919, both men were enjoying great success. They had managed not only to defeat their enemies on the battlefield but also to convince the international community that it was these same enemies who were responsible for the war. Although France and England had won that war with much help from America and Russia, their diplomatic victory in Paris meant that Clemenceau and Lloyd George reaped most of the rewards. Russia and the United States sacrificed a great deal but received very little in return; all annexations and indemnities went to France and Britain. Freud and Bullitt emphasized Wilson's role in these events, using the strongest imagery they could conjure: "The whole stream of human life may be deflected by the character of a single individual. . . . All life would have been a different thing if Christ had recanted when He stood before Pilate." Blaming Wilson for betraying his own convictions, Freud and Bullitt were unforgiving: "Wilson preached magnificently, promised superbly, then fled. . . . The Western world will not find it easy to wipe from memory the tragic-comic figure of its hero, the President who talked and ran."[18]

On May 17, 1919, Bullitt resigned his post in the State Department, breaking protocol and submitting his resignation directly to Wilson:

I was one of the millions who trusted confidently and implicitly in your leadership. . . . But our Government has consented now to deliver the suffering peoples of the world to new oppressions, subjections, and dismemberments—a new century of war. . . . Russia, "the acid test of good will," for me as for you, has not even been understood. Unjust decisions of the Conference . . . make new international conflicts certain. It is my conviction that the present league of nations will be powerless to prevent these wars, and that the United States will be involved in them. . . . I am sorry that you did not fight our fight to the finish and that you have so little faith in the millions of men, like myself, in every nation who had faith in you.[19]

Bold and touching, it is one of the most eloquent documents in the history of international relations. On the same day Bullitt wrote a letter to House, the man who hired him. He wrote that his resignation was a protest not against the fact that Wilson had ignored his Russian project but against the Versailles treaty as a whole. House asked Bullitt to stay on at the State Department, but Bullitt refused. Wilson did not respond, of course, and Bullitt passed his letter on to the newspapers. The *New York Times* reported him saying that he was heading to the French Riviera and there, lying on the sand, would be watching the world going to hell.

Bullitt received a formal approval of his resignation from Lansing. Although not happy with his subordinate's decision, Lansing was also, like Bullitt, disappointed with the outcome of the Paris talks. Writing about Bullitt's resignation in his memoir, Lansing said that the five leading members of the American delegation had also sent him letters protesting the treaty. Wilson and House shaped their foreign policy staff to fight for a peace that would end all wars, because only this idea could justify America's participation in the war. Unsurprisingly, their staff was unhappy when the treaty fell short of this goal, but Bullitt was the only American who actually resigned over it. According to Bullitt's memo, Lansing told him, smiling: "I really believe that there is very little difference between our points of view on the treaty." When Wilson proclaimed that the League of Nations would correct any shortcomings of the peace, even Lansing objected, noting that because Wilson's charter gave the great powers the right to veto, the League would be helpless were any great power to violate the peace. The League, Lansing said, would not make the world better than the Paris Conference did. He resigned less than a year after Bullitt, in February 1920.[20]

But one member of the British delegation, John Maynard Keynes, made the same choice as Bullitt, and for similar reasons. Keynes quit Paris nine days after Bullitt and explained his decision in his extraordinary work, *Economic Consequences of the Peace* (1919). Keynes depicted the peace conference as a "nightmare"; like Bullitt, he personally blamed Wilson for betraying the peoples of Europe. Keynes also argued, like Bullitt, that Germany and her allies had signed not an unconditional capitulation but a truce that was conditioned on Wilson's Fourteen Points. Moreover, Keynes pondered the fact that, during the Paris talks, the European allies were entirely dependent on American aid for both food and loans. For all his idealism, Wilson had real power over Europe at the end of the war. Keynes was able to demonstrate that Germany would not pay its indemnities because it simply could not. Like Bullitt, Keynes predicted that the peace that had been signed in Versailles would cause a new, bloody war in Europe. And Keynes's response to the "nightmare" of the Paris Peace Conference was also personal and tragic: "A sense of impeding catastrophe overhung the frivolous scene; the futility and smallness of man before the great events confronting him . . . —all the elements of ancient tragedy were there."[21]

Rarely has a political prognosis been more accurate. A witness of the debates in Paris, Keynes suggested that Wilson had not stood a chance against the experienced strategist, Clemenceau, or the ruthless manipulator, Lloyd George. Both these politicians had overwhelmed the American leader, who had been forced to take refuge in his eloquence. Keynes psychoanalyzed Wilson earlier than Freud and Bullitt did, producing similar results: "In the language of medical psychology, to suggest to the President that the Treaty was an abandonment of his professions was to touch on the raw a Freudian complex. It was a subject intolerable to discuss, and every subconscious instinct plotted to defeat its further exploration." Uncharacteristically, Keynes did not temper his feelings about Wilson: "The President was not a hero or a prophet; he was not even a philosopher."[22]

Keynes and Bullitt shared so many insights about Wilson's role in Europe that it is difficult to believe they did not discuss the matter in Paris. In any case, Bullitt published a detailed and glowing review of *Economic Consequences of the Peace*. Keynes was "an authentic master of English language and he has depicted the scene with the skill of a great artist. No more truthful picture has ever been drawn. No more tragic acts have ever been recorded," he wrote.[23] Years later, Bullitt gave a copy of Keynes's book to Freud; it was probably from Keynes that Bullitt and Freud adopted the idea of Wilson's "moral collapse" and garnered some statistical detail about America's leverage over Europe. But Bullitt and Freud produced sharper and more bitter responses to this "collapse"; unlike Bullitt and Freud, Keynes had never been captivated by Wilson, whom he viewed as a hypocrite and a provincial. In his review of Keynes's book, Bullitt compared the Paris Peace Conference to the Congress of Vienna, which decided the fate of Europe after the defeat of Napoleon, and drew an analogy between Wilson and Alexander I, another well-meaning leader who "talked and ran." These three authors, different in so many respects, all regretted that the most intellectual of the American presidents had failed to take advantage of the exceptional situation at the end of the First World War. "Never had a philosopher held such weapons wherewith to bind the princes of this world," Keynes wrote.[24]

The Treaty of Versailles had to be ratified by the US Senate for it to enter into force. The Republicans had a majority at the time. Ratification would provide a non-American body with the right to decide on matters of American military intervention. The Senate guarded its prerogatives ferociously, but Wilson refused to compromise on this point. His popularity was high, and his victory in the war widely admired. In September 1919, the Senate Committee on Foreign Relations invited Bullitt to testify about his trip to Russia and subsequent resignation; one of Wilson's leading detractors, Senator Henry Cabot Lodge, chaired the hearings. As their long exchange revealed, Bullitt and Lodge agreed about the futility of the Versailles treaty, and Lodge was particularly interested in Bullitt's mission to Russia. The members of the Senate committee took delight in hearing about the incompetence of the American delegation to the Paris Peace Conference. According to the official record, "laughter" interrupted this part of the hearings four times. Bullitt accused Lloyd George of dissembling to the British people; divulged private conversations with Secretary of State Lansing; and revealed deep dissatisfaction with his former duties. "The League of Nations at present is entirely useless," said Bullitt, citing Lansing. "The great powers have simply gone ahead and arranged the world to suit themselves."[25]

Moreover, Bullitt recited Lansing's remarks in which the secretary of state described some senators who were present at the hearings. On May 19, 1919, Lansing had told Bullitt in Paris that if the Senate could only understand what the Versailles treaty actually meant, the treaty would have been defeated "unquestionably"; but, according to Lansing, nobody could understand the treaty except Senators Lodge and Knox.[26] On September 12, 1919, Bullitt repeated Lansing's words to a committee hearing in Washington at which Knox and Lodge were present. He cited Lansing as having said that Mr. Lodge would probably understand the treaty but that his "position would become purely political, and therefore ineffective." At this point, the chair of the committee, Senator Lodge, calmed the audience: "I do not mind," he said. After another burst of laughter, Bullitt asked "to be excused from reading any more of these conversations." Senator Frank Brandegee said, "We get the drift," and the committee erupted again. Providing a comic twist to his understanding of what had happened in Paris, Bullitt seemed to deliberately spark a scandal. At the end of the hearings, Knox asked Bullitt what he was going to do next. "I expect to return to Maine and fish for trout, where I was when I was summoned by the committee," Bullitt answered.[27]

He was glad to learn in November that the Senate had failed to ratify the treaty. However, Bullitt's testimony in the Senate had spoiled his relationships with many people in power. During this testimony, Wilson was still president, Lloyd George was British prime minister, and Lansing was secretary of state. Interestingly, Bullitt's revelations did not target Colonel House, who at this point had also lost his faith in Wilson's diplomacy. Shortly after the hearings, Bullitt published a book, *The Bullitt Mission to Russia*, which compiled the documents related to his trip, concluding with the notes of the hearings before the Senate committee. The advertisement for his book read, "If you would know how near the world was to peace with Russia, how Lloyd George, Col. House and others all favored it, how Lenin met all the Paris proposals, and how the whole affair was then abandoned—read Mr. Bullitt's startling testimony that has set two continents talking."[28] In response, the *New York Times* published a long and hostile essay by Edwin James, "The Fall of Bullitt," which accused the former diplomat of excessive ambition and naive trust in the Bolsheviks. Another newspaper clipping, which Bullitt also preserved in his papers, compared him to a typical Henry James protagonist, an ambitious and dishonest American in Europe. In fact, the cosmopolitan, multilingual Bullitt was the opposite of James's provincial fools. An editor of the *Nation*, Lincoln Colcord, wrote to Bullitt on May 29, 1920, that he was pleased by Bullitt's letter to the president and by the fierce discussion that it provoked. Later, on September 16, Colcord lamented the fact that their mutual friends believed Bullitt was a "dishonorable young man. ... I can imagine that you will run into this kind of criticism everywhere in the crowd in New York which calls itself liberal. Don't for Heaven's sake take this seriously."[29]

President Wilson and his beloved creation, the League of Nations, had many enemies. But Bullitt was the first American diplomat to publicly criticize the injustices of the Versailles Treaty and predict that it would lead the world into a new war. Bullitt's testimony helped conservative senators prevent the ratification of the Versailles treaty and the Charter of the League of Nations. The United States did not become a member of the League, and without America the organization was unable to advance peace or prevent war. Although this was not the only factor, Versailles's humiliation of Germany contributed to the next world war. Freud and Bullitt were probably right that Wilson's refusal to consider the Bolshevik peace proposal was the most significant mistake made at the Paris Peace Conference. But the United States learned from its mistakes and eventually ended the Second World War completely differently from the way it had ended the First World War. America and its allies—with the exception of the Soviet Union—refrained from seizing territory and demanding compensation; the Bretton Woods financial system protected the desolated belligerents from postwar inflation; and the Marshall Plan financed the reconstruction of Europe with American money, creating a flourishing though divided Germany. The bitter experience of Versailles inspired these measures, which were decided by veterans of the First World War and the Paris Peace Conference. The generation of Roosevelt, Bullitt, Marshall, and Keynes was determined not to repeat Wilson's mistakes.

In April 1922 Germany and Russia signed a new treaty. Gathering in the Italian town of Rapallo after Mussolini's election, they renounced the Brest-Litovsk Treaty, voided their mutual claims, and pledged to cooperate economically and militarily. The Treaty of Rapallo allowed Germany to avoid some of the harm done by the Versailles treaty because Soviet resources—grain, coal, ore, and oil, among other raw materials—compensated for the loss of Alsace, an important mining and industrial region given to France. After Rapallo, American journalist Herman Bernstein conducted an interview with Walter Rathenau and Bullitt. The head of the German delegation to Rapallo, Rathenau denied that there was a military component to German-Russian cooperation and emphasized the peaceful reconstruction of both countries. Bullitt disagreed; he was confident that Rapallo was a prelude to a military alliance between the two states. "All that the Allies have done with regard to Russia and Germany necessarily forced these two nations to combine." The day would come, Bullitt said, when the Atlantic powers would confront a new coalition of forces: an axis of Germany, Russia, Japan, perhaps China, and parts of the Islamic world. Their conflict with the Atlantic powers within twenty-five or thirty years would be a "situation too terrible to contemplate."[30] The new war would occur, Bullitt prophesied, around 1950. In fact, the Molotov-Ribbentrop Pact was signed, and the new war started much earlier—in 1939.

Many Europeans saw no value in the imperialist ambitions of the First World War, and even less in the Treaty of Versailles. But it was not Bullitt, Keynes, or Rathenau who voiced the most vehement opposition to the Treaty of Versailles. It was Hitler, Mussolini, and Stalin who turned resentment into practical politics. In Tehran and Yalta, President Roosevelt paid close attention to Communist Russia, which President Wilson had refused to take into consideration. But when the next, post–Second World War generation of Russian, European, and American politicians set about dealing with the dismemberment of the socialist bloc, they forgot the lessons of Versailles. Like the First World War, the Cold War ended in the emergence of a revanchist Russian elite, which threatened the world with the prospect of a new war.

6

IT'S NOT DONE

Bullitt resembled, in many ways, his richer but less fortunate peer Jay Gatsby, who came to embody the postwar generation as protagonist of F. Scott Fitzgerald's great novel. "I see Bill Bullitt, in retrospect, as a member of that remarkable group of young Americans . . . for whom the First World War was the great electrifying experience of life," George Kennan wrote in 1972. "They were a striking generation, full of talent and exuberance, determined—if one may put it so—to make life come alive. The mark they made on American culture will be there when many other marks have faded. But in most of them there seems to have been a touch of the fate, if not the person, of the Great Gatsby."[1]

For Kennan, Bullitt's generation derived its talent from the legacy of the First World War. Theirs was not a "lost" generation, as Ernest Hemingway described it. Mourning for friends who perished in the fight fueled a desire to "make life come alive," to revive themselves and the world, to return to a prewar condition. The lasting influence of the war in civil life was one of Fitzgerald's central themes. In *The Great Gatsby*, Jay desperately resists this impact; throughout the novel, he tries to rewind time so that he and Daisy, the woman he loves, can regain their prewar innocence. It does not work. Facing the irreversibility of time, Gatsby is killed, and only the narrator mourns him. To both the protagonist and the reader, the plotline demonstrates that time cannot be reversed, war is irrevocable, and the beloved is not innocent: a mother and the wife of a jealous husband, Daisy is eager for a different kind of relationship—an affair, but not one of love.

Kennan carefully chose a key word to describe how the war affected the Gatsby generation: far from exhausting or paralyzing them, the war was an "electrifying experience" for its survivors. The incomplete revolutions in Europe energized them and gave them hope, while the unjust peace that concluded the war mingled mourning and anger. While fighting in Europe, American soldiers came upon discoveries that addressed civil life in America; after many trials and errors in postwar America, the disappointed survivors returned to the memories of the Great War. Now they mourned not only the loss of human lives but also the loss of humanistic ideas that the war obliterated. Electrified by war, these people failed to realize this energy in peace; as Kennan put it, "they knew achievement more than they knew fulfillment." Their ends were mostly "tragic," wrote Kennan, but their experience was "electrifying"—in other words, both painful and productive.[2]

It so happened that Bullitt published his first novel, *It's Not Done*, in 1925, the same year Fitzgerald published *Gatsby*. Ironically, Bullitt's novel was more successful than Fitzgerald's at the time of publication. The first printing of *Gatsby* totaled just 20,000 copies; *It's Not Done* was rapidly republished many times, selling 150,000 copies. Bullitt's more traditional novel conformed to readers' expectations, making it an easier sell than Fitzgerald's innovative masterpiece. Only during the Depression did *The Great Gatsby* emerge as a complex portrait of the American man, a model through which Kennan and millions of other readers would come to understand the country they had lost. For now it was easier for the public to appreciate Bullitt's novel, which tracked the development of the protagonist from privileged childhood to disappointed maturity in a traditional psychological manner. Emulating the classical realism of Dickens and Balzac, the novel detailed the historical life of the protagonist typical of America's upper-middle-class, East Coast urban elite. During and after the First World War, the United States resembled Bullitt's rapidly changing, strife-filled, lusty Philadelphia rather than Gatsby's Long Island, a playground for the rich and beautiful captured in a rare moment of catharsis and death.

At the center of *It's Not Done* are a dozen families who know one another all too well, and together rule over the large and prosperous city that Bullitt chose to name Chesterbridge. The name has classical connotations (English schools still teach their pupils that cities containing "chester" in their names were established by the Romans) and is a certain allusion to Bullitt's native

Philadelphia. With their inheritances and black servants, the protagonists live luxurious, lazy lives. But to their surprise, they often lose their financial, legal, and even marital battles to the new rich, whom they do not consider "gentlemen." The protagonist's father is a prominent doctor who owns properties in the city and the country. His children have horses; when they grow up they have personal servants. When the son causes trouble at school, his father intervenes and dismisses the teacher; when the mother hints that the sermons at church are too long, the pastor makes them shorter. The family's tough practices are inherited from the good old times. When the son brings home a new friend, the daughter of a French artist, the servants feed her in the kitchen because she is too low-class to enter the living room. If anything threatens to undo the family, it is philanthropy: the family opens a free clinic for blacks and it drains the accounts. These American aristocrats are concerned about the sudden emergence of rivals from the lower classes, but nothing in this idyllic picture warns them of the forthcoming catastrophes of the First World War and the Depression. The central protagonist, journalist John Corsey, is overwhelmed by anxiety about the new century, in which automobiles were replacing horses, department stores ruining nice little shops, movies replacing the theater, and blackmail replacing duels. "The country is running away as fast as it can from every standard it ever had, from every ideal of Washington or Hamilton or even Jefferson. Yes, and of Walt Whitman, too," Corsey remarks.[3] It helps a bit that Corsey's brother-in-law becomes the mayor of Chesterbridge. "We're colonials, that's all, who've made a bit of money and built up our own brand of snobbery," he says in the novel. Corsey's understanding of the local elite is instructive; they are not aristocrats, he says, just snobs. "Not one of them will receive a manufacturer. . . . Can anyone tell me why it's respectable for us to own coal mines and to deal in coal but not to manufacture saws or rope?" (171).

This untitled nobility, owing everything to their ancestors who chose the right time and place to emigrate, nevertheless believe that their own education and virtue secure their well-being. The novel depicts the protagonists from both good and bad families of Chesterbridge falling in love, getting married, committing adultery, and divorcing. Very few of them are happy, least of all John Corsey. His wife prefers social pleasures to his company, and their son leaves for voluntary service in the British army. The novel takes a critical, even satirical view of American society. It depicts the wartime administration in Washington as a helpless bunch of crooks who are easily manipulated by a depraved, witty beauty who spies for Germany. When America entered the war, the patriotic Corsey was a fan of Woodrow Wilson, who told him with tears in his eyes, "I hate this war, I hate all war, and the only thing I care about in life is the peace I'm going to make at the end of it" (263). With time, Corsey grows to detest the Versailles treaty as much as Bullitt.

Bullitt's novel depicts a world that preached, though it did not always practice, family values, good education, and fair competition. The world of *It's Not Done* is one in which election results remain unknown until the last vote is counted; a world in which the editor of a local newspaper could get an audience with the president, or have a prisoner released from the city jail; a world in which the people from the lower classes compete, sometimes successfully, with old money; a world in which Wagner and Schopenhauer come up in small talk; a world that denied women equality but supported their efforts to keep themselves occupied by singing opera, writing book reviews, working in military hospitals, and even spying. Education and prestige had cachet; the author never misses an opportunity to point out who graduated from Princeton and who from Harvard. Corsey's uncle is the president of the University of Chesterbridge (which, we are told, ranked sixth among American universities). Like Bullitt, John Corsey becomes a journalist after failing to finish Harvard Law School, is promoted to editor-in-chief of the local newspaper, and then becomes ambassador to Italy (ten years after writing this novel, Bullitt would become ambassador to France). Corsey has some of Bullitt's biographical traits, but he also resembles Bullitt's older friends, like Steffens. At the end of the novel, however, Corsey becomes a weak, restless man who does not know what to do with his unfaithful wife, corrupt power, and wasted life.

It's Not Done is a psychological novel rather than a bildungsroman. Corsey's maturity brings him major problems. Smart, rich, and lucky, Corsey is unsatisfied in his marriage, though still in love with his wife and too moral to pursue any affairs. The novel suggests that Corsey's emotional problems are symptomatic of his generation, class, and nation—of a new, "modern" condition. Blaming modernity for betraying high moral principles, Corsey is nostalgic for the bygone world satisfied by simple morality. Still, he believes in progress. "We sit up and . . . blame modern life. But you weren't killed by modern life and I wasn't killed by modern life; we were killed by our inherited ideas," he says in conversation with his uncle (370).

Throughout his life Corsey remains in love with two women, the French girlfriend of his youth, who gave birth to his illegitimate son and then left for Europe, and the American wife who (it so happened) fell pregnant almost at the same time as the girlfriend. Both women ultimately reject him, but this double misfortune earns Corsey the attention of both the author and the reader. The novel follows him across three decades, starting from his sensitive adolescence and ending with his frustrated middle age, when, after an attempted suicide, he decamps to Italy. This move conveniently occurs in 1921, so Bullitt's imagination let Ambassador Corsey watch Mussolini come to power and deal with the fallout. But the novel ends shortly before the Mussolini era, giving just a hint of Corsey's involvement in the seminal events of the century. Politics aside, the reader witnesses Corsey's erotic passions, which he usually fails to bring to consummation. Various women—ladies of his circle, his secretaries, or just street prostitutes—continuously tempt him. Sometimes he tries to approach this or that woman, but he shies away at the last moment. Meanwhile, the men around Corsey—his friends, enemies, and even his beloved brother—all indulge in affairs, cheat on their wives, buy sex, divorce, and marry again. Involved in various intrigues, not too scrupulous in his journalism, and increasingly disillusioned in his "principles," Corsey remains sentimental to the end.

In his combination of unscrupulousness in business and unusual selectivity in matters of love, Corsey does indeed look and act like Fitzgerald's Gatsby. Both live among peers engaging in old and new kinds of debauchery, but both remain loyal to the lovers of their youth. For Fitzgerald and Bullitt, their stories exposed the excessive, decorative decadence that their protagonists erroneously took for modernity. Their alienation does not prevent Corsey and Gatsby from participating in the business and politics of modern life; it only stops their participation in social and sexual pleasures, the only realm of modernity in which they both feel vulnerable. When Corsey's son goes off to fight in Europe, Corsey mostly fears that his son would pick up a disease from European women. He attempts to talk to his son about the need for precautions, but the words fail him. His son would be killed in battle.

If anyone in Bullitt's fictional world knew how Chesterbridge really worked and what could help it, it was doctors like Corsey's father. His best friend is also a doctor, who interprets Corsey's little diseases as manifestations of one big problem, his sexual dissatisfaction. The diagnosis is unmistakably Freudian: "You will never let yourself feel right about anything short of marriage with a girl your mother approves of. And you will want her to be a virgin nymphomaniac. Unfortunately, they do not exist" (98). Corsey's mother is confident that he would never deliberately publish a lie or blackmail, if only because he is a gentleman of Chesterbridge. In the course of the novel Corsey betrays those expectations, but he religiously follows his mother's rules about women.

The author persistently depicts the conflicts between Corsey's ideas about sexuality and "modern life," and the reader feels that this is the author's unresolved question, the "it" that's "not done."

But women are not the only threat to the fashionable world of Chesterbridge, however much the town operates like a gentlemen's club. Coming from the best family of this booming but still provincial town, Corsey observes the unprincipled parvenus capturing power, wealth, and influence. A permanent theme of the novel is the failure of people from good families who lose their old money to the more cynical nouveau riche. One example comes in the form of a casual acquaintance from Corsey's youth, the son of a drunken manufacturer, who finishes college, turns into a journalist and businessman, becomes the indispensable deputy editor of Corsey's newspaper, and wins the sympathy of Corsey's wife. The war intensified the generational conflict, and when it concluded, new people like Gatsby claimed Corsey's women and assets.

Bullitt's novel tragically culminates in the death of Corsey's son in battle after he volunteers to join the British army well before America enters the war. Mourning him, Corsey manages to save his illegitimate son, Raoul, from jail. Raoul, who grew up in France, has come to America as a socialist agitator. Calling himself a Bolshevik, he is imprisoned in Chesterbridge after lecturing to striking miners about the Soviet constitution. Corsey does not share his interest in this subject, but he does see irony in the fact that the last heir to the bourgeois Corseys is a Communist. During the war, Corsey makes a second career as an intelligence officer in Washington, where he exposes (and sometimes shields) the German spies embedded in the federal government.

At the end of the novel, Corsey admits that he feels closer to the ancient Greece he studied in school than to the generation returning from war. These young veterans brought with them new technologies, new money, and a tectonic shift in tastes and values. "Paris has become a suburb of New York, London is trying to become one." But instead of accepting this new responsibility, the privileged Americans from Chesterbridge abhor it: "We are brought up in the age of horses.... Happiness to you and me is quiet country beauty," Corsey tells his uncle while they sit in the police station trying to rescue Raoul from prison (370). Corsey cautiously acknowledges the possibility that his pro-Bolshevik son, Raoul, could be right: "The whole world has passed into the new machine age and you and I are as alien to it as if we were fifth-century Athenians," his uncle says, to which Corsey responds, "And all we have to look forward to is Raoul's world. Communism! But who in hell knows anything!" (371).

Corsey is more conservative than his author, who ironically shows how Corsey misunderstands the new French art practiced by his girlfriend. But the novel's struggle to resolve issues of love, family, and sexuality in a postwar world of capitalism and Cubism is a problem that Corsey and Bullitt both share. The theme is a common one in the great literature of the late nineteenth and early twentieth century, explored by Tolstoy, Freud, Joyce, and Fitzgerald. Despite the half century separating them, Tolstoy's Karenin would find much in common with Corsey; and his wife, Anna, would probably feel at home in the salons of Chesterbridge and Washington as Bullitt described them. Even the title of *It's Not Done* refers to the mainstream tradition of Russian socialism. The title is Bullitt's response to the bible of Russian radicalism, Nikolai Chernyshevsky's novel *What Is to Be Done?* In his novel Chernyshevsky calls for social protest by focusing not on economic inequality but on the unresolved issues of family and sexuality, on the impossibility of divorce, on the woman question, and prostitution. He offers hazy solutions—such as the organization of a sewing cooperative for street girls or emigrating to America for unhappy husbands. It was not these recipes that brought Chernyshevsky's novel its fame, but a timely question: What is to be done? Writing from across the ocean half a century later, Bullitt offered an oblique, somewhat bitter reply: It's not done.

7

WIVES

After the Senate hearings, Bullitt went back to Maine to catch trout and had no regrets about his scandalous revelations. In a private letter to Nancy Astor, the American woman who later became the first female member of the British Parliament, Bullitt explained the reasons for his resignation using lofty arguments not dissimilar to Wilson's rhetoric: "I am not at all surprised that you were horrified by my testimony. Yet I am certain that if you had been in my place you would have done just what I did—only more. . . . I knew well that if I did give a full account of the Russian business I would be hated bitterly. . . . I knew that I should throw away [the] chance of a normal, advancing political career—such as most of your friends will have." Lying to the Senate was as unacceptable to him as lying under oath to the court, he wrote. Still, Astor was appalled by Bullitt's testimony.[1]

Retracing Bullitt's unorthodox path begs the same question that he asked himself: Are we right to put faith in those who lie about the past, cheat in the present, and are confused by the future? Philip Kerr, a mutual friend of Astor and Bullitt, did not correct his boss, British prime minister Lloyd George, when Lloyd George told the House of Commons he had heard nothing about secret negotiations with the Bolsheviks. The prime minister lied as if under oath, and Kerr knew it. As Lloyd George's personal secretary, Kerr had helped Bullitt prepare his mission, for which he had received Lloyd George's approval.

Kerr went on to have a "normal, advancing" career and later became the British ambassador to the United States and a member of the House of Lords.

Bullitt's testimony did not entirely destroy his career: he returned to public service thirteen years after this event. Still, Bullitt's early resignation was so unusual for a public figure that it surprised even his brother. An experienced surgeon who spent years collecting and publishing Bill's letters, Orville Bullitt later wrote that Bill was an "idealist with a strong feeling for the romantic [who] liked to dramatize his purpose."[2] Bill's first biographer, Orville understood that his brother's idealist feelings and dramatic foresights were by far more rewarding than those of his friends and enemies with more conventional careers.

Bullitt tried and failed to find consolation in his wife, Ernesta—"a striking beauty with dark hair, brilliant eyes, and a slender figure," as Orville described her.[3] After Bullitt's resignation, the couple bought an apple farm near Ashville, Massachusetts. They refurbished the attic into a large living room and added a few bedrooms in the old barn. For a while, they socialized happily and arranged musical parties for their friends. In 1923 they divorced. Bill passionately wanted a child, but Ernesta miscarried. They had other problems, which Bullitt portrayed in his novel *It's Not Done*. In the novel the wife of the protagonist, a cold but sociable beauty, has lost interest in her husband. The conflict is damaging to both husband and wife, but in the novel the couple finds their way to reconciliation, unlike Ernesta and Bill.

Divorce in their social circle was rare. Ernesta's good conduct was beyond doubt, but Bill's reputation became even more scandalous. While the protagonist of *It's Not Done* was painfully faithful to his wife, Bullitt often sought and easily found the company of women, usually those of high society. His talent for friendship applied to women as well as men: his love affairs, short and long, often turned into friendships that lasted for decades.

In 1922 Bullitt began an affair with Eleanor Medill Patterson, one of the richest American heiresses, known as Cissy. Their relationship was short-lived; Bill was almost ten years younger than Cissy and was still married to Ernesta. Yet Cissy wrote that Bill was the most attractive of the men she met, "at least to me."[4] They both were considering writing novels. Her novel, *Glass Houses*, was published in February 1926, a little before Bullitt's novel, *It's Not Done*; both works drew upon their relationship. They also shared an unusual interest in Russia. Cissy's second novel, *Fall Flight* (1928), depicted the royal court and high society of St. Petersburg. She also wrote for newspapers; her Chicago family, the Medills, owned a significant portion of the American press.

In the early twentieth century, Washington, DC, entertained the gossip about the "three Graces" who reigned at the balls of the capital: Alice Roosevelt, Cissy Patterson, and Marguerite Cassini. Alice was the daughter of President Theodore Roosevelt; Marguerite was the daughter of Count Arthur Cassini, the ambassador of the Russian Empire to the United States; Cissy was the heiress of the Medill family, one of the wealthiest families in the country. Her life story was quite unusual and no less cosmopolitan than Bullitt's. In 1904 she married, against the wishes of her parents, the Polish-Russian count Joseph Gizycki (1867–1926). The count proposed in St. Petersburg, where Cissy was visiting her uncle Robert McCormick, the US ambassador to Russia. Gizycki was a Russian officer and the owner of two vast, mortgaged estates in Ukraine—"halfway from Warsaw to Odessa," as Americans situated them.[5] After her wedding, Cissy, like all American women who married foreigners before 1922, was deprived of her American citizenship and became a Russian subject. The Gizyckis remained at their Ukrainian estate in Volyn until the autumn of 1905, when they moved to Vienna because of popular unrest and cholera epidemics in Ukraine. They had a daughter, and both loved horse races and hunting in the grand English style. After four years of marital life, Gizycki beat her, and Cissy ran away bleeding. The count did not give Cissy access to their daughter until President Taft wrote a touching letter to Nicholas II, asking him to intervene. Appealing to the Austrian judge, Gizycki demanded compensation of four hundred thousand rubles; in the end, he gave their child to Cissy in exchange for a regular subsidy from her parents.

Tall, red-haired, with a pale face and widely set eyes, Cissy Patterson looked as though she had stepped out of a John Singer Sargent or Valentin Serov painting. Her excellent figure, poisonous wit, and wicked reputation were magnetic. After her miserable years in Ukraine, Cissy was still proud to own a black pearl necklace that had belonged to the tsar's niece, Irina Yusupova (whose husband, Felix, succeeded in murdering Rasputin). In fact, Cissy's life was always complicated. For a while she was in love with her cousin, Medil McCormick, who entered therapy with Karl Jung at his Swiss clinic in March 1909. Jung also counseled her then. Later, she had an affair with Johann von Berstorff, the German ambassador to the United States (1908–1917), and they continued seeing each other even after the United States entered the First World War (Bullitt depicts a similar love story on the edge of espionage in *It's Not Done*). A little later, Cissy had an affair with Nicholas Longworth, the husband of her friend Alice Roosevelt (Longworth later became the Speaker of the House of Representatives). Cissy's affair with Bullitt followed all this.

There were rumors that Bill even proposed marriage to her but was refused. Another rumor suggests their relationship was periodically renewed, even after Bill's second marriage.

Their extensive correspondence, as Bullitt preserved it, sounds business-like. Cissy Patterson took ownership of the *Washington Herald* in 1930, becoming the only woman in America to be the chief editor of a major newspaper. Unlike Bill, Cissy was an opponent of America's involvement in the Second World War. She attacked Bullitt for pulling Roosevelt into the war, both in her private letters and in public in her newspaper. Later, in the early 1940s, Roosevelt suspected that Bullitt used his friendship with Patterson to discredit a rival. This could be true: Bullitt used women, and the newspapers called Cissy the most powerful woman in America.

In December 1923 Bullitt married Louise Bryant, the widow of John Reed. The choice was extraordinary. Louise was six years older than Bill but he didn't know it; she lied about her age. He understood all too well, however, that Louise belonged to a different world. The daughter of a Pittsburgh miner, Louise grew up in Nevada and graduated from the University of Oregon, where she wrote a thesis in American history. She went on to teach in a modest school in a California town and was connected to the women's suffrage movement. Orville Bullitt remembered Louise as a woman of extraordinary talent and beauty; he mentioned her "large luminous eyes."[6] Still, the marriage of Bill and Louise was incredible.

Louise had been married twice before, first briefly and then, famously, to John Reed. "As American as apple pie," as Bertram Wolfe put it, Reed had just graduated from Harvard, where he created the Socialist Club together with his classmate Walter Lippmann and competed with another classmate, T.S. Eliot.[7] Jack, as his friends called him, lived in Greenwich Village, worked for his father's friend the journalist Lincoln Steffens, and was entertained by the lioness of Village society, Mabel Dodge (a millionaire's widow, eight years older than Reed, she was his lover for a while). Jack published in the monthly *Metropolitan*, where his stories about the Mexican Revolution appeared beside the latest works by Kipling and Conrad; the magazine touted Reed as the "American Kipling." He later worked for the journal of the extreme left, *The Masses*, whose editor, Max Eastman, would go on to become the translator and literary agent of Trotsky. Through *The Masses*, Reed met Louise Bryant, an enthusiastic reader and radical activist. The couple lived a bohemian life; almost immediately, Louise developed a whirlwind affair with Eugene

O'Neill, later a famous playwright. But they practiced free love, and the couple married in August 1916.

Eastman wanted a correspondent in revolutionary Russia. In the summer of 1917 he raised money for such a mission from Wall Street capitalists; Jack and Louise both went to Petrograd. He wrote for *The Masses* about the hunger in Russia and the helplessness of the Provisional Government. She interviewed leaders from Kerensky to Trotsky and was intensely interested in the women of revolution: the "grandmother of the Russian Revolution" Breshkovskaya, already well known in America; the rebellious Spiridonova; and the seductive Kollontai. In November, Jack and Louise witnessed the occupation of the Winter Palace in Petrograd, which marked the beginning of the Bolshevik Revolution. Reed became close to Trotsky, worked in the People's Commissariat of the Enlightenment, and gave a memorable speech at the Second All-Russian Congress of the Soviets, in which he promised the Bolsheviks the support of American workers. In January 1918 Trotsky appointed Reed to be Soviet consul in New York. Both hoped that the United States would speedily recognize the Bolshevik government, but this would not happen until fifteen years later.

Back in America Jack and Louise each wrote a book about their revolutionary experience: Jack's was called *Ten Days That Shook the World*, Louise's was called *Six Red Months in Russia*. Both books were successful but did not bring in much income. However, between their apartment in Greenwich Village and their farm in Croton-on-Hudson, they lived a comfortable life. Louise brought back furs, shawls, and high boots from Russia; she loved to dress brightly and exotically—they called it the "Russian style" in Manhattan. The ascetic Emma Goldman, the star of the American left, remarked that Louise was not a Communist herself, she only slept with a Communist.[8]

Reed helped create the Communist Labor Party of America, which was meant to be very different from the Communist Party of America, its rival for official recognition by the Bolsheviks. In the spring of 1920 Reed again sailed to Russia in hopes of securing recognition of his party by the Communist International. The Comintern not only agreed with his arguments but also donated 102 diamonds to Reed's Communist Labor Party. Carrying these diamonds, a false passport, and Lenin's preface to the new edition of the *Ten Days*, Reid was arrested in Finland. Some New York newspapers reported his execution (later, they denied it). Jack spent three months in solitary confinement before he was released to Petrograd. He wrote to tell Louise that he was dying and begged her to come. Amazingly, she did, also carrying forged documents. From the United States, she first sailed to Sweden and then to Murmansk, which was still occupied by the Allies. There, she crossed the front line and, miraculously, arrived safely in Petrograd. By then, however, Jack was on his way to Baku, where he was to take part in the Bolshevik Congress of the Peoples of the East. "There is nothing that Uncle Sam gives for free. He comes with a sack of oats in one hand and with a whip in another hand. Who believes in his promises pays with blood," he said in Baku.[9] While there, Reed got into a conflict with a ruthless leader of the Comintern, Grigory Zinoviev. Later, Bullitt—likely relying on what Louise told him—wrote that during this last month of his life, Reed was severely disappointed with the Comintern and the Bolsheviks. He also contracted typhus and returned to Moscow sick.

Louise found Jack in Moscow on September 15, 1920. A month later, he died in her arms, a hero of the American and international Left. Reed was buried in the Kremlin wall with unprecedented honors and remains the only American interred there. "Courage" was the key word in the stories about the young, prosperous man who told the world about the Russian Revolution, and his wife who stayed with him in life and death. Very few had learned of Reed's conflict with Zinoviev and his disillusionment with the Soviets; Reed's biographers were mostly sympathetic to the Left and did not trust this allegation.[10]

After Jack's death Louise remained in Moscow, where she cabled reports to the American newspapers almost daily. In 1921 she made a pilgrimage to the Soviet East—like Jack had done before her, but with more success. For two months she traveled through the Kazakh steppes and Turkestan, interviewing the activists, observing the life of local women, and cabling her reports to America. She was the only Western journalist to visit those places in the early 1920s. In Central Asia Louise began an affair with Enver Pasha, an Ottoman officer who had masterminded the Armenian genocide and now advocated an alliance between Bolshevism and Islam; a year after their short romance he was killed in battle with Red Army cavalry.

In the spring of 1921 Louise returned to America. This was no simple matter, given that the State Department knew she had left the country under a false name and passport. The following year she again sailed to Moscow to collect material for her new book, *Mirrors of Moscow*, which featured an interview with Felix Dzerzhinsky, organizer of the Soviet apparatus of terror.[11]

In 1922 Max Eastman, editor of *The Masses* and Louise's employer, followed her to Moscow. After spending two years in revolutionary Russia, he wrote a romantic travelogue, *Love and Revolution,* and married Elena

Krylenko, the sister of the future chief prosecutor of the Moscow show trials, Nikolai Krylenko. Upon his return to the United States, Eastman published *Lenin's Testament*, in which Lenin named Trotsky his heir and severely criticized Stalin. In the 1930s, Eastman had been working as Trotsky's literary agent and translator. He and Elena were living happily in New York while her brother was busy accusing his hapless, tortured victims of Trotskyism, high treason, and contacts with foreigners. As one might expect, Nikolai Krylenko was arrested in 1938 and, after a ten-minute trial, executed. One might also expect that his Trotskyite brother-in-law, Max Eastman, gradually became disappointed in Marxism and, like Bullitt, turned into a Cold War hawk.

"President Roosevelt, Jack Reed and I—we are of the same blood," Bullitt told a journalist in 1933. The tragic fate of Jack Reed had a particular meaning for Bullitt. Witnessing the Russian Revolution and dying a heroic death in Moscow had turned Reed into a hero of the Left, a model of courage and determination. Going to Moscow, meeting Lenin, and trying to stop Russia's catastrophe, Bullitt could have hoped to win Jack Reed's friendship, or even to surpass Reed's writings with real deeds. But Bullitt's Russian mission failed, and Reed's death ended their short-lived rivalry. The two men were often mentioned together by their contemporaries, and sometimes these comments suggest that Bullitt felt inferior around Reed, something that was unusual for Bullitt. His brother quoted Bullitt writing in February 1918: "I wish I could see Russia with as simple an eye as Reed. I am unable to win through the welter of conflicting reports about the Bolsheviks to anything like a solid conviction." Immediately after this citation, Orville Bullitt wrote: "During his entire life Bill never had a sense of inferiority in his personal relations."[12]

John Reed was emblematic of the generation electrified by the First World War. When Kennan compared Bullitt to these peers he listed several outstanding persons who also met "frustrated and sometimes tragic end[s]."[13] Though all were frustrated at some points, and some eventually committed suicide, they all lived to old age. Only Reed's death was truly tragic, a heroic death of a young man who fought for his ideas in a distant land and sacrificed himself for a foreign people.

In *It's Not Done*, Bullitt ascribes Louise's features to a French woman with whom young Corsey, the protagonist of the novel, shares moments of passion. They soon part, and she gives birth to their son, who grows up to be a socialist agitator and sounds a lot like Reed. At the end of the novel, this son is arrested for inciting a strike, and Corsey and his friends bail him out from the American jail, as in real life Bullitt and his friends bailed out George Andreychin (see Chapter 9). But even after saving his son from prison, Corsey cannot bring himself to feel close to him. The whole novel feels like the author's reflection on a feeling of inferiority, as he grapples with the new generation of Americans, who might prefer Jack Reed to Bill Bullitt.

Harold Stearns, an American who lived for years at the expense of his countrymen in Paris (he is believed to be the prototype for Harvey Stone in Hemingway's *The Sun Also Rises*), said of Bullitt: "Bill was intelligent, friendly, rich—yet sometimes he made me uncomfortable, and I think it was what used to be a curious inferiority complex. I mean, Bill envied what he couldn't have been, even had he tried, for he had too much money...—that is, a Bohemian."[14] Did Bill really have such a complex, and did this inferiority underlie his complicated feeling toward Jack Reed? Some mutual friends explained Bullitt's second marriage this way.

Bullitt married Louise Bryant three years after Reed's death. Ernesta did not give her consent for this divorce for a long time, so Bill and Louise lived in sin in Istanbul. By the time Ernesta agreed to divorce Bill, Louise was pregnant, and the wedding ceremony was held in secret. Louise was collecting material for a book about the new Turkey. She was particularly interested in the status of women and the role of religion. As in Russia, Louise solicited meetings with top officials: the woman who had interviewed Lenin and Mussolini wished to secure an interview with Ataturk. The couple rented an old sixteenth-century mansion on the Bosporus with fresco ceilings; they seemed happy. A visiting friend, the American sculptor George Biddle, described their relationship as a "passionate love affair." He wrote that they definitely had common interests—for example, both were "very serious about Russia."[15] Despite all this, Biddle did not believe the couple was fit for family life. "Bill's friends always discounted much of what he said; at most, fifty percent of it could not be taken seriously," he said of Bullitt. As for Louise, Biddle knew that "Jack Reed was the real love of Louise's life, and she talked a lot about Jack. Instead of minding it, Bill seemed to make Reed *his* love mystique, too."[16] George's brother, Francis Biddle, the future attorney general, would later handle the couple's divorce.

Loyal to the "love mystique" of Jack Reed, theirs was an ideological marriage. Although Louise's charm, talent, and radicalism were beyond doubt, the fact that she was Reed's widow was important to Bullitt. Marrying the widow of an American insider of the Russian Revolution, Bullitt symbolically brought Reed back to life, gave them both the opportunity for a new friendship. Bullitt's second marriage did not bring him money or connections, but it did move him to the center of the international Left. The Bullitts' views at this moment were markedly different from what Reed had believed in 1920, however. Since the Paris Peace Conference, Bullitt saw the moderate Left as the only force that could prevent catastrophe in postwar Europe. In political terms, Louise remained to the left of Bill, particularly where women's rights were concerned. This unusual family adopted the memory of Jack Reed and worshiped Lincoln Steffens as a common, symbolic father. But they were not more radical or more bohemian than their Parisian contemporaries, who included F. Scott Fitzgerald with his wife, Zelda, Ernest Hemingway, Harold Stearns, and their drinking buddies.

A few years prior, in Istanbul, Hemingway had unsuccessfully courted Louise and gossiped about her in his letters from Paris. Together, their circle enjoyed the cheap Paris and its distance from Prohibition-era America. On Sundays, the Bullitts served lunch in their chic apartment, with their Basque chef and Albanian barman catering to their guests. With his typical anti-Semitism, Hemingway wrote about Bullitt as a half-Jew, though the two men regularly played tennis and attended horse races together nonetheless.[17] Bill was an expert in horses and made the right bets, which impressed Hemingway. The Bullitts had much in common with the Fitzgeralds. The husbands wrote novels that would compete on the American market. The wives, both southerners and journalists, were brilliant, but both contracted serious and unusual diseases quite early on. If Fitzgerald's *Great Gatsby* could be read as a novel about Bullitt, *Tender Is the Night* could be read as a novel about Bryant (in fact, it is a precise clinical history of Zelda Fitzgerald). Despite all this, Fitzgerald and Bullitt became neither friends nor foes. Bullitt was a stranger to modernist experiments, Fitzgerald's specialty. But Bullitt eagerly socialized with fashionable artists; in 1931, he traveled across France together with Henri Matisse.[18]

In Istanbul, Bill and Louise had adopted a child, ten-year-old Refik, the son of a noble Turkish family whose parents had been killed in the war. He lived with them in Paris and, at some point, impressed Hemingway with his ability to throw knives. He would go on to attend school in Massachusetts—he grew up American. After Refik's adoption, the couple conceived their daughter, Anna, who was born in February 1924 in Paris. Lincoln Steffens came to be with the couple at her birth.

In 1928 Louise Bryant fell ill with a strange disease. Painful swellings developed under the skin on various parts of her body. Surgically removed, they tended to reappear. The condition, known as Dercum disease, is still incurable.

Louise drank more and more often. Doctors explained that this was a side effect of the disease, but alcoholism was common among the Americans who sought adventure in Paris. Various doctors, including the Philadelphian Francis Dercum himself, treated Louise, but her condition only worsened. Louise and Bill often quarreled, torturing each other with mutual jealousy.

They lived together for about six years. Winters they spent in a rented apartment in Paris, summers at Bullitt's farm in Ashville. The farm had horses; Bill was a good horseman and particularly loved jumping. In the fall of 1926, he fell from his horse and blamed the fall on his unconscious death wish, which he had read about in psychoanalytic books. In a letter to a friend, he wrote that because of this fall, he had realized that only Sigmund Freud could help him.[19] His conflicts with Louise were probably another motivation for his desire for analysis. Thus, Bullitt visited Freud in Vienna the same winter. To his delight, he learned that the famous Viennese professor remembered his name from the time of the Treaty of Versailles.

Psychoanalytic ideas were then becoming increasingly popular among American intellectuals. Bullitt's left-wing friend Max Eastman, the former editor of *The Masses* who became Trotsky's translator, wrote that Freud was his teacher "in many things" and his "Father Confessor." Eastman also visited Freud in 1926 and found him "smaller" than he thought, "slender-limbed, and more feminine." They talked about the unconscious and about America, which inadvertently brought them to the First World War: "You should not have gone into war at all," said Freud. "Your Woodrow Wilson was the silliest fool of the century, if not of all centuries." Eastman thought that Freud was "both a scientist and demonologist," but he did not tell him that, nor did Bullitt. Freud charmed these young American visitors; their experiences were very distant from his, but he knew how to challenge and inspire them. He wanted Eastman, who was busy writing about Russia, to write about America, and even suggested the title for a future book: *The Miscarriage of American Civilization.*[20] Freud's initial approach to Bullitt was very similar.

After several consultations, Bill decided that Freud's psychoanalytic method would help him settle his relationship with Louise. In a letter dated February 19, 1928, sent to Louise who was in the sanatorium in Baden-Baden, Bill outlined a detailed plan of treatment: "You have a neurosis which is just as definite a disease as appendicitis. And you have Dercum's disease. That you will finish off at Baden. The neurosis you will get rid of with Freud. There is in my mind not the slightest doubt but that you will be entirely well by next

autumn. . . . When you get rid of your neuroses you will want me, I am absolutely sure."[21]

Bullitt still hoped to save their marriage, but he could not hide his anxiety.
He wanted to help Louise, but Freud would start with himself. Those who
knew him offered alternative explanations for this analysis. Sculptor George
Biddle said that "Bullitt's phobias were many and powerful." Writer Vincent
Sheean believed that Freud treated Bullitt in "a very long analysis" that dealt
with "Bill's intricate muddle of complexities and silliness."[22]

On December 7, 1928, Bill sent a long letter to Louise: "For some reason or
other, you seem to need tension and disputes and explanations. It is no good.
Particularly by mail. I would have much preferred to have been hit by a taxi
[the] night before rather than have received your telegram." In the telegram
in question, Louise accused Bill of dining with a certain young woman—"Rami"—too often; Bill responded by using psychoanalytic language that
seems to be his primary means of private communication in this period.

> Unfortunately, I am still so dependent on you emotionally that you can
> destroy me. And you always do. Perhaps you take as your model the disputes
> you imagine took place between your father and your mother when you were
> a small child. Next time please try to remember that I am neither your father
> nor your mother. . . . It is all really dumb and makes me more than ever
> realize that the only salvation for me is to achieve indifference. Nothing on
> earth could be harder for me to do than that, but you make it absolutely
> necessary. I cannot endure the business of feeling very close to you and then
> having you bang me over the head. You always bang me on the head, so the
> only answer is not to feel close to you. Perhaps, fundamentally, that would
> suit you much better.[23]

Bullitt loved good manners, and one could imagine that he did suffer from his
wife's alcoholism and bursts of jealousy. His therapy with Freud, if there was
a therapy, was short-term; Bullitt was satisfied and wished Louise would
undergo the same treatment: "I would have nothing more to do with your
analysis than you had to do with mine. . . . He only takes two persons in summer and it would be an extraordinary piece of luck if he should be willing to
take you. He would only do it because he really likes you and myself." He really
hoped Freud would help, and he wished Louise to want the same thing. "You
may be sure that he will refuse unless he is certain that he can cure you and

that you need the analysis profoundly." Louise was concerned that Freud would be prejudiced against her, and in response Bullitt wrote her: "I used to say to Freud that you were the most normal person I had ever known." He was trying to convince her that "the drinking is just a symptom—it is not at the bottom of the neurosis." He could not absolve himself from this therapy, but he tried and tried: "I can't help you to find the baby experiences and you cannot find them by yourself. Freud can help you to find them, but it will be your own intelligence and your own will that will do the work. I am enormously glad that at least you will go and talk to him."[24]

Louise postponed her visit to Freud, but Bullitt continued trying to persuade her. His main argument was Freud's success with his own analysis. On April 6, 1929, Bill wrote to Louise: "perhaps in a very few days with Freud you might get down to something immensely useful. After all it only took me about two days to discover that Ernesta represented Jack [Reed] and to lose all neurotic feeling about her. You might discover the root of your feeling about drink just as quickly." This striking confession reveals how Freud understood what drove Bullitt from one failed marriage to another. His identification with John Reed—his role model, the former husband of his wife, and the source of his feelings of inferiority—was the center of his therapy with Freud. One need not be a psychoanalyst to discern the identification and substitution that determined Bullitt's marriage to Reed's widow. Indeed, that's how their strange marriage was understood everywhere, from conservative Philadelphia to leftist New York and to drunken American Paris. Louise and Bill openly discussed their feelings for Jack, their memory of him, and his impact on their lives. But judging from this letter, Freud took a more radical step: he discerned Reed's influence in Bullitt's marriage to Ernesta. According to Freud, Ernesta also "represented" Jack to Bill, and this identification was the source of Bullitt's "neurotic" desire. Sculptor George Biddle detected "love mystique" in Bullitt's feelings toward Reed; Freud saw in Bill's passion for his male friend, the hero and victim of the revolution, both ideological and erotic dimensions. Bullitt claimed that this interpretation helped him to get rid of his "neurotic feeling" toward Ernesta: from this we know that Bullitt agreed with Freud's idea and that Bryant was aware of it.

Bill's passion for the cold aristocratic Ernesta did not vanish after his marriage to the temperamental, exotic Louise. His novel, *It's Not Done*, portrays this situation in detail: the protagonist, also a journalist and diplomat, cannot act on his unrequited longing for his beautiful but cold-hearted wife. Louise's friend Kitty Cannell, whom Bullitt sometimes took out for dinners in Paris together with Louise, said that Bullitt's actual problem was impotence, and this problem brought him to Freud. "Another thing," Connell said, was that Louise was a feminist, and "the marriage itself began to seem hollow to her. I began to feel that she thought of it as a threat to her identity. Perhaps that was why she fantasized [about] Jack even more obsessively."[25] This sounds more plausible than impotence: Louise fought for her independence from Bill, and both of them thought about Jack obsessively. Freud's interpretation focused on the importance of an idealized image of Reed, as a rival and internalized mediator, in Bullitt's world. Perhaps Freud talked to Bullitt about a latent homoerotic desire and explored how this desire contributed to the destruction of his first marriage, shaped his second marriage, and was now threatening to destroy it. Discussions of this latent desire and its manifestations left a perceptible imprint on Freud and Bullitt's joint work on Wilson's biography.

Freud's meeting with Louise Bryant was finally scheduled for April 23, 1929. According to the plan, Freud and Bryant would meet several times and then agree on the duration of the treatment. Bullitt would pay the expenses. On April 16, Louise sent a letter to Bill from Baden-Baden; she had talked to Freud, and she was going to travel to Vienna and asked Bill to send her money. But then the correspondence breaks off; she probably never did go to visit Freud after all.

For Bill, Louise's failure to comply with his plan for psychoanalysis was the last straw. In September they met in New York, but Louise was so drunk that he checked her into the hospital. While she was there, Bullitt perused her private letters and found her correspondence with the sculptor Gwendolyn Le Gallienne, which alluded to a homosexual relationship between the two women. In December 1929, while Louise was again in the Baden-Baden sanatorium, Bill began divorce proceedings in Philadelphia, accusing his wife of lesbianism. His archived testimony blames Louise for alcoholism, sexual "perversion," and for having a detrimental influence on their daughter. The court, chaired by Francis Biddle, awarded Bill a divorce and gave him full custody of his daughter, Anna. Bullitt wrote to Louise to inform her of the court's decision, writing that it was "a horrible defeat, the worst defeat I have ever had in my life. But it is a defeat and we won't make matters better by closing our eyes to the fact."[26] She long suspected him of hiring a detective to follow her; he denied it.

Bullitt never married again. An elegant bachelor, he had multiple relations with women after the divorce. He did not see Louise and did not allow her to see Anna. For the rest of her life, he regularly sent her money. For a while,

Louise openly lived in Paris with Gwendolyn Le Gallienne, setting new standards of bohemian life. The two separated a year later, in 1931, after Louise accused Gwen of trying to poison her. She was constantly looking for a chance to see her daughter, but Bill would not allow visits.

Louise's last passion was, strikingly, piloting airplanes: she took lessons, learned to fly and used to fly alone, without an instructor, over Paris. She began many literary ideas and projects but soon stopped working on all of them except the one most important to her: the biography of Jack Reed. But again, Bill turned out to be an obstacle: the relevant documents were in his possession, and he did not wish to deliver them. Still, the last years of Louise's life were dedicated to her return to Reed. In 1934 a Marxist graduate of Harvard, Granville Hicks, began to work on Reed's biography.[27] Louise helped him but also suspected him of informing on her. John Reed's memory was inspiring and divisive to the end.

8

FREUD'S COAUTHOR
AND SAVIOR

The late 1920s was the time of Bullitt's midlife crisis, which coincided with the horrible events in America and Europe that, he felt, were materializing his worst expectations. His career was stuck, his family had collapsed, and his novel was quickly forgotten. In this spirit, Bullitt wrote his second novel, *The Divine Wisdom*. Based on Freud's ideas about incest, religion, and the origins of humanity, *The Divine Wisdom* applied them to a modern though exotic situation. The action is largely set in Istanbul but begins in St. Petersburg. Peter Rives, an American steel and railroad magnate, falls in love with Ursula Dundas, the daughter of the American ambassador to the Russian Empire. Ursula, described as cold and beautiful, was based on Bullitt's first wife, Ernesta. In the novel Peter and Ursula marry and, for some time, live happily together with Anna, Peter's daughter from his first marriage. Then Ursula starts an affair with a British diplomat, and she tells her husband. The betrayal shakes Peter, and he is estranged physically from his wife. When he finds out that she is pregnant, he knows that this is not his child. Wanting to save face, he accepts the child as his own but divorces Ursula.

The divorce has a profound impact on Peter: he becomes devoutly religious. Obsessed with stamping out immoral behavior, this newly formed Puritan begins lobbying for harsh laws aimed at redeeming America. His children grow up separately—Anna with her father and David with his mother. Both children participate in the First World War: David serves as an officer and

Anna as a nurse. After the war, they accidentally meet in Istanbul, when an assassin wounds David and Anna nurses him back to health. They fall in love, but then they find out they are brother and sister. Anna learns about Ursula's adultery and tells David. Knowing they have different fathers and different mothers, they happily consummate their love. In the eyes of the law, however, they remain brother and sister, and their enraged father pursues them with an armed gang. Fleeing into tunnels under the Byzantine part of the city, David and Anna find Aladdin's treasure, make love under a statue of Dionysus, and discover the lost secrets of Julian the Apostate. At the climax of the novel, David dies heroically in Anna's arms.

The plot of the novel isn't entirely believable. Tired of Byzantine wonders, the reader is left speculating about how the two central themes—incest taboo and American Puritanism—are related. Bullitt completed, printed, and proofread the text, but he left it unpublished.[1] He could easily have found a publisher, and it is not clear why he decided not to share his fantasy with the reader. Probably, he hoped to return to the civil service and was worried that the publication of another scandalous novel would jeopardize his plans.

Freud did help Bullitt, and his influence went far beyond the quick therapy Bullitt received in 1926 in connection to his suicidal thoughts and marital affairs. A little later Bullitt visited Freud in a Berlin hospital; preparing for surgery, Freud was depressed. He said that he had written everything he wanted to and that he was ready to die. Trying to entertain him, Bullitt mentioned that he was working on a book about the Treaty of Versailles, which would consist of historical portraits of Lenin, Lloyd George, Wilson, and several other leaders. Excited about the project, Freud offered to write the Wilson chapter with Bullitt. Having recently finished books about Leonardo da Vinci and Michelangelo, Freud wanted to write an analysis of the modern man.

It was a dramatic proposal, and Bullitt loved it. In the moment, he had been working with papers of Prince Max von Baden, the former chancellor of the German Empire, but now abandoned this project in favor of the Wilson biography. Both Wilson and Freud were role models for Bullitt, and with this book, he allied with one father figure against the other. At the start he was afraid that Freud's chapter in his book would "produce an impossible monstrosity: the part would be greater than the whole." But he also believed that Freud's psychoanalytic study of Wilson would be as important as "the analysis of Plato by Aristotle." It was a lofty goal, but Bullitt was also thinking about the market for this book. He wanted to write it for foreign affairs experts; with Freud's participation, he hoped that "every educated man would wish to read it."[2]

Freud wrote a separate introduction to this book, explaining the project from his perspective. He had followed Wilson from the moment the American president appeared on the European horizon, which, for Freud, meant in the Austrian newspapers. Explaining his attitude toward Wilson, Freud quoted from *Faust*: Mephistopheles, Goethe wrote, "always desires evil and always creates good." Wilson, Freud wrote, was "almost the exact opposite, . . . the true antithesis" of Mephistopheles: the President wanted good but always did evil.[3] Though opposites, they both did not know what they were doing. Psychoanalysis turned this interplay between the moral (good-evil) and the epistemic (being aware or unaware of what one does or wants) into the central drama of human subjectivity. In choosing Mephistopheles as his metaphor, Freud affirmed his desire to write a history of modern humankind. Unknown to the Scriptures, Mephistopheles is the modern—cynical and cunning— incarnation of devil.

Combining Bullitt's memories with Freud's theories, their book founded an emerging genre of psychobiography that peaked in the 1970s, about fifty years after they started the work. It was the first psychobiography of a modern man and also the first book-length psychoanalytical study of politics. The coauthors expected that the book would change historical understandings of Wilson, the First World War, and the Versailles treaty. They did not hide their personal feelings toward the subject, President Wilson. Although this book, Freud wrote, "did not originate without the participation of strong emotions, those emotions underwent a thorough subjugation." More specifically, Freud wrote about his antipathy for Wilson and his aversion to the president's "intrusion into our destiny."[4] Later, in October 1930, Bullitt wrote that Freud wanted him to return to politics and hoped that their book would help him to do so. Indeed, Freud's sympathy for Bullitt and his antipathy for Wilson seemed to be driving forces behind the book.[5]

For different reasons, Freud and Bullitt were both bitter about the Versailles treaty and the outcome of the First World War. Freud's two sons, Ernest and Martin, served in the Austro-Hungarian army, one on the Eastern front, and the other in the West. Martin was injured and, for a time, missing in action, until he was found as a prisoner of war in Italy after the armistice. Having survived the war, the threat of revolution in Vienna, fear for his sons, the collapse of the empire, and the postwar inflation that had impoverished him, Freud changed the deepest of his views. During and immediately after the war, Freud's works expressed cultural pessimism, dissatisfaction with civilization, and an uneasy acknowledgment of those forces that he called the death drive—psychic forces that lead individuals to obsessive repetition and that lead societies to war. Learning from his patients, Freud was also looking for a scientific explanation of homosexuality and the various ways in which people suppress it. He formulated a theory of "psychological androgyny" according to which gender differences are neither a given nor a constant; an individual constructs them according to her or his desires, fears, and circumstances. The unconscious is androgynous; it does not know gender.

In 1927 Bullitt regularly traveled to Vienna to see Freud, for whom America was a land of great promise that eventuated in a civilizational "miscarriage." Indeed, Freud's most profitable patients were Americans. Freud was personally interested in his young friend who had been an active participant in the final events of the war that had destroyed the world Freud loved. For Bullitt, Freud was a "great man" who had a clue to his personal problems and probably could help with his professional frustration as well. A single father who had just gone through a scandalous divorce, Bullitt was a failed diplomat and an aspiring novelist who was struggling with his second book. He had much to learn from Freud. Although his two novels feature frank discussions of male and female sexuality, the book he coauthored with Freud demonstrates a much more sophisticated—and for its time pioneering—understanding of the individual, sexuality, and their interplay in politics. Bullitt's knowledge of the documents and personalities of Wilson's era provided Freud with rich evidence that he had not had when he wrote about great figures of the distant past. The prospect of publishing a polemical book in English about the American president offered Freud an entirely new perspective and readership. Starting their intellectual journeys from very different places, Freud and Bullitt met in the devastated, nostalgic capital of the former empire. Both were cosmopolitans, true citizens of the world. The men shared an interest in global politics and enjoyed the depths of the psyche. Their worldliness united them.

Working on this book, Bullitt respectfully translated and edited the drafts of his senior coauthor. He also wrote his own chapters, which reflect his knowledge of Wilson's administration. The coauthors confronted the task of integrating Bullitt's chapters on Wilson's politics with Freud's chapters on his psychological development. In fact, synthesizing their prose and ideas was impossible, and the chapters of the book remained clearly different. Bullitt wrote in the fast precise style of American journalism, Freud wrote in a wordy and repetitive way that turned complex concepts into protagonists of a tragedy. But "for the analytic part we are both equally responsible," Freud stated in his introduction.[6] Though both men wrote certain parts of the book, Freud read and approved them all.

They worked together for two or three years with Freud reading biographical literature on Wilson, and Bullitt collecting interviews with those who worked with the president. During Bullitt's visits to Vienna, they discussed these materials. Finalized and edited by Bullitt, the book documents his profound understanding of psychoanalytic theories as they emerged in this late period of Freud's work. This joint effort was friendly and respectful; rather than ignoring the authors' obvious differences, the work capitalized on their complementarity. In a sense, this friendly partnership between the coauthors so different in age and experience transcended the theory of Oedipal aggression against the father that they imposed on their hero.

The coauthors agreed to share the royalties, with two-thirds of the profits going to Bullitt and one-third to Freud. They agreed that the book would be released in English before being published in German, which left control over the publication of the book with Bullitt. In the spring of 1932, Freud and Bullitt finished the manuscript, but they ran into a problem that could have been foreseen from the outset. Rereading the finished text, Freud added several paragraphs with which Bullitt could not agree. In these additions, Freud diverted his attention from Wilson and gave a detailed interpretation of Christianity's relation to bisexuality and castration anxiety. One of these fragments was published recently, and indeed, it deepens the text of the book.[7] However, these and other—still unknown—additions from Freud ground the publication to a halt. At Bullitt's suggestion they postponed the publication. In the meanwhile, both of them signed each chapter of the manuscript.

By 1938 the book had still not been published. Bullitt was the American ambassador in Paris, and Freud a sick Jewish doctor in Nazi-occupied Vienna. He did not want to leave Vienna, even though staying meant almost certain death. Together with Freud's daughter, Anna, Bullitt convinced Freud to leave, and it was certainly Bullitt who organized their departure from Vienna. Saving Freud was a surprisingly complex operation that required considerable diplomatic effort, fund-raising, and coordination. The American consul in Vienna, John Wiley, Bullitt's former subordinate in the Moscow embassy, telegraphed Bullitt immediately after the Anschluss, on March 15: "Fear Freud, despite age and illness, in danger."[8] Bullitt called Roosevelt. The next day, Secretary of State Hull telegraphed Wiley to tell him that the president wanted Wiley to raise the question of Freud's emigration with the new Viennese authorities. Hull asked Wylie to act quickly, but said that Wiley should not mention Roosevelt in his conversations with the Nazi authorities. On March 17, rumor spread that Freud had been arrested, though Wiley reported to Bullitt that this was not true. Freud was still at home, but his home was searched by the Nazis. Wiley sent two American officials from the consulate along with Irene Wiley, the consul's wife, to Freud's apartment; they were present during the search. The Nazis confiscated Freud's passport and a large sum of money. Consul Wiley talked to the head of the Vienna police, who assured him that Freud was not in any danger.

Austrian Jews had to pay the Nazis a significant sum for each person's departure; in addition, the Nazis demanded that Freud pay the thirty-two thousand shillings that his psychoanalytic publishing house owed to its suppliers. Bullitt cabled the State Department to say that he was personally willing to pay for Freud's emigration. Cabling back, Wylie informed Bullitt that the costs would be considerable: Freud wanted to take sixteen people, including ten members of his family, as well as a maid, a personal doctor, and the family of this doctor. In response, Bullitt wrote that he could not pay for sixteen people, and asked Wylie to persuade Freud to take with him only his wife and daughter. Freud's relatives who stayed in Austria, including four of his sisters, perished in the Holocaust.

Bullitt offered Freud and his family ten thousand dollars, a huge sum in those days, and promised to come up with more money on top of this. To this end, Bullitt contacted Marie Bonaparte, who was a psychoanalyst, the translator of Freud into French, and a descendant of Napoleon; she came to Vienna and resolved the financial issues with the Nazis at her own expense. But on March 22, the Gestapo arrested Freud's daughter, Anna. Wylie immediately informed Bullitt and contacted the authorities in Vienna. Anna was released the same day, and Wylie again telegraphed this news to the State Department, which cabled it to Bullitt in Paris. Through diplomatic channels, Bullitt took care of procuring French visas for Freud and his family. On April 12, 1938, a month after the Anschluss, Secretary Hull sent Wylie a telegram, which again asked the consul about Freud's emigration plan.[9] In the end, on June 4, Freud and his family left Vienna by train. An agent of the American Secret Service followed them, with instructions to help Freud should they encounter difficulties at the border. Ambassador Bullitt and Princess Bonaparte were waiting for Freud at the train station in Paris. Freud did not know the details but was aware of the tremendous support he was receiving; he later wrote from London an eloquent thank you note to Bullitt. He loved the calm and beauty of his new home in London, and he was sure Bullitt had played a significant part in his escape.[10]

In Paris Bullitt reminded Freud of their unresolved dispute about the additions to their book. A little later, he visited Freud's new home in London and brought the manuscript with him. The frail and grateful Freud allowed Bullitt to remove the disputed passages; once again, he looked through the chapters and approved the last version of the whole text. But it was still impossible to publish the book, because it contained some details that were critical of Colonel House and his family. House had died in the spring of 1938, but Wilson's widow, whom the book portrayed quite negatively, was still alive. Bullitt seems to have been in no hurry to print the book, perhaps realizing that the publication of the text would threaten his political career. He finally published the book, the most enduring of his writings, in 1966, shortly before his death.

Freud's heirs agreed to the publication and received their share of the royalties. Later, however, they would come to doubt Freud's authorship. The book appeared when the genre of psychobiography came into vogue in America; psychoanalyst Erik Erikson penned the most famous books in the genre, writing psychobiographies of Luther (1958) and Gandhi (1969). Freud and Bullitt, as it turned out, had invented this genre much earlier than Erickson. Moreover, they applied the psychobiographical method to a contemporary American, employing it not only as an analytical tool but also as a political weapon. Their book was a rare criticism of Wilson in the liberal decade that saw Wilson's reputation rehabilitated. While in the interwar period Wilson's legacy was undermined by criticisms of the Treaty of Versailles and the fate of the League of Nations, by the 1960s Wilson the idealist and internationalist was seen as an alternative to the Cold War consensus. With its contempt for Wilson, the book was immediately criticized; Eric Erickson attacked the book most vehemently, accusing Bullitt of dishonestly representing Freud's work and questioning whether Freud had authored it at all. It was only when Bullitt's papers became available to researchers that Freud's signatures, manuscripts, and other documents proved his involvement beyond any shadow of a doubt.[11]

About half of the book addresses Wilson's second term, and specifically the Paris Peace Conference. The authors explore the events in Paris in great detail, offering a day-by-day narrative. They also analyze Wilson's entire life, his "passive" and "active" sexuality, and his relationships with his father, mother, brother, and wives. Throughout the book the authors assess Wilson's political decisions in light of his psychosexual development. "We feel that we need not apologize for the closeness of our scrutiny.... In so far as any human being is ever important, Wilson in those months was important. . . . All life would have been a different thing if Christ had recanted when He stood before Pilate."[12]

The book focuses on Wilson's religious imagination, which, according to the authors, exerted a significant influence on his political activities. Wilson was a Presbyterian, and Freud and Bullitt offer a radical interpretation of his faith. According to the authors, Wilson saw his father as God and himself as Jesus Christ, the Savior of mankind. These identifications are, they argue, not unusual: "a large number of little boys" draw parallels between religion and their own lives.[13] Freud and Bullitt found it plausible that Wilson's identification with Jesus Christ was central to his personality; moreover, this identification was key to his political career. Identification with Christ formed a special kind of puritanical Super-Ego, "whose ideals are so grandiose that it demands from the Ego the impossible." This analysis resembles German sociologist Max Weber's depiction of the Protestant ethic: no matter what the Ego reaches in real life, the Super-Ego can never be satisfied. "It admonishes incessantly: You must make the impossible possible! You can accomplish the impossible! You are the beloved son of the Father! You are the Father Himself! You are God!"[14]

It was not easy for the authors to agree on these conclusions. They held different religious beliefs, and they were both "stubborn." In Bullitt's words, Freud "was a Jew who had become an agnostic; I have always been a believing Christian. We often disagreed but we never quarreled."[15] For Freud, a Jewish agnostic, Wilson's Presbyterianism was alien. But Bullitt, a descendant of the Huguenots who grew up among Philadelphian Quakers, saw Wilson's experience as close to his own. The Freud and Bullitt book developed through the transformative years of the century, and the drama surrounding Freud's emigration unfolded as the two were working on this book. Importantly, Freud used his comparison of Wilson to Mephistopheles in his own introduction to the book, and not in the text of the book that he shared with Bullitt. Freud thought that Wilson "unconsciously" identified with Christ. Tempting Freud with emigration, did Bullitt do to Freud what Mephistopheles did to Faust? Did Bullitt—consciously or not—identify with Mephistopheles?

Religion plays a surprisingly big role in this psychobiography. Wilson's father was a priest, and Wilson himself an ardent believer. In Scotland and North America, Presbyterianism was a common branch of Calvinism; it became known as "high church" in the United States; and Princeton University—where Wilson served as president—was founded as a Presbyterian College.

Max Weber, a contemporary of Freud and Wilson, located "the spirit of capitalism" precisely in Presbyterianism and other Puritan denominations. Weber ascribed particular importance to the idea of predestination. God determined every event, but no man could learn God's purpose and the path to salvation. As God's instrument, a person would act on the basis of his or her own conceptions of good and evil and thus increase God's glory. Earthly criteria of success such as victory in battle, wealth, or political success—all this is an indirect sign of future salvation. Thus, in combining the belief in predestination with the inability to comprehend it, Weber derived from Protestantism the necessity of trial, error, hopeless frustration, and endless progress—the spirit of modernity. A German patriot, Weber admired and at the same time resisted the global power of the Puritan—Anglo-Saxon and Dutch—versions of capitalism; it brought the "iron cage" of responsibility and loneliness, he wrote.[16]

In Freud and Bullitt, these features of Presbyterianism produce interesting effects. They see Wilson's belief in predestination as the cause of his political isolation and weakness, which led to the tragedy of Versailles and the collapse of the Progressive movement. The authors write about Wilson the president: "His identification with Christ was so powerful that he could not ask for war except as a means to produce peace. He had to believe that somehow he would emerge from the war as the Savior of the World." Like his father the pastor, Wilson hoped to resolve his problems—now the problems of the world—by his sermons. Only when he called the war a crusade did he become strong and happy.[17]

Freud and Bullitt's portrait of Wilson was in many ways a condemnation of provincial, fundamentalist America. Connecting Wilson's politics with his religion, the authors explain this conundrum as the "feminine" resolution of the universal bisexuality that Freud attributed to human nature. With his feminine "passivity to his father," Wilson realized himself in his speeches and was unable to see the world outside them. Everywhere—at Princeton, in Washington, and in Paris—he created discussion clubs that failed to replace the "masculine" action. His brainchild, the League of Nations, also implemented this vision. At the Paris Peace Conference, the president refused to fight treachery, as if he were a woman; he responded with sermons to lies and threats that came from his partners in the negotiations, as if he were a pastor. In Freud and Bullitt's reading, the nonconformist tradition of the British sectarians who moved to America was responsible for Wilson's crusade and capitulation. He was "born in a nation which was protected from reality during the nineteenth century by inherited devotion to the ideas of Wycliffe, Calvin and Wesley."[18]

British economist John Maynard Keynes and diplomat Harold Nicolson—both present at the Paris Peace Conference—also saw Wilson's Presbyterianism as the key to his politics.[19] Trying to explain Wilson's failure in Paris, Keynes used the same rhetorical tools as Freud: "His thoughts and his temper was such which are peculiar to a theologian, not an intellectual." Wilson would not understand this distinction, but for the generation of the First World War—arguably the first secular generation—it was crucial. The agnostic Europeans were surprised to see religion dominating politics. First enchanted and then disappointed by Wilson, they never understood him. In England and Scotland, one could still find some Presbyterians, Keynes wrote mockingly, but they were mostly beggars; in America these people were rich, educated, and wielded political power.[20] Keynes compared Wilson to Don Quixote; Freud contrasted him to Mephistopheles. It is important, of course, that both these characters deny what they are actually doing: one denies his own good deeds, the other denies the evil he has caused.

More compassionate than Bullitt or Keynes, Harold Nicolson saw in Wilson "not a philosopher but only a prophet," someone on par with Tolstoy and Gandhi. Along with these great populists, Wilson "believed in all sincerity that the voice of the People was the voice of God." By his standards, international politics "should be as high, as sensitive, as the standard of personal conduct." In fact, Wilsonism was interesting for Nicolson precisely because "this centennial dream was suddenly backed by the overwhelming resources of the strongest power in the world." Nicolson also hated "violence in any form," but he detected in Wilson's statements "a touch of methodical arrogance" and "a strain of fanatical mysticism." It was a true surprise and deep disappointment when Wilson's spiritual power betrayed him at the very moment that American military power peaked: the president "possessed unlimited physical power to enforce his views.... It never occurred to us that, if need arose, he would hesitate to use it."[21]

Like Max Weber, Freud and Bullitt saw a particular religious tradition as the key to understanding modernity. They explained Wilson's career through his identification with Christ—his ambitious energy (he was the savior of humanity, after all), his quarrels with his closest associates, including House (who became Judas), and finally, his League of Nations (the establishment of heaven on earth). For them, Wilson embodied two aspects of America they did not like: the weak and feminine on the one hand and the provincial and fundamentalist on the other. Freud and Bullitt seriously underestimated the gravity of choices that Wilson made while he was heading the talks toward his ultimate purpose, the establishment of the League of Nations.[22] He had to make deals both in Paris and in Washington to get the treaty ratified, and the League instituted. He was a man who believed in structures to contain conflict; thus the League of Nations could constrain tyrants from overstepping the boundaries of peace by extending the principles of the US Constitution to world affairs. This project was political rather than religious, and so was its fate. Freud's disappointment with the unfulfilled promise of Wilson's Fourteen Points and the collapse of Austria-Hungary and Bullitt's failure in Paris after the stunning promise of his trip to Russia both played roles in shaping their bitter perspective.[23]

William C. Bullitt Sr., the father of Bill and Orville, from the obituary in *Harrisburg Telegraph*, March 23, 1914.

Bullitt in 1916, as contributor to the *Evening Ledger*

The Paris Peace Conference, 1919. Courtesy of the Library of Congress
Prints and Photographs Division, Washington, DC.

which has prevented the countries south of the Rio Grande from being, like Africa, pawns in the diplomacy of Europe.

"That each power should covenant

independent condition which they have assumed and maintain, are henceforth not to be considered as subjects for future colonization by any extrinsic powers."

Bullitt Says Lenine Agreed to Terms, Then Allies Repudiated Their Offer

New York Tribune
Washington Bureau

WASHINGTON, Sept. 12.—An agreement with the Soviet government of Russia, whereby trade relations would have been resumed, fighting halted on all fronts and the Red Guard demobil-

Mr. Bullitt explained, "was that Kolchak had made a 100-mile advance."

Contradicts Lloyd George

Senator Knox asked Mr. Bullitt if he had seen the statement of Lloyd George in the House of Commons that he knew nothing of any proposals submitted to

A page of the *New York Tribune*, September 13, 1919.

Edward House, 1920. Courtesy of the Library of Congress Prints and Photographs Division, Washington, DC.

Eleanor (Cissy) Patterson with her daughter, Felicia Gizycki.

John Reed, circa 1915. Courtesy of the Library of Congress Prints and Photographs Division, Washington, DC.

Louise Bryant, circa 1920s.

Bryant at Reed's funeral in the Kremlin, 1920.

Lincoln Steffens. Courtesy of the Library of Congress Prints and Photographs Division, Washington, DC.

Bullitt as the American ambassador to the Soviet Union, 1933. Courtesy of the Library of Congress Prints and Photographs Division, Washington, DC.

Bullitt with Soviet officials.

Bullitt talking to Mikhail Kalinin and Maxim Litvinov.

Bullitt with his daughter Anna, a screenshot from a Soviet documentary.

Young George Andreychin.

Andreychin in prison.

Olga Lepeshinskaya

Mikhail Bulgakov, 1928.

Bullitt and H. G. Wells in Moscow.

Marguerite LeHand between FDR and Bullitt.

George Kennan, 1947. Courtesy of the Library of Congress Prints and Photographs Division, Washington, DC.

Bullitt and Marie Bonaparte are meeting Freud in Paris, June 5, 1938.
From the collection of the Sigmund Freud Museum.

Diplomats in 1938: William C. Bullitt, envoy to France; Acting Secretary of State
Sumner Welles; US Ambassador to Germany Hugh R. Wilson; and William
Phillips, Ambassador to Italy. Courtesy of the Library of Congress Prints and
Photographs Division, Washington, DC.

Bullitt visiting the White House, 1939. Courtesy of the Library of Congress Prints and Photographs Division, Washington, DC.

"Why are we sleeping, Americans?" Speech in Philadelphia, August 1940.

Bullitt in 1941, from *Life* magazine.

Bullitt in retirement, from *Life* magazine.

Bullitt visiting China, 1947, from *Life* magazine.

9

HONEYMOON WITH STALIN

One summer day in 1932 three strangers drove a car up to the wall of the Kremlin. Surprising the guards, they spoke English. One of them produced a permit, and the guards let another man, an impeccably dressed foreigner, proceed toward the grave of John Reed, who was buried in the Kremlin wall among Bolshevik heroes. The two other men watched from a distance as William Bullitt, "sentimental to the core," laid a large wreath on the grave of John Reed. Head bowed, Bullitt stood before Reed's grave "for many minutes"; when he returned to his companions, "tears were rolling down his cheeks and his features were drawn with sorrow."[1]

This was Bullitt's third visit to Moscow—surprising for an American who was, though related to John Reed, never a Communist. It is not clear what else Bullitt was doing in Russia, besides weeping at the grave of his ex-wife's former husband. He wrote to Colonel House that he wished to sort out Lenin's papers in the Moscow archive, but nothing came of these plans. The presidential campaign had just started in America, and Bullitt was on his way back from Vienna to campaign for Franklin Delano Roosevelt. Counting on Roosevelt's victory and anticipating his turn to the left, Bullitt expected that relations with the USSR would be on Roosevelt's agenda. From 1917 to 1933 there were no diplomatic relations between the Bolshevik government of Russia and the United States. In the midst of the Great Depression, Roosevelt declared that he would resume these relations. Bullitt saw an opportunity to use his connections to rekindle the US-Soviet relationship.

George Andreychin, a Bulgarian Communist who got Bullitt permission to visit John Reed's grave at the Kremlin, was a longtime friend and a helpful guide in Moscow. On the eve of the First World War, Andreychin emigrated to the United States, fleeing conscription to the Austria-Hungarian army. There he befriended Charlie Chaplin, Reed, and other leftists. In Minnesota in 1918 Andreychin organized a miners' strike and was facing twenty years in jail under wartime laws. Released on bail thanks to Chaplin, Andreychin fled to revolutionary Russia. Later, Max Eastman thanked Andreychin for helping to obtain Lenin's "Letter to the Congress," the Bolshevik leader's political testament that was essentially an anti-Stalin pamphlet and one of the major assets of the Trotskyite movement. In the 1920s Andreychin worked in important but prosaic positions in the State Planning Committee in Moscow and in the Soviet Embassy in London. He received Soviet citizenship but preserved his American citizenship as well; still, he could not go back to the States because he was a fugitive from justice. A convinced Trotskyite, he was exiled to Kazakhstan in 1927 but continued to correspond with Trotsky. In 1932 he wrote a letter of repentance and returned to Moscow. When he brought Bullitt to Reed's grave, he was working at Intourist, the Moscow travel agency that was filled with informers and seductresses.

In September 1932 Bullitt started working at Roosevelt's campaign headquarters. He met Roosevelt in October, and they immediately took a liking to each other: both were "brilliantly and boldly intuitional," recalled their mutual friend Louis B. Wehle, who organized the meeting. Colonel House also supported Bullitt's return to politics; still, it was "a temperamental congeniality," as Wehle put it, that made these two men "warm friends" after their first conversation. Bullitt immediately started correspondence with Roosevelt and donated one thousand dollars to his campaign. More importantly, he flattered Roosevelt from the very beginning. After listening to one of Roosevelt's radio addresses, Bullitt wrote: "It was the most inspiriting address that I have heard since Wilson's speeches in 1918. You not only said the right things but also said them with a 1776 spirit."[2] Promising a New Deal to Americans, Roosevelt saw himself as launching the new revolution, and Bullitt honestly shared his hope for a transformation of the political system. But Bullitt detested Wilson and his speeches in 1918, while Roosevelt was, in contrast, grateful to Wilson, with whom he began his public career. He probably took

Bullitt's praise at face value, while in fact it was a tongue-in-cheek one-man show, Bullitt's specialty.

In his letters to Roosevelt, Bullitt combined flattery with irony in a way that both entertained the addressee and educated him about the world affairs that were becoming crucial to his job. Bullitt's girlfriend and Roosevelt's secretary, Margaret LeHand, admired these letters—"a confidential dispatch which reads like a most exciting novel."[3] Historian David Fromkin noted that Bullitt "tended to discuss events in terms of personalities."[4] As ambassador, Bullitt fully realized this journalistic skill in his diplomatic dispatches, which matched Roosevelt's lively, intuitive, and personal way of directing world affairs. Aware of his lack of international experience, Roosevelt could not stand the tedious advisers. "Moments of boredom were a desperate ordeal" for Roosevelt. "His mind was sure to range ahead of any slow speaker," recalled Louis Wehle.[5] Secretary of State Cordell Hull was boring and logical; Roosevelt respected his experience but preferred to receive his information about foreign affairs from more exciting interlocutors, like Bullitt. At this moment Bullitt's career depended on matching Roosevelt's tempo, wit, and thirst for detail.

One of Bullitt's talents was his ability to cooperate with older and more powerful people such as House, Freud, and Roosevelt. In dealing with these "substitutes for a father figure," as Freud would have called them, Bullitt did not obey or rebel but established friendship—a relationship of equals. He was not so good at cultivating his relationships with those whom he mentored, his symbolic sons; this asymmetry in his relationships would become worse, much to his own dismay, in his later years. Generally sincere despite his routine mischievousness, he was also less successful at forging more formal relationships among the British elite and the Soviet bureaucratic class, though he made lasting friendships with leaders elsewhere on the Continent. In America his personal diplomacy seemed to work well. While he seemed dramatic to some and sentimental to others, Roosevelt nicknamed him "Bill Buddha," which indicated an even-tempered, smiley, and all-accepting kind of character.[6] To pull all of these various traits together, Bullitt had to show an unusual self-control—what his friend Charles Bohlen described as his ability to turn his brilliance on and off at will.[7]

Roosevelt was elected in November 1932. Two months later, Hitler became chancellor of Germany. Attacking the Treaty of Versailles was one of Hitler's favorite themes. In America and England the success of German revenge-seekers signaled the death of Wilson's idealism, and the old opponents of the

Treaty of Versailles experienced a bitter moment of truth. Roosevelt's inauguration took place in March, and in April Bullitt was appointed assistant secretary of state—roughly the same position that he had left almost fifteen years earlier.

Bullitt's first assignment was to prepare for the World Economic Conference, which was held in London under the auspices of the League of Nations in the summer of 1933. Bullitt worked on this event together with James Warburg, one of Roosevelt's financial advisers and a nephew of Jacob Schiff, the Wall Street tycoon who years earlier had financed the émigré Bolsheviks fomenting revolution in Russia. Warburg's portrait of Bullitt was delightful: "he is a naughty boy; he loves to create a scene and he can put on an act of indignation such as I've rarely seen, and come out roaring with laughter over it. He had little concern about the success of the conference; he had no concern about anything economic. He's one of these curious people to whom the drama is more exciting than the results." Warburg characterized Bullitt as a maverick, but appreciated his contribution to the conference because Bullitt was "the only person on the horizon a) who knows Europe thoroughly, and b) who has real talent as a negotiator."[8]

The World Economic Conference ended in failure. A little earlier, Roosevelt had abandoned the gold standard, which paved the way for what is known today as "quantitative easing." The sudden fall of the dollar spawned chaos in international finance. However, Keynes applauded Roosevelt's decision, and Bullitt also supported it. Surprising everyone, Alfred Hugenberg, the German minister of economics and a longtime ally of Hitler, announced on the conference that the global Depression would end when Germany received its African colonies back and acquired new "living space" in Eastern Europe. According to historian Arthur Schlesinger, Bullitt made mistakes in London that had become characteristic: he angered one British statesman by suggesting that the American delegation room had been wired by the British and enraged another by taking his secretary out for a dinner and trying to pry British state secrets from her.[9]

The New Deal needed money, which could only come from the federal state. Implementing his revolution from above, Roosevelt dramatically increased governmental spending, abandoned the Prohibition laws, and created millions of jobs. The radicalization of Germany, the turn toward greater state involvement in the economy, and vague expectations of a new war, all drew attention to Russia and its socialist experiment. Despite the absence of diplomatic relations, trade between the United States and the Soviet Union had been thriving.

As unemployment rose in the United States, thousands of pro-Soviet Americans immigrated to the Soviet Union. Many of them wanted to build state socialism, while others simply sought employment. From the Karelian woods to the Dnieper dams to the Ural mines to the Volga plants, the talent and skills of these Americans made a big contribution to Stalin's industrialization. Over time, many of these people perished in the Gulag, but the American government and the press either did not know or refused to believe that this was happening. The Soviet Union was a significant potential market for American goods and a possible military ally, a counterweight to Germany in Europe and to Japan in Asia. An alliance between the United States and the Soviet Union could change the balance of power in Europe and the world; looking back, one could easily see how the timely formation of such an alliance could have prevented or alleviated the worst catastrophes of the Second World War. Some New Dealers also saw in the Soviet Union a model for their domestic reforms. These progressive Americans believed that collectivization, industrial experiments, and five-year plans would bring peace, growth, and a thriving culture to the Soviet Union.

In the absence of diplomatic relations, Soviet-American trade was largely controlled from Moscow. Bullitt stated later that the Soviets needed many American industrial products, but in the 1920s, the sales of these products were supported by "strange financing. . . . We found that we had given away our products when we thought we had sold them" (76). Amtorg, the Soviet trade agency, had operated legally in the United States since 1924. From its offices in Manhattan and Moscow, Amtorg ran huge import-export operations. Its agents also collected technical and military intelligence and were quick to use force if money did not work. The FBI watched the Soviet agency closely, but strange Russian stories nonetheless unfolded on American soil. Ephraim Sklyansky, the first head of Amtorg and a close friend of Trotsky, sank in a boat on a lake in New Jersey in 1925; murder was never proved.[10] In 1930 a special congressional committee investigated Amtorg. The committee reported that most of the agency's correspondence was encoded, and the American Navy specialists were unable to crack the code. Still, American exports to Russia were large and growing: from trucks to turbines, tractors to airplanes, rails to cranes, American technology had become the backbone of Soviet industrialization. In return Russian exports to the United States comprised mostly gold and furs, sometimes supplemented by works of classical art that had been confiscated from their prerevolutionary owners. The United States did not have a trade agency in Russia, and importing Soviet goods to America was an obscure business that attracted eccentrics like oilman Armand Hammer and fur trader Motty Eitingon. Surprised by this situation, Secretary of State Cordell Hull wrote that the establishment of regular relations would be more profitable to the United States than the Soviet Union: "It was easier for Russians to do business in the United States without diplomatic protection than it was for Americans to do business in Russia."[11]

However, the Soviet-American rapprochement was attractive for Kremlin strategists as well. The establishment of diplomatic relations with the United States would ensure the triumph of the Soviets in their long, successful campaign for international recognition. It would mark the victory of the People's Commissariat of Foreign Affairs, which was led by Maxim Litvinov, a cosmopolitan Bolshevik who, before the revolution, had spent ten years in London. America was also a source of technical information and, possibly, military and economic assistance. Moscow was very much concerned about possible conflict with Japan. Generals always prepare for the wars of the past, and the Kremlin remembered the grave lessons of the Russo-Japanese War of 1904–1905. Soviet commissars saw the rapprochement with the United States as a counterweight to the Japanese threat on the Soviet Pacific Coast, which they could not defend alone. In the long run these hopes proved to be surprisingly pertinent, though Japan would attack the United States and not the Soviet Union, and the Kremlin would end up needing American help in Europe, not Asia.

From an American perspective, there were many obstacles to the recognition of the Soviet Union. In a memorandum dated October 4, 1933, Bullitt listed them in order of significance. First, in 1917 the Bolsheviks had disavowed Russian debts to the American government; Bullitt hoped to return these debts by offering restructuring and deferrals. Second, the Soviet governmental organizations, the Comintern and Amtorg, spread Communist propaganda in the United States; as a condition for diplomatic relations, Moscow had to stop this propaganda. Finally, the USSR also had to ensure the protection of civil and religious liberties of Americans in Moscow and across the country. Tactically, Bullitt detected a vicious circle: to discuss controversial issues with Russia, America needed the diplomatic relations, but these relations could not be established until the Soviets resolved the disputed issues.

Breaking this circle, Bullitt worked with Boris Skvirsky, the head of another Soviet agency in Washington, the Soviet Information Bureau. They agreed on the text of two identical letters that were exchanged between Roosevelt and the "Soviet president," Mikhail Kalinin. Litvinov came to Washington and opened the first telephone line between Washington and Moscow. On November 18, 1933, newspapers reported the establishment of diplomatic relations between the USSR and the United States. The president nominated Bullitt as American ambassador to the Soviet Union. In a rare interview with the *New York Times*, Stalin praised the establishment of diplomatic relations with the United States and Bullitt's role in the process. Stalin said he had heard "much" about Bullitt from Lenin, who also "liked" him. The Soviet leader appreciated that Bullitt was "a direct man who says what he thinks" and did not talk "like an ordinary diplomat." Stalin also complimented Roosevelt: he was "a realist," Stalin said, and saw the world as it was.[12]

On December 3, Bullitt's old friend George Andreychin congratulated him from Moscow. "I am genuinely distressed," he wrote, "not to be the first to welcome you as the first American ambassador to the Russian Revolution. You are certainly the man for the job." In response, Bullitt expressed the hope that they might "consume some vodka and caviar together soon."[13] Reminiscing about their joint trip to Russia some fifteen years earlier, Lincoln Steffens congratulated Bullitt with an unusual parable: "There was a man who was after a guy who was in prison, so he had himself sent to this prison, but his enemy was in another prison. So he served out his term, had himself convicted of another crime," and then did it for the third time—but finally stabbed his enemy. So, concluded Steffens, that man beat Bullitt's record, but Bullitt was "the second most persistent son-of-a-gun in my history." Bullitt could relax, Steffens added: the third most persistent man was Litvinov.[14]

Bullitt did not expect problems with his nomination in the Senate. Only the British diplomats, who remembered him in Paris or had heard about his Anglophobia, were unhappy. One of them reported from London: "I think Mr. Bullitt may do less harm in Moscow than in Washington, though he is a kind of man who does harm anywhere." From Washington, the British ambassador responded that Bullitt was "completely unscrupulous where there is question of taking his objective" (58).

Bullitt's counterpart, who had been nominated Soviet ambassador to the United States, was Alexander Troyanovsky. Characteristically, he was the former ambassador to Japan (1927–1933); in his youth, Troyanovsky, an artillery officer by training, took part in the Russian-Japanese war of 1904–1905. The appointment of a Japan specialist to serve as ambassador to Washington showed that the perceived Japanese threat was much stronger in Moscow than in Washington: Bullitt was an expert in Europe, not Japan. But in Moscow, he talked about the Japanese threat regularly.

Bullitt based his selection of employees solely on "intuition," and this faculty rarely betrayed him. In November 1933 George Kennan found the new ambassador packing up his luggage at the State Department. Learning that Kennan spoke Russian, Bullitt immediately offered him a job in Moscow. Kennan had been serving in Riga with a small group of "observers" who monitored developments in the Soviet Union and wrote reports to the State Department. Bored there, he was thrilled by the new appointment. The posting started in a few days and would launch the stellar career of Kennan, who became one of the most influential diplomats of the Cold War. Just as quickly, during a short meeting in Moscow, Bullitt recruited Charles Thayer. Thayer did not even speak Russian, but he turned into an excellent translator and an accomplished career diplomat.

With a small entourage, Bullitt sailed from New York aboard the *President Harding* to Le Havre. Winter was approaching, the ocean was stormy, and Bullitt called for the red wine to be replaced with champagne, which he thought would be better during the storm. Kennan could not leave his cabin out of sickness, and Bullitt visited him. Kennan recalled:

> He talked to me with that charm which was peculiarly his own. It was our first really personal conversation and I was naturally curious about the character of this brilliant and fast-moving man who had so suddenly become my immediate superior. I carried away from the talk an impression of enormous charm, confidence, and vitality. But I also had an impression of quick sensitivity, of great egocentricity and pride, and of a certain dangerous freedom—the freedom of a man who, as he himself confessed to me on that occasion, had never subordinated his life to the needs of any other human being. (xv)

In Moscow the delegation stayed near the Kremlin, at the Hotel National, where the American flag was flown. Bullitt was touched that he was placed in the very same room where he had stayed with his mother in 1914, nearly twenty years earlier. *Pravda* wrote enthusiastically about the establishment of diplomatic relations with the United States; the new ambassador was "a longtime friend of the Soviet Union" and "Lenin's partner in the negotiations." It was Bullitt's fourth time in Moscow, and he loved every bit of it. After he presented his credentials to Kalinin, he wrote to Roosevelt that he thought Kalinin was "a simple-minded old peasant," endowed with "a delightful shrewdness and sense of humor" (63). Kalinin told Bullitt that the American president was "completely out of the class of the leaders of [other] capitalist states" because Roosevelt really cared about American workers and farmers. Kalinin also told Bullitt that Lenin "many times" expressed his sympathies for Bullitt, in conversations and also in his "Testament." This is what Bullitt wrote to Roosevelt; in fact, Lenin's "Testament" does not mention Bullitt, and Kalinin would have been unable to cite the document, which was directed against Stalin and was not acknowledged as genuine during the entire Soviet period. Bullitt also wrote that the Soviet diplomat Ivan Divilkovsky told him: "You cannot understand it, but there is not one of us who would not gladly have his throat cut to have had such things said about him by Lenin." To help Roosevelt understand this passage, Bullitt offered an analogy that he could have borrowed from his book about Wilson: "Lenin's present position in Russia [was] not unlike that of Jesus Christ in the Christian church," and therefore he, Bullitt, enjoyed something similar to "the personal endorsement of the Master recorded in St. Mark" (64). One could only imagine Roosevelt's laughter when he learned that the natives treated his ambassador as a local saint who had been endorsed by the founder of their religion and mentioned in their gospel. Impressing Roosevelt was Bullitt's task in Moscow, and he initially succeeded. Demonstrating his influence and friendship with important people in the Soviet Union was a constant theme in his official dispatches; but over time their addressee, Roosevelt, grew tired of this. On the other hand, it was true that Bullitt befriended some of the most important Europeans in the twentieth century. Moreover, some of these important men and women made their careers or physically survived thanks to Bullitt's efforts.

When Bullitt arrived in Moscow, he shared his sympathy for the socialist experiment with leftists like Lincoln Steffens and Henry Wallace. During his first months in the Soviet capital, he often spoke about the Bolsheviks with enthusiasm. He persuaded Wallace, then secretary of agriculture, to pay attention to the Soviet achievements in his field; for some reason, he emphasized their successes in artificial insemination.[15] According to Wallace, Bullitt had a free and liberal mind, and he could not stand surveillance. As a result of his life in Moscow, Wallace noted, Bullitt's attitude toward the Soviets changed radically, and he described the Communist Party as an institution similar to the Spanish Inquisition. However, Bullitt told Wallace that he was fond of the Russian people, particularly the women: even in the construction of the Moscow subway, he noted that women worked harder than men. A supporter of further rapprochement with the Soviets, Wallace worried about Bullitt's anti-Soviet instincts; people like Bullitt brought on the Cold War, Wallace said later. He added that Bullitt was a wonderful man but given to sudden mood swings.[16]

Even the Soviet spies in Washington acknowledged the unusual qualities of the American ambassador. In October 1934 they managed to read Bullitt's memos to the State Department and passed them on to Moscow. Soon Bullitt learned about the leak from his Moscow friends and reported it back to the State Department. Closing the circle, in an encrypted message to the NKVD (the Soviet secret police), Soviet agent Yitzhak Akhmerov wrote from Washington, DC: "We ask you to observe maximum caution in sending reports from B[ullitt] to offices neighboring yours. The cunning of B[ullitt], his abilities, social disposition, and contacts with high-ranking persons in your city [Moscow] give him opportunity to touch many people. An indirect hint in a conversation may be enough [for him]."[17]

Despite his concerns about security and secrecy, Bullitt had unusually egalitarian, even anarchic ideas about the work of an American embassy. According to one of his closest associates, Loy Henderson, Bullitt did not recognize the traditional hierarchy. The ambassador believed that prior experience in the diplomatic service was a hindrance to good service in the Moscow embassy. This informal playful atmosphere shocked some guests. Having visited the embassy shortly after it was opened, Professor Samuel Harper, a son of the president of the University of Chicago and the founding father of Russian Studies there, strongly disapproved of the "tone" he discerned in the embassy, which he described as "too frivolous and even flippant"; this tone, Harper said, was set by the embassy's leader, whom Harper had disliked since the Paris Peace Conference.[18]

For a while Bullitt was delighted with the Kremlin leadership. "The men at the head of the Soviet government today are really intelligent, sophisticated, vigorous human beings." They fully embodied these qualities in greeting the American ambassador, who was distinguished from the ordinary Western diplomats with whom the Soviet leaders could not "be persuaded to waste their time." As Bullitt informed his president, Soviet leaders habitually ignored European ambassadors in Moscow, but they were "extremely eager to have contact with anyone who ha[d] first-rate intelligence and dimension as a human being. They were, for example, delighted by young Kennan" (65). The Soviets seem to have gone out of their way to make Bullitt happy. Litvinov organized a "superb banquet" featuring "nearly all" members of the government and resembling one of Jay Gatsby's parties: "food and wines were of a quality that no one in America would dare to serve nowadays," wrote Bullitt to the president; "many toasts were drunk to you and me and the United States" (64).

It was easy to talk to the English-speaking Litvinov, and Bullitt shared with him his wish that the Moscow high quarters would treat him as an insider: he would not stay in Russia, Bullitt said, if this didn't happen. When conversation turned serious, they talked about the Japanese threat, a theme Bullitt brought up regularly. "Attack by Japan upon the Soviet Union is regarded as certain by all members of the Government and communist party with whom I talked in Moscow," Bullitt wrote to Roosevelt in December 1933 (60). Litvinov considered the war with Japan so probable that he wanted an urgent pact with the European powers that would secure the Soviet Union's western frontiers. He was particularly concerned about a possible anti-Soviet coalition consisting of Japan, Germany, and Poland, and he told Bullitt he knew about some "preliminary conversations" among these powers. To counter these preparations, Litvinov talked about the possibility of a coalition consisting of the Soviet Union, the United States, Japan, and China; he asked Bullitt to take part in organizing this alternative alliance.[19] On December 15, Bullitt met the Soviet prime minister, Vyacheslav Molotov, who shared Litvinov's fear of a forthcoming Japanese attack and suggested that if Soviet-American relations had been established a couple of years earlier, the Japanese threat would have been averted. Bullitt agreed with this counterfactual analysis. In late 1933 Bullitt met the Bolsheviks who were in charge of Soviet foreign relations, trade, and defense. They all agreed about the threat of war with Japan and wanted American help. Interestingly, the only high-ranking official who did not believe in the Japanese threat was Karl Radek, a shrewd and ruthless leader of the Communist International. Bullitt befriended him but did not trust his opinion.[20] The fear of Japan was the reason for the unexpected Soviet decision to join the League of Nations in September 1934. Even though the United States was not a member of the league, Litvinov asked Bullitt to support the decision, and Bullitt responded positively. Litvinov also asked for Bullitt's word that America would not lend to Japan, and that France and England would not give the country credit either.

The American ambassador engaged in a friendly competition with People's Commissar of Finance Grigory Grinko over who could learn the other's language better. The plan was that six months after the deal was struck, in June 1934, Litvinov would judge which of the two men had achieved the greater level of linguistic proficiency. The prize would be a medal with Roosevelt's profile, Bullitt informed the American president. Bullitt never did learn to speak Russian, and Kennan and others translated for him while he was in Moscow. It is not known whether Grinko learned English, but Bullitt liked him anyway. Three years after the agreed date, Grinko was arrested, tortured, and tried; on March 2, 1938, at the end of his trial, he confessed to being a Trotskyite and cooperating with the German, Japanese, and American intelligence services. After sharing with the judges his "joy at the fact that our villainous plot has been uncovered and those unprecedented troubles that we had prepared, are now prevented," Grinko was executed.[21]

Always sympathetic to the military, Bullitt enjoyed the company of the People's Commissar of Defense, Kliment Voroshilov, "one of the most charming persons I have ever met." Voroshilov grew up in the metal factories in Luhansk and started his career in the Red Army during the Civil War in Ukraine. He would become the longest-serving member of the Central Committee of the Communist Party (thirty-four years), and his native city would be named after him. Voroshilov knew how to engage with Americans: Thayer also wrote about Voroshilov as a charming fellow who looked like a "cherub," and recorded how Bullitt danced "some sort of a medley" of the Caucasian *lezginka* and American foxtrot with Voroshilov.[22] At their first meeting, Voroshilov asked Bullitt to bring to the embassy American naval and aviation experts so that his commissariat could use their advice. Passing this request to Roosevelt, Bullitt offered his support: "It is obvious that our representatives in the Soviet Union today can have a really immense influence." He advised Roosevelt to send the best men, "who will be absolutely on the level with the Soviet Government"; if these American officers in Russia would "refrain from spying and dirty tricks of every variety," they could play a role of the military advisers to the Soviet leaders, which might be "very useful in the future" (65).

On December 20, 1933, Voroshilov invited Bullitt and his translators to a gala in the Kremlin. Stalin was there, and with him "the whole gang that really runs things—the inside directorate," explained Litvinov in his rich English. Bullitt was introduced to Stalin for the first time. "He was dressed in a common soldier's uniform," Bullitt observed. Surprised by the Soviet dictator's small stature, he admired Stalin's "shrewd humor." In a dispatch to Roosevelt, Bullitt dedicated a long passage to a detailed account of Stalin's pipe, eyes, hands, nostrils, and mustache. Evidently, Bullitt was taken with Stalin, and he eagerly shared his feelings with Roosevelt: "With Lenin one felt at once that he was in the presence of a great man; with Stalin I felt like talking to a wiry Gypsy with roots and emotions beyond my experience" (66).

Stalin and Bullitt spoke across the hostess, Voroshilov's wife. The toasts at the table followed a tradition that Bullitt thought was Russian but was actually Georgian. Stalin began by proposing a toast to President Roosevelt, "who in spite of the mute growls of the Fishes dared to recognize the Soviet Union." Hamilton Fish, a congressman and the First World War veteran, was an opponent of the New Deal and of recognition of the Soviet Union. Stalin knew it and he knew the word "fish"; the table appreciated the joke with "considerable laughter." In response, Bullitt proposed a toast to the health of President Kalinin. Molotov offered the third toast, "To the health of one who comes to us as a new Ambassador but an old friend" (67). The memory of his unsuccessful mission to Bolshevik Russia, which had for a time ruined Bullitt's career, was helping him now.

After the tenth toast, Bullitt tried to sip rather than drain his glass, but Litvinov explained that it would offend the gentleman who proposed the toast. Bullitt continued to drink in Russian-style, bottoms-up. "I have never before so thanked God," Bullitt wrote to Roosevelt who also loved to serve his guests a few too many cocktails, "for the possession of a head impervious to any quantity of liquor." Gradually, everyone at the table reached a condition that Bullitt compared to the all-male banquets at Yale, where "discretion was conspicuous by its absence." The intoxicated Soviet leaders discussed the Japanese threat. Introducing Bullitt to General Alexander Egorov, chief of general staff, Stalin said: "This is the man who will lead our army victoriously against Japan when Japan attacks" (promoted to the highest military rank of marshal, Egorov was tried and executed in 1939). Near the end of the dinner, Stalin asked Bullitt for assistance in a massive economic deal: he wanted to buy 250,000 tons of old railroad from the United States, which the Soviets needed for a new line to Vladivostok. Stalin explained that he would beat the Japanese anyway, but used American rails would make it easier. Stalin then grabbed Georgiy Piatakov, the deputy commissar of heavy industry, marched him to the piano and ordered him to play. While the organizer of Soviet industrialization played "wild Russian dances," Stalin stood behind him and hugged him "affectionately" (67–68). Piatakov was tried, tortured, and executed in 1937.

After hours of eating and drinking, Stalin and Bullitt sat down and talked through an interpreter. "Stalin was feeling extremely gay, as we all were, but he gave me the feeling that he was speaking honestly," Bullitt reported to Roosevelt. Wanting Bullitt to feel at home in Moscow, Stalin asked him to tell Roosevelt that, "in spite of being a leader of a capitalist nation," the American president was "one of the most popular people in the Soviet Union." Passing these niceties on to Roosevelt, Bullitt added some flattery of his own for Stalin, calling the Soviet leader a man of "great shrewdness and inflexible will"; the conversation convinced him that Stalin also had "intuition in extraordinary measure." Finally, Stalin had another gift: "the quality of being able to treat the most serious things with a joke and twinkle in his eye. Lenin had the same quality. You have it," Bullitt wrote to Roosevelt. In these semi-official dispatches, Bullitt never missed a chance to inform, boast, entertain, and flatter; reporting on a drunken party with Stalin was a great chance to practice this diplomatic art. Saying goodbye, Stalin promised Bullitt something that he did not offer to any other ambassador or, in fact, to anyone but his bodyguards: access "any time, day or night. You have only to let me know and I will see you at once." Bullitt saw this offer as an "extraordinary gesture" and had no doubt it was sincere and true (69). Despite his intuition, Bullitt did not suspect that he would never see the Soviet leader again.

Before leaving, Stalin asked Bullitt whether there was "anything at all in the Soviet Union" that Bullitt wanted. Bullitt replied modestly, saying that he wanted nothing but to continue "the intimate relations" with Stalin. But when Stalin persisted in offering his help "with a genuinely friendly emotion," Bullitt revealed what he really wanted. The new embassy needed working and residential space, and Bullitt had his eye on a neoclassical mansion that was built in 1915 for Moscow banker and industrialist Nikolay Vtorov, one of the richest men in prerevolutionary Russia. The mansion was not big enough for the embassy, though its central hall was "colossal," wrote Bullitt, who later used this hall to its limit. The mansion, which would be the ambassador's residence, later became known by the hybrid Russian-English name "Spaso House."

For the embassy itself, Bullitt chose a different place: Sparrow Hills, a high bluff on the bend of the Moscow River. There was a lake and wooded areas, and the best views of the river and the city. "We were not modest in our demands and asked for the entire bluff containing some fifteen acres of ground," Bullitt wrote to Roosevelt, who approved the idea. They did not know that more than one hundred years earlier, on this plot of land Alexander I started but never finished the "Cathedral of Christ the Savior," which would have served as a monument to Russia's victory over Napoleon. Nor could they have foreseen that after the Soviet Union's victory in the Second World War, Moscow State University would be built on the same land—the "temple of science," as the Russian press called it, which belatedly imitated the skyscrapers of New York but was, at the time of its construction in 1948, the tallest building in Europe. Unaware of this, Bullitt had his own grand project in mind. He wanted to build at Sparrow Hills an expanded replica of Monticello, Thomas Jefferson's manor in Virginia. "I can conceive of nothing more perfect for an American Embassy than a reproduction of Monticello in that setting," Bullitt wrote to the president (65). For both of them, Jefferson's estate in Virginia, a masterpiece of neoclassical architecture, was a symbol of the American Revolution, pilgrimage site, and a monument to American democracy. Several high-ranking officials in the State Department were southerners, and Bullitt hoped that they would like his idea of a Monticello on the Moscow River.

And so, Bullitt asked Stalin to give the American government fifteen acres of land in Sparrow Hills for the construction of the American embassy. Stalin agreed, and Bullitt held out his hand to shake hands with the Soviet Leader. To his astonishment, Stalin took his head in his hands and gave him "a large kiss." Then Stalin turned up his face for kiss in return, and Bullitt kissed Stalin. "This evening with Stalin and the inner circle of the Soviet Government seems almost unbelievable in retrospect," wrote Bullitt to Roosevelt (69).

Bullitt immediately started corresponding with Soviet authorities about building the embassy. Troyanovsky, the Soviet ambassador in Washington, confirmed the deal in an official letter. Roosevelt requested funding for the project from Congress, which allotted money with the understanding that the American government would rent Spaso House while the embassy in Sparrow Hills was under construction. Bullitt's daughter, Anna, later described Spaso House: "It was a Russian Victorian pomposity, badly proportioned and cold, enormous with no room for anything. It was built around the central ballroom with a glass dome like the Capitol, so I crawl from my bedroom and lie on the floor upstairs and watch between the marble balustrade what was going on below, like Voroshilov and Budyonny doing Russian dances after polo." Indeed, the residence was not entirely comfortable, and the ambassador knew about the unfortunate history of his new home: in 1918, the owner's son killed his father, a fabulously rich industrialist, in the central ballroom. After the revolution, the commissars used the mansion for entertaining; according to Anna, they added "an enormous dining room in red marble, incorporating the hammer and sickle in the Corinthian columns" (81).

Bullitt noticed surveillance every time he left Spaso House. At home he was always concerned about wiretapping; he routinely instructed his assistants to look for taps and hidden microphones, and often they found them. He invited naval experts to set up professionally designed codes to encrypt his communications and to eliminate bugs and leaks. Ironically, years later Bullitt would find out that Tyler Kent, the person to whom he entrusted the codes, was a Soviet agent.[23]

After much effort Bullitt managed to get permission from the Kremlin to fly an airplane over the Soviet Union. He even planned to fly to Siberia, though this ambitious project did not materialize. He had a personal pilot, Thomas White, who had been recommended by General MacArthur. White was tall, elegant, and spoke Russian, but he did not fly well. Once he lost his control of his plane and landed upside down in a swamp near Leningrad while flying with Bullitt, though both survived the accident. But like other Bullitt's employees, White made a stellar career during the Cold War: from 1957 to 1961, he served as Chief of Staff of the US Air Force and in this capacity, convinced conservative generals to produce the first ballistic missiles. Another smart appointment was Roscoe Hillencoetter, a sailor and naval courier whom Bullitt named his security chief. Hillencoetter followed Bullitt to Paris and served as assistant naval attaché. Later he worked with the French Resistance, and after the war became the first director of the CIA.

Bullitt's initial successes evoked a mixed response from the diplomats who had more extensive experience with the Soviets. The British consul in Leningrad wrote, "The new ambassador, Bullitt, was appointed by Roosevelt as being a friend of the Soviet Union—a dangerous position to be in. The other foreign missions are watching with *Schadenfreude* to see how long the honeymoon will last."[24] George Kennan also mixed warmth with caution when talking about Bullitt. He was "a fine ambassador," Kennan wrote in 1972. "We took pride in him and never had an occasion to be ashamed of him. . . . Bullitt, as I knew him at that time in Moscow, was charming, well-educated, imaginative, a man of the world." Kennan emphasized that Bullitt was able to argue with the great intellects of the Communist movement, such as Radek and Bukharin. He spoke excellent French and German, which compensated for his inability to speak Russian. Most importantly, "he was outstandingly a buoyant disposition. He resolutely refused to permit the life around him to degenerate into dullness and dreariness. All of us who lived in his entourage were the beneficiaries of this blitheness of spirit, this insistence that life be at all times animated and interesting and moving ahead."[25]

However, Bullitt was impatient, which was a weakness for a diplomat, Kennan argued. The ambassador "came to Russia with high hopes, and he wanted to see them realized at once." Kennan also believed that Bullitt had underestimated the difference between Stalin and Lenin, and this misperception was the reason for his excessive disenchantment with the Soviet Union. Nonetheless, Bullitt and his staff still accomplished a great deal. "We were in many respects a pioneer enterprise—a wholly new type of American diplomatic mission, the model and precursor of great many missions of a later day. . . . We were the first to cope seriously, for example, with the problem of security . . . in a hostile environment. But we were also the first to take a primarily intellectual and scholarly attitude to our work. . . . We regarded ourselves as a lonely and exposed bastion of American governmental life, surrounded by a veritable ocean of official Soviet ill will."[26]

Although this description of the ambassadorial lifestyle does not sound very appealing, Kennan remembered his years in the Soviet Union as the best, most productive time in his long life. Even the Moscow winters were "healthy and exhilarating." He was lonely at first, especially in the winter of 1934, when Bullitt left for Washington and made Kennan the acting head of the embassy. Unlike his colleagues, who were mostly bachelors, Kennan was married but kept his wife away from Moscow. Like Wilson, Kennan was raised a Presbyterian; like Freud, he claimed he was agnostic. The problems of moral choice tormented Kennan, and like Bullitt, he often discussed them in theological and demonological terms. Before his appointment to Moscow, Kennan had served as an intern at the diplomatic station in Riga. He practiced his Russian with Vladimir Kozhevnikov, a homosexual and a cocaine addict. Embarrassed, Kennan wrote to his sister, "My Puritan origins [are] rising in relentless revolt against the non-puritanical influences of the last few years," and the victory was with the former. As he put it, "prolonged and intimate association with the devil does not lie in the Kennan character." That summer he fell in love and, a few months later, married a woman who would remain his wife for seventy-three years. Referring to *Faust*, young Kennan wrote that his biography should be called "The story of the man who tried to sell his soul and could not" (in fact, his biography, written by John Gaddis, is subtitled *An American Life*).[27] As a connoisseur of Russian literature and theater, Kennan was able "to drink in impressions of Russia itself: of its life, its culture, its aspect, its smell." He socialized with American journalists who were based in Moscow, such as Walter Duranty and Eugene Lyons. Most of them sympathized with the regime, enjoyed its support, and lived with Russian girlfriends. Together they organized, as Kennan put it, "uproariously informal parties."

Sharing abundant drinks and meals with their Russian friends, the American diplomats and journalists passionately discussed the absurdities of both Russian and American life. But Kennan knew he was different from other Americans in Moscow: he was never enchanted with Marxism and avoided the sharp disappointment with it that became familiar to many, including Bullitt. For Kennan, there was something in Russia for which he could not find words, and he was in love with these inexpressible qualities: "words would fail me if I were to try to convey in this context the excitement, the enjoyment, the fascination, and the frustration of the initial service in Moscow."[28] This was a remarkable confession for someone who built an outstanding career on his ability to shape vague political ideas into precise diplomatic formulae. He believed that his colleagues also felt an unusual satisfaction with their Russian life: "Most of us look back at these days, I suppose, as the high point of life—the high point, at least, in comradeship, in gaiety, in intensity of experience."[29]

Still, the Moscow entries in Kennan's diary are full of uncomfortable experiences that he tried to control. On September 3, 1934, Kennan wrote that in Moscow "human flesh lives in one seething, intimate mass—far more so even than in New York. . . . And it is human life in the raw, human life brought down to its fundamentals—good and evil, drunk and sober, loving and quarreling, laughing and weeping—all that human life is and does anywhere, but all much more simple and direct, and therefore stronger."[30] Discussing the frequent question, "How do the Russians stand it?" he responded: "Many of them didn't." All those vital people he saw on the streets, "they are the elite, not the elite of wealth . . . but nature's own elite, the elite of the living, as opposed to hoi polloi of the dead."[31] This survivors' elite captivated him, "an over-civilized, neurotic foreigner" who would have difficulty enduring there, he wrote, even for a few months. Bitterly critical of the Soviet regime, Kennan loved "the tremendous, pulsating warmth and vitality of the Russians." This was also Bullitt's perspective, though young Kennan articulated it better—and exaggerated to an extent. They both would remain "distrusted outsider[s]" of Soviet life, which they explored with undiplomatic vigor and disdain; but a deep, illusionary sense of belonging was solely Kennan's: "I would rather be sent to Siberia among them (which is certainly what would happen to me without delay if I were a Soviet citizen) than to live on Park Avenue among our stuffy folk." Here were unusual views for someone who would lay the foundations of American politics toward the Soviet Union for decades to come. Deeply concerned about escalating problems in the Soviet Union, he never blamed the people—this "human life in the raw," the surviving "elite of the living," "one of the world's greatest people." Only the government was responsible for the terror, devastation, and despair—a "ruthless authoritarian regime which will stop at nothing."[32]

This uneasy mix between two deep emotions—love for the Russian people and culture and deep contempt toward the Soviet regime—infused Kennan's reports, articles, and books, including the famous "Long Telegram." Balancing one another, these two feelings secured the flexibility of Kennan's strategy of containment, which did help the world avoid a new world war. Kennan's friends knew that his love for Russia was unconditional; Isaiah Berlin described this passion as "a kind of unhappy love affair, where love grows deeper and more desperate the more obviously it is unrequited."[33] They also knew about Kennan's critical attitude toward the US government; after reading his *Soviet-American Relations*, Berlin remarked: "How typical of George Kennan to accuse America of all recent misdeeds."[34]

Kennan's service at the Bullitt embassy in Moscow fundamentally shaped his political views. In his dispatches from there, he focused mainly on the arrests, deportations, and sheer terror of Soviet life; for him, it was "a sort of liberal education in the horrors of Stalinism." When he wrote his memoirs many decades later, he said that his understanding of the events in the mid-1930s had not been "inaccurate."[35] His dislike for Soviet-style Marxism made him a particularly shrewd observer: "My own case was perhaps unusual in that there were no pro-Soviet sympathies to overcome." Unlike his fellow Americans in Moscow, he had never gone through a Marxist period; moreover, he harbored a complete distaste for Russian Marxism. He explained this distaste as a result of his experience living in the Baltic countries; his happy marriage to a Norwegian helped as well. As he saw it, after Kirov's murder in 1934 a "terrible cloud of suspicion and violence, of sinister, unidentifiable terror" came over the USSR, and it was a new thing rather than a continuation of a tradition. In Washington, the New Dealers believed in the virtues of planned economy and were not particularly interested in his depictions of the Soviet terror; Kennan soon realized that his views of Stalin's Russia did not match the official line in Washington. However, Bullitt saw in Kennan his most capable employee and fully supported him.

The regime invested its power in isolating the foreigners who lived in Moscow from its native population. Still, opportunities for contact were many:

according to Kennan, the members of the embassy talked with ordinary Russians at the theater, during public events, and while traveling. Focused on the political terror, investigative torture, and mass arrests that he had seen in Moscow, Kennan did not think that they were logical consequences of socialism. On the contrary, his views in this period were shifting to the left, and he was becoming more critical of American capitalism, even in the relatively watered-down version articulated in the New Deal.

Despite Moscow's charms, Kennan developed ulcers that everyone agreed were the result of the bad food and hard life in Russia. In his memoirs Kennan connects the worsening of his ulcer to the murder of Kirov, which, he thought, initiated the Soviet terror. Bullitt sent him to Vienna, and his condition improved under the supervision of the pioneering doctor Frieda Por, a Jewish Hungarian therapist who suggested he read Freud.[36] As Bullitt did for Freud, Kennan helped his doctor emigrate to the United States. Upon his return to Moscow in 1935, Kennan watched the show trials and purges for two more years. He reported them to Washington in great detail. "Now we know more about the background of these events than we did then; but then, on the spot, our ideas were quite adequate," he wrote in 1972. In the Russia of the mid-1930s, Kennan saw "the purges, cynicism, shamelessness, contempt for humanity—all triumphantly enthroned." The country was in the hands of a monstrous tyrant, he wrote, and the evidence of human degradation was everywhere. "The effect was never to leave me. Its imprint on my political judgment was one that would place me at odds with official thinking in Washington for at least a decade thereafter."[37]

Kennan's extraordinarily successful career during the Cold War was a result of his early experiences in Moscow and with Bullitt. "I couldn't be the sort of smooth, self-contained type of Foreign Service officer who advanced because he'd made no waves," Kennan wrote. In February 1946, Isaiah Berlin wrote that he was surprised to find in Kennan a very unusual kind of diplomat. Unlike many colleagues whom Berlin met in Washington during his diplomatic service in the Second World War, Kennan was thoughtful and gloomy; Berlin explained Kennan's "melancholy" by the fact that he was intellectually "absorbed" by the nature of the Stalinist regime.[38]

But in early 1934, Bullitt and Kennan still hoped that the difficulties of socialism would be temporary and the honeymoon of Soviet-American relations would produce serious results that would change Russia and the world. That spring, Bullitt brought a new group of employees to Moscow. His new secretary, Carmel Offie, was known as a very capable man (Kennan described him as a "Renaissance type"), but he did not speak Russian. For many years, he took care of Bullitt's correspondence, financial affairs, and health issues. Loy Henderson was Kennan's friend at the Riga consulate; after his work in the Moscow embassy, he became an influential desk officer at the State Department. The pinnacle of his career was to predict the 1939 pact between the Soviets and the Nazis. But later during the war, the State Department purged the officials whose expertise sounded too anti-Soviet, and almost all of these people were former members of Bullitt's embassy. Roosevelt sent Henderson to Asia, and he served as the ambassador to Iraq, India, and Iran.

Another expert on the Soviet Union, whose career Bullitt launched to the top of American politics, was Charles Bohlen. He had also learned Russian in Riga with Kennan and then became Bullitt's close associate in Moscow. More diplomatic than other members of the embassy, Bohlen survived several changes in American policy towards the Soviet Union. During the war, he came to Moscow with Harry Hopkins, and was Roosevelt's translator in Tehran and Yalta. Later he wrote the most important speeches for Marshall and was Truman's adviser on Soviet affairs. Isaiah Berlin knew both diplomats, Bohlen and Kennan, and noted interesting differences between them. To Bohlen, Soviet-American relations were something like a game of chess; for Kennan, it was a struggle of "ideas, traditions . . . forms of life."[39] In 1953 Bohlen replaced Kennan, whom the Soviets had declared persona non grata, as the head of the US embassy in Moscow. Then, like Bullitt, Bohlen was appointed ambassador to France in 1963.

Two of the top diplomats of the Cold War, Bohlen and Kennan were close friends. "Life has made us the intellectual and professional brothers," wrote Kennan. Depicting his friendship with Bohlen but, as usual, lacking English words to describe all things related to Russia, Kennan cited Nikolai Bukharin, an early Bolshevik leader and a victim of the Moscow show trials (1936–1938). Kennan admired Bukharin and his friends and was shocked by the trials. Tortured and possibly drugged, the erstwhile leaders of the revolution confessed to espionage and high treason and denounced their friends in incredible detail. According to Kennan, Bukharin said in his last speech before being convicted and shot, "intellectual friendship was the strongest of the bonds between men."[40]

In this rhetorical construction, Kennan described a friendship with an American colleague using the words that one Bolshevik said about another in the most extraordinary circumstances, after torture and before death. The

American observers saw the people who made the Russian Revolution and became its victims as fabulous figures, heroes of ancient tragedy, hostages of fate. Those few Muscovites who met the Americans in Stalin's Moscow also saw them as mythical heroes—powerful aliens who could bring either danger or salvation. This trade in extraordinary and unrealistic expectations was one of the secrets of Stalin's Moscow.

10

BLUFF

E verything had changed when Bullitt returned to Moscow in early 1934 after a trip to Washington. "The honeymoon atmosphere had evaporated completely before I arrived," he wrote in a letter to Roosevelt.[1] In an effort to save face, he said he had anticipated this turn of events, though he evidently had not. In March 1934 Bullitt reported the unexpected détente in Soviet-Japanese relations to the State Department: "In December the Soviet Government was so fearful of an immediate attack by Japan that cooperation with us was eager and immediate. The Soviet Government is now convinced that Japan will not attack and we are therefore simply one among the capitalist nations." As a result, the ambassador was having "the greatest difficulty in getting anything done" in Moscow.[2] A joke began circling around the embassy: "The Japanese have let us down badly."[3] Bullitt formulated a general rule: "The Russians' love for us at any moment will be exactly [in] proportion to their fear of Japan."[4]

Years earlier Roosevelt and Bullitt had made a bet about where the next war would break out, wagering "one red apple." Roosevelt picked Europe and Bullitt picked the Far East. In the spring of 1935 Bullitt reminded the president of this old bet, noting with his usual flattery that Roosevelt had been right again. Austria was about to explode, while the Far East was then "momentarily quiet."[5] Still, the coming war with Japan was Bullitt's central concern in Moscow. Whose war would it be? Bullitt knew how weak the Soviet Union's

immense eastern borders were. Russian naval forces in the Pacific were min-
iscule. The Russo-Japanese War of 1904–1905 resulted in the destruction of
the Russian navy, the humiliating peace that Theodore Roosevelt brokered
in Portsmouth, and mass protests all over Russia that foreshadowed the collapse of the Romanov empire.

In a July 1934 dispatch to the State Department, Bullitt told his side of the
story. "The fear which still obsesses all the leaders of the Soviet Government
is that of a war on two fronts." According to this script, the war would start in
the East and continue unpredictably. "Every member of the government is
convinced that if Japan should attack the Soviet Union in the East, Poland
would, at a favorable moment, attack in the West." Although there was no
formal agreement between Poland and Japan, Bullitt referred to the words of
the Polish leader, Józef Piłsudski, who said that a Japanese attack on the
Soviet Union would give Poland a chance that comes but once in a thousand
years. Moreover, Bullitt wrote that Hitler was aware of the Polish-Japanese
plans and that the Soviet government was aware of Hitler's cooperation with
the Poles. In December 1934 Nazi foreign minister Konstantin von Neurath
told the American ambassador to Berlin, William Dodd, that "Japan would
invade Russia in case of war and that the result would be chaos in Russia";
Dodd was "surprised" by these words.[6] Bullitt's good friend in Moscow, the
French ambassador Charles Alphand, told him that the forthcoming
Franco-Soviet Treaty of Mutual Assistance would relieve the tensions in the
Far East.[7] Concluded in May 1935 this pact failed to have much of a global
impact, however. Soviet-American rapprochement would have done more,
and peace in the Pacific was clearly in the interests of the two countries. But
unlike Theodore Roosevelt in 1905, FDR did not want to engage America in
complex multilateral talks.

Bullitt was right that the Bolsheviks were worried about a possible war
with Japan, but he underestimated their self-preservation skills. Precisely
because of its fear of Japan, the Soviet government was planning a major
diplomatic retreat. Already in May 1933 Litvinov had made a secret proposal
to the Japanese government about selling the disputed Chinese Eastern
Railway, a strategic asset in any future war in the Far East. As in Brest-
Litovsk in 1919, the Bolsheviks withdrew from positions that their predecessors had successfully defended; after the Russo-Japanese talks in 1905—
and mostly because of American help in these talks—the Chinese Eastern
Railway remained a Russian, and later a joint Soviet-Chinese, property.
Selling the strategically important railway, with adjacent territory, towns,

and industries, to Japan was a dramatic undertaking. The railway was about one thousand kilometers long, and about seventy thousand Russians lived in the rail corridor. Soviet and Japanese diplomats kept the talks secret until the sale was announced in March 1935. Russian engineers and their families were deported to Siberia; by 1937 the NKVD had shot twenty-eight thousand of them.[8]

Bullitt's counterpart, the Russian ambassador to Washington Alexander Troyanovsky, started his career as an officer in the Russo-Japanese War. Praising Troyanovsky in his letters to Roosevelt, Bullitt believed that like those proverbial generals who are always prepared to fight the last war, Stalin's diplomats would do everything to avoid the worst defeat of their recent past. In his very first telegrams from Washington in January 1934, Troyanovsky repeatedly asked the Commissariat for Foreign Affairs about the negotiations with Japan and the decision about the Chinese Eastern Railway. Like Bullitt, Troyanovsky understood that Soviet-Japanese tensions would define American-Soviet relations. But Troyanovsky knew what Bullitt did not know: key to the Soviet-Japanese relations was the Chinese Eastern Railway. During Troyanovsky's first meeting with Roosevelt in February, the president started the conversation by asking the ambassador about the Japanese position toward Russia. Assuring Troyanovsky that American intentions in the Pacific were peaceful, Roosevelt warned him about the strength of the Japanese navy. Troyanovsky did not mention the negotiations about of the Chinese Eastern Railway.[9] Bullitt learned about the secret talks between the USSR and Japan in July 1934 from Boris Stomoniakov, the Bulgarian revolutionary who was the Bolshevik deputy commissar for foreign affairs (he was arrested and executed in 1938). But Stomoniakov also told Bullitt that the Japanese would not attack the Soviet Union because they feared the power of Soviet aviation. To prove this point, Stomoniakov "insisted" (wrote Bullitt, with some irony) that the Japanese people had some racial defect in their "ear channels" that damaged their sense of equilibrium and "made it physically impossible for the Japanese to develop aviators of the highest ability."[10] Feeling the Soviet-Japanese détente and interviewing his counterparts in Moscow about it, Bullitt underappreciated the real explanation, the forthcoming sale of a huge and strategically important territory. Even a year later, the Soviet consul in San Francisco told the commissariat that "many Americans" disbelieved the rumors about the forthcoming sale of the Chinese Eastern Railway; they thought that Soviet diplomats were trying to buy time by dragging on talks with Japan.[11]

After two years of negotiations, the Soviet Union sold the Chinese Eastern Railway and dramatically changed the situation in the Far East. Of course, Stalin and Litvinov did not know how successfully they had redirected their old enemy, Japan, against their new friend, the United States. However, they understood the importance of their secret negotiations with Japan. Stalin's request for the colossal purchase of old American rails was forgotten, as was Bullitt's idea of sending a group of American navy vessels to Vladivostok for a friendly visit. The sale of the Chinese Eastern Railway was presented as a major victory for Soviet diplomacy; it could be the reason that, when the whole of Litvinov's commissariat was purged and his deputies were executed on the eve of the Molotov-Ribbentrop pact, Litvinov was allowed to survive. Redirecting Japanese aggression toward the United States, the Soviets cherished their new peace with Japan even though this peace was interrupted by several border conflicts in 1938–1939. Even when the Second World War was at its peak, the Soviet Union preserved diplomatic relations with Japan and remained neutral with respect to Japanese-American hostilities.

Soviet-American diplomatic relations were first established in anticipation of a coming war in the northern Pacific, and they shaped in a different way when war seemed unlikely. In this new situation, the Soviets refused to discuss the settlement of Russian debts, even though that had been a condition for establishing diplomatic relations between the two nations. Revising its decision, the Moscow City Council agreed to give to the US Embassy not the fifteen acres of the Sparrow Hills that Bullitt had requested but a low and marshy part of them instead. Bullitt was outraged, along with the State Department officials. According to their calculations, the American embassy in Moscow needed 280 office rooms and 220 residential rooms, while in fact, it had 72 rooms for all purposes.[12] Eventually, Congress transferred the funds it had allocated for the construction of Monticello in Moscow, Bullitt's ambitious project, to the embassies in Central America. In April 1934 Roosevelt signed the isolationist Johnson Act, which prohibited the government and private banks from granting loans to nations that failed to pay their wartime debts (Finland was the only country that had paid them). Bullitt's position in talks with the Soviet leaders deteriorated sharply. On his part Litvinov could no longer hope—and promise the Kremlin—that they would persuade the American ambassador to grant a loan to the Soviets. Disappointed, Litvinov accused Bullitt of a "tendency to blackmail."[13]

Bullitt developed a new narrative that spring. According to the story he repeated to various Soviet officials, the resolution of Soviet-Japanese tensions was the result of newly established Soviet-American diplomatic relations. Bullitt's negotiations in Moscow, he said, had alarmed Japanese leaders and pacified them. He started spreading this story before he learned about the negotiations about the Chinese Eastern Railway, but he did not stop after he learned of it. The first time that Bullitt tested this narrative was during a visit to one of the top Soviet diplomats in Moscow, Ivan Divilkovsky, on March 7, 1934. Divilkovsky was a relatively young French-speaking diplomat who was then the general secretary of the Commissariat of Foreign Affairs; his memos reveal that Divilkovsky and Bullitt understood each other well. Bullitt told Divilkovsky about "a significant reduction of tensions in Soviet-Japanese affairs," and his Soviet interlocutor agreed. According to Divilkovsky's memo, Bullitt said, "ostensibly, the Japanese were convinced that during his first visit to Moscow [as the ambassador in December 1933], he reached with us an agreement that the United States would provide us with military aid in the case of conflict with Japan."[14] Divilkovsky's language in this memo shows that he did not believe Bullitt's story.

On March 13, Bullitt repeated the same line to the deputy Commissar for Foreign Affairs, Nikolai Krestinsky. The former ambassador to Germany (1922–1930), Krestinksy was an old Bolshevik who would be executed in 1938 as a leader of a supposed Trotskyite organization in Moscow. "Bullitt said that the Japanese have developed an explanation for his recent visit to and quick departure from Moscow. They believe that he and the Soviet government agreed on some kind of treaty that was directed against Japan, and that this treaty was so important and secret that he could not trust it to the telegraph and had to go to report the news personally to the President."[15] Krestinsky asked what further consequences these events would bring. Bullitt told him, "the Americans did nothing to refute these suspicions of the Japanese. They chose to let them [the Japanese] think that we have agreed about something. Let it be a situation that constrains them."[16]

The next day, Bullitt discussed the same issues with Litvinov, who only three months earlier had anticipated an imminent Japanese attack. Again, Bullitt told Litvinov that Japan would not attack that spring because it was concerned about a possible intervention by America. Clearly, Bullitt wanted Litvinov to understand that peace in the Far East was, essentially, the result of American diplomatic efforts. But the Soviet commissar, who had been fully involved in the negotiations about the Chinese Eastern Railway, did not take the bait. "Bullitt said nothing interesting but the fact that America will not come out with its own initiatives," he wrote to Troyanovsky.[17] On March 26,

Bullitt repeated his message to deputy commissar, Grigorii Sokolnikov (previously the head of the Bolshevik delegation in Brest-Litovsk, Sokolnikov would be arrested as a Trotskyite leader and murdered in 1939): "the Japanese are confident that I brought from Moscow to Washington the terms of our secret [American-Soviet] deal against Japan and discussed them with Roosevelt." However, Sokolnikov wrote in his memo, Bullitt added that, in fact, America had "no intentions of going to war with Japan."[18]

Having no assurance from the president that the United States would help Russia if war broke out with Japan, Bullitt realized that all he could do in this respect was a diplomatic maneuver that amounted to a bluff. With limited means, he needed to show that his bluff was credible. In March 1934 Bullitt suggested to Walton Moore, assistant secretary of state, that Moore could "intimate" to the Soviet diplomats that, if they did not want the service of the American Import-Export Bank, this facility would be offered to the Japanese. "A mere hint in this direction will, I believe, produce agreeable results," Bullitt wrote.[19] With Divilkovsky, he discussed the forthcoming Second Naval Disarmament Conference in London; Bullitt wanted to attend it and was hoping the Soviets would take part in this event alongside the United States, European powers, and Japan. The problem was that the Soviet navy was too small to qualify for the conference. Acknowledging the situation, Divilkovsky told Bullitt that the Soviet Union could not compete with Japan in building dreadnoughts. In response Bullitt proposed "half-seriously" that the Soviet government "publish a monstrous program of naval development," which would secure its place among the great oceanic powers.[20] Bullitt could not offer any actual aid for the project, so he tried to act by stirring up publicity.

Bullitt correctly identified the Japanese threat to the USSR as the key issue in his negotiations with the Soviets. The threat continued for years to come, but the perception of it was changing. In December 1933 Litvinov told him that "everyone" expected a Japanese attack on Vladivostok.[21] Several months later, in April 1934, Bullitt wrote Roosevelt that "the Russians are convinced that Japan will not attack this spring or summer," and that was the reason that their "underlying hostility" was palpable "through the veneer of intimate friendship."[22] Still, the perceived threat was diminishing, and Litvinov believed this to be his major success in office. Whether or not Bullitt understood the reason for this change in the Bolsheviks' mind, he still hoped that this development would not damage his interests in Moscow. In October 1934 he told Roosevelt about a "most belligerent" conversation he had with Litvinov, who "still under-estimates completely the influence that the United

States can have in preserving peace in the Far East." To his relief, Bullitt had a better understanding with Bolshevik military leaders, who wanted to beef up their garrisons in the Far East. "Fortunately Voroshilov is putting a great deal of energy into this job" of preserving peace in the Pacific, Bullitt wrote to Moore.[23]

In March 1934 Litvinov fell ill and received Bullitt in hospital. Bullitt wanted to discuss the project on Sparrow Hills and the payment of the old debts, but Litvinov wanted new loans. Bullitt could not promise them, and Litvinov chose to ignore Bullitt's hints about Japan. Both sides were irritated, and Litvinov referred Bullitt to the head of the Protocol section of the commissariat, Dmitrii Florinsky. After two stressful conversations on March 25 and 26, 1934, Florinsky wrote a memo in which he recorded their discussion with some irony. Florinsky said that the previous agreement about the land on Sparrow Hills was the "greatest and extremely sad misunderstanding" and blamed Troyanovsky for this misunderstanding; there was a certain typo in the document signed by Troyanovsky, he said, and this typo was the cause of misunderstanding. His apologies, Florinsky noted, put Bullitt "into a state of extreme exaltation, which he barely tried to conceal"; his face turned red and his tone became "ruthless." Bullitt said that it would be impossible to build the American embassy on the remaining seven acres because the president and Congress had already approved the project, which was slated to reproduce "the best examples of American architecture" (he meant Monticello). Bullitt had discussed the plan for the new embassy with everyone from Stalin to Roosevelt; he "categorically refused" to accept the new and diminished offer. Florinsky responded "that there are troubles that could always happen, that could be neither predicted nor avoided. This is what happened with the misprinted order. One should courageously look at the failures as they are. One cannot ignore the facts." Understandably, this made Bullitt even more furious. He stated that the United States would either build the embassy beautifully and according to the approved plan or not build it at all. Finally, Bullitt changed the subject to Japan. Again, he "confidentially" told Florinsky that the Japanese government believed that during his visit to Moscow in December, Bullitt had signed a secret pact with the Soviet government that obliged the United States to enter the war should hostilities emerge between Japan and the Soviet Union. Bullitt insinuated that this was secret information he had learned directly from the Japanese. Surprised by Bullitt's unexpected sincerity, Florinsky informed his superiors about this conversation in detail.[24]

It so happened that we know more about Florinsky than we know about

Bullitt's other counterparts in Moscow. A relatively sophisticated person who started his career as Litvinov's secretary, Florinsky was the son of the former head of Kiev University. The Bolsheviks had shot his father. When the British consul in Leningrad asked Florinsky how he could work with them after this, Florinsky asked in response, "if one's father was run over by a tram should one cease to ride trams?"[25] However, the Soviet Terror was not a tram. On October 5, 1934, Florinsky was playing bridge with Irene Wiley, the wife of the Counselor of the American Embassy, when he was called to the telephone; he came back smiling and said that he would soon return and resume the game. Irene never saw him again. Florinsky was accused of organizing a homosexual ring within the Commissariat for Foreign Affairs. Presumably threatened or tortured, he outed many Moscow homosexuals—most of them within the commissariat—who were also arrested. After serving five years in the notorious Solovetsky camp, Florinsky was tried again, this time for espionage, and executed.[26]

In August 1934 Bullitt greeted his friend, French financier Jean Monnet, at Spaso House, the new home of the American embassy in Moscow. Monnet had just come from China, where he was advising the government of Chiang Kai-shek on financial reform. Curious and energetic, Monnet shared with Bullitt his "creatively intimate picture of China and Japan." On Monnet's suggestion, Bullitt decided to go to Japan. "I was very anxious to fly to Vladivostok but decided that it was foolhardy and shall, therefore, take the train." When the trip was at risk of being delayed, he shared his impatience with Evgenii Rubinin, an official with the Commissariat for Foreign Affairs. In a memo Rubinin wrote that Bullitt had "connected some ambitious plans with this trip to the Far East."[27] Rubinin was probably right: Bullitt's ambitious plans were definitely connected to the "secret pact" between the United States and the USSR, Bullitt's own invention.

In September 1934 in Washington Bullitt met his old friend Boris Skvirsky, a Soviet diplomat who had been instrumental in establishing diplomatic relations with the United States. Skvirsky in a memo recorded what Bullitt told him: "Decisive for the establishment of relations was the situation in the Far East and the efforts to avoid the war between the Soviet Union and Japan. The recognition of the Soviet Union by the United States played a major role because it cooled down the Japanese, who thought that in the case of war, the United States would help the Soviet Union." Bullitt told Skvirsky that once the political situation changed and a Japanese attack seemed less probable, the Soviet Union had started making "impossible demands" on the United

States.[28] Later, Bullitt told Skvirsky that, because of the dangerous situation in the Far East, "the Americans consciously chose such a political course that the Japanese would believe that the USSR and the U.S. are much closer than they actually are." Even if that was not true, said Bullitt, it would create the illusion of stability, which was a "desirable" and even "necessary" element of Soviet-American relations. Skvirsky reported that this was not the first time Bullitt told him his story about misleading the Japanese.[29] When Soviet Ambassador Troyanovsky reported to Litvinov about the souring of Soviet-American relations, he blamed Bullitt's mythmaking. Troyanovsky said that the improvement of Soviet relations with Japan had "seriously disappointed some Americans, who made their bets on our forthcoming war with Japan and on the fact that America would dictate to us the conditions of its aid."[30]

When Bullitt visited Vyacheslav Molotov, the chairman of the Council of People's Commissars, in October 1934, they both expressed much concern about the state of Soviet-American relations. As Rubinin, who was present at the meeting, wrote in his memo, "Bullitt apologized in advance for his excessively rude comparison, and then said that Soviet-American relations are like a small and very weak flower, and that it is not good to pee on it. Comrade Molotov responded that the Soviet Union had been always absolutely polite. Then he agreed that Mr. Ambassador's observation applied to both sides equally."[31]

Bullitt left Moscow on October 10, 1934, traveled across the Trans-Siberian Railway, and arrived in Japan two weeks later. He noted that the double tracks ended well to the west of Vladivostok and decided that this would be the point where the Red Army expected to meet the Japanese: he was still anticipating a Japanese attack. He had talks with the emperor and with senior Japanese officials, but he was disappointed: "All these conversations were so polite and formal in nature that they contained nothing of interest," he wrote.[32] Judging from what he chose to share with Roosevelt, he was most interested in the conversation with the Soviet ambassador in Tokyo about the Japanese navy. It was much stronger than the American fleet, Bullitt reported to Roosevelt. From Tokyo, Bullitt traveled on to China, where he had long and sincere talks with Chiang Kai-shek, which were interpreted by the Chinese leader's beautiful, Wesleyan University–educated wife. Bullitt admired Chiang Kai-shek: "his foresight and wisdom have rarely been surpassed in the annals of statesmanship." The two men spoke mostly about the Japanese threat to China. The Chinese leader correctly predicted that Japan would attack China in 1937. He said he would never make peace with the Japanese and would eventually defeat them. He also said, however, that China would face its greatest difficulties after the Japanese defeat.[33] Bullitt concluded that the United States and the Soviet Union should have worked together to create a strong, independent China that could be their ally against the real and imminent Japanese threat. It was still unclear whether the Japanese threat would be directed against the Soviet Union, the United States, China, or a combination of those. This uncertainty created space for diplomatic maneuvering.

Bullitt's leaks about the imagined secret Soviet-American alliance annoyed the Bolshevik leadership because they could alarm the Japanese and destroy the Soviets' expected deal with them. In November 1934 Litvinov told the Council of People's Commissars that Bullitt was "determined to frighten us" and suggested that his overtures be firmly rejected.[34] In the classified report on the state of Soviet-American relations in 1935, the Commissariat of Foreign Affairs expressed satisfaction with the "sobering" of the Roosevelt administration that followed "the collapse of their serious hopes and bets on the forthcoming war between the Soviet Union and Japan." The commissariat personally blamed Bullitt for "heating those hopes up." It was Bullitt, the report said, who had consistently informed Roosevelt and European diplomatic circles that Japan would attack Vladivostok.[35]

Litvinov presented the sale of the Chinese Eastern Railway as his personal diplomatic victory. Indeed, that deal shifted the focus of Japan's military preparations away from the USSR and toward the United States. In November 1935 Bullitt dined with Litvinov and reported to the State Department that the commissar "felt sure Japan planned the domination of China, but would not attack the Soviet Union."[36] Feeling as if they were on top of the game, Bullitt's interlocutors in the Commissariat of Foreign Affairs perceived him as being "confused," "pessimistic," and "depressed." In November 1935 Bullitt told Troyanovsky that their "joint failure in developing American-Soviet friendship was the biggest failure in the diplomatic history of recent years."[37]

As Bullitt understood it, if Japan was an actual threat to the Soviet Union and the United States, and if the Red Army could fight hard against this threat, then playing on tensions between the Soviet Union and Japan would be of central interest to the American government. Conversely, the Soviet-Japanese détente increased the risk of the Japanese attack against the United States. Again, Bullitt was right, but he had to play his card against all odds. In January 1936 the Soviet agent who oversaw Martha Dodd, a Soviet spy and the daughter of the American ambassador in Berlin, wrote to his superiors in Moscow:

"She told me about Bullitt's swinish behavior during his sojourn in Berlin. According to her, Bullitt severely scolded the USSR in the American Embassy, arguing that in the next few months the Japanese would capture Vladivostok and the Russians would do nothing about it."[38] In April 1936 Bullitt wrote to the Secretary of State: "The only actual threat to the Soviet Union is the Japanese." Praising the strength of the Red Army, he criticized Soviet diplomacy and propaganda. "All Litvinov's propaganda trumpetings to the contrary, the Soviet government knows very well that Germany can not be in a position to make war on the Soviet Union for many years." In Bullitt's opinion the Soviet Army was not ready for offensive operations, because the country's railways were "still inadequate" and there were "literally no highways in the entire Soviet Union." However, "on the defensive, the Red Army would fight hard, well and long."[39] The State Department did not listen to his advice and failed to support Bullitt's game. In December 1937 Bullitt told Roosevelt in a letter from Paris, "I still believe, as I have for several years, that conflict between Japan and Russia is inevitable."[40] After the Second World War, Bullitt personally accused the president of having failed in the Far East. Roosevelt, he said, "inaugurated unwisely the policy of appeasing Japan which led us by devious paths to the disaster at Pearl Harbor."[41]

Bullitt's strategy was to play off the American-Soviet-Japanese diplomatic triangle, and he pursued it to the very end of his term in Moscow. But, while trying hard to manipulate the future, he made serious mistakes in the present. From the start, the ambassador knew that Soviet-American rapprochement depended upon the Japanese threat to both nations. He saw that the degree of Soviet hospitality to America tracked the ebbs and flows of this threat, as it was perceived from Moscow. Acting in the interest of American security, he tried to make himself a part of the big game in the Far East. Clearly Bullitt thought that if he could convince Soviet leaders that he could either stop or defer Japanese aggression, he could get them to agree to the construction of Monticello on Sparrow Hills. Major agreements in trade, security, and armaments could then follow. If he could secure a rapprochement with Russia without breaching the limits that Roosevelt set for him, that is, without promising actual military or economic aid, it would strengthen American positions in the Pacific and also boost Bullitt's political career in Washington.

In reality there were two problems with Bullitt's strategy. First, Japan did not in fact wish to attack Vladivostok, setting its sights on Pearl Harbor instead. Second, the Soviets had their sources in Japan, and they were excellent. Bullitt was developing his bluff precisely when the best of the Soviet spies, Richard Sorge, had settled in Tokyo. From September 1933 Sorge was informing the Kremlin about the Japanese and, later, German plans and intentions; he correctly informed the Kremlin about the German invasion in 1941. He was also a former librarian of the famous Institute for Social Research, the cradle of the Frankfurt School of Critical Theory, a polyglot, and a womanizer. He was Bullitt's rival even though the American ambassador never heard his name.[42]

Bullitt wrote to his patron and friend in the State Department, Walton Moore: "The next twenty years will be as filled with horror, I believe, as any that the world has traversed, and we shall need not one FDR but a succession of Presidents of his quality to keep us out of the shambles."[43] Bullitt's ambitions were frustrated on both sides. His detailed and challenging letters to Roosevelt make up a volume, but it is not clear how much of what he wrote Roosevelt was ever actually read or appreciated. The president's responses were encouraging but random, short, and mostly ironic—"trivial," as Kennan characterized them.[44] In Moscow Bullitt's plan to communicate with the top leadership failed; he was reduced to ordinary contacts with officials of the Commissariat for Foreign Affairs, whom he detested. "It is difficult to conduct conversations with the Soviet Foreign Office because in that institution the lie is normal and the truth abnormal."[45]

Soviet diplomats in Washington started a personal vendetta against Bullitt. In early 1936 Troyanovsky informed the Kremlin of Bullitt's ambition to run for president in 1940, or at least to be appointed secretary of state. Troyanovsky commented that any such appointment would not favor Soviet interests.[46] In May 1936 Konstantin Umansky, new acting head of the Soviet mission to Washington who also coordinated espionage in America, suggested that the time was ripe to commence "invisible efforts" against Bullitt. Specifically, he proposed to launch a personal campaign against Bullitt in American newspapers, which, he said, for the Soviet embassy "would not be a hard thing to do." Umansky also plotted ways to "increase the appetite" of Bullitt's rivals in the Democratic Party.[47] Bullitt knew about Umansky's intentions; when the Kremlin sent Umansky to Washington Bullitt warned the State Department that Umansky was a "Bolshevik intriguer of the lowest kind" who would try to interfere with the presidential campaign.[48]

Surrounded by spies, Bullitt detested them and shunned espionage, which he considered to be a European thing. Preaching such American values as "efficiency, sincerity, and straightforwardness," he was proud of American diplomacy. There was no government in the world, Bullitt wrote, that "was so fully informed with regard to relations between Stalin and Hitler as the American government," and US diplomats achieved this success "without an expenditure of one cent for spies or agents."[49] The first American ambassador to the Soviet Union wrote to his boss, Secretary of State Cordell Hull: "We should never send a spy to the Soviet Union." These were his own terms of the trade, and he was confident of their superiority. He did not think about his own bluff when he beautifully wrote, "There is no weapon at once so disarming and effective in relations with the communists as sheer honesty. They know very little about it."[50]

11

THE THEATER OF DIPLOMACY

"**D**id you murder someone that your fingers are dipped in blood?" a pedestrian asked Irene Wiley, the newlywed wife of the counselor at the American embassy.[1] It was April 1934 in Moscow. Irene went home and cleaned the red polish from her nails—a Russian-speaking cosmopolitan artist of Polish-Jewish origin who, as the wife of the second in command at the American embassy, became its first lady. Soviet officials called her "pilsudchitsa," a class enemy and follower of Polish president Joseph Piłsudski.

Greeting the Wileys, who came straight from their wedding in France, Bullitt filled their sitting room with white chrysanthemums. The only flowers he could get in the city, they created a "funeral parlor atmosphere," Irene later wrote. The Wileys got an apartment in the National, a luxurious but dilapidated hotel next to the Kremlin. The food in the hotel was "very appetizing but highly lethal," and Irene learned to cook in the bedroom. She found out, however, that even if consumed the same day it was butchered, "the underfed Soviet cow" was inedible. Desperate, she bought crawfish and left them to soak in the bathtub until dinner, but they were so lovely that she decided to release them into the Moscow River. Even this was difficult in Moscow: the police immediately approached her, suspecting foul play. It became her responsibility to instruct the embassy's waiters, whom she found entirely untrained. She spent hours teaching them which glasses were for the wine and which for the water, and heard one of them telling another, "Madam Wiley must be very superstitious, she wants us to do everything the same way all the time." She had to endure long Russian dinners, from ten o'clock in the evening to two in the morning, and usually found herself "between the Japanese ambassador, who spoke only Japanese, and the British Ambassador, who refused to speak at all." Sometimes, the Soviet leaders were more entertaining. Kalinin once asked her over champagne in the Kremlin: "You are an artist, why aren't you a Bolshevik?"[2]

Concerned about the psychological state of Bullitt's embassy, Roosevelt acknowledged that Soviet agents continually and illegally monitored the American diplomats. Proposing new security measures, the president asked Bullitt not to recruit anyone who was not born in America and to encourage members of the staff to study Russian language. He also instructed Bullitt to prohibit "spying of any kind" by everyone employed by the embassy, including military experts, even though they would be "spied upon constantly." To keep the diplomats entertained during their difficult mission, Roosevelt sent Moscow the latest movie projector that was able to show sound films—a "talking picture machine," as he called it.[3]

Unexpectedly, the embassy began to run out of money. The official ruble exchange rate was vastly different from its real value, the fact that every foreigner in Moscow knew well. Most foreigners exchanged their dollars or francs on the black market, which secured them a good life for little money. But foreign embassies could not use the black market for official dealings with the Soviets such as paying for construction projects and other expenditures. For their everyday necessities such as food and drinks, the Americans in Moscow could only go to stores that accepted rubles. At the start Bullitt forbade his associates from using the black market. However, the official rate made living prohibitively expensive. Bullitt told Litvinov that a bouquet of flowers in Moscow would cost him 130 dollars, and a piece of chocolate would cost 13 dollars. He also complained that it cost twenty times more to send a telegram from Moscow to Washington than from Washington to Moscow. The seductive availability of the black market surfaced even in Bullitt's correspondence with Roosevelt. The British consul in Leningrad, Reader Bullard, followed the situation with pleasure; he had relied on the black market for years, and now he saw that his American peers tried to survive without it. As he expected, Bullitt soon gave up: "As for the Ambassador, the friend of the Soviet Union, the more rubles he can buy illegally, the better pleased he is."[4]

The embassy wanted the Soviet government to respect intellectual property. Specifically, Bullitt asked the Soviet publishing houses to pay royalties to the American writers who had been translated in the previous years. The Commissariat for Foreign Affairs prepared a list of these American writers, most of them left-wing novelists, and estimated the overall debt to be about 20,000 convertible rubles. It was a relatively big sum; in 1933, the USSR paid 4,500 convertible rubles to translated authors in all foreign countries combined.[5] After making this calculation, the officials at the commissariat realized that they had forgotten about the Russian translation of John Reed's *Ten Days that Shook the World*, which sold 733,000 copies. The royalties for Reed's book would have come out to 175,000 convertible rubles alone. Moreover, the Soviets would have to pay this money to John Reed's widow, Louise Bryant, who had recently divorced the American ambassador, and they expected that this money would be another area of conflict with Bullitt. Passing Bullitt's concerns to Stalin, Litvinov proposed a financial scheme that would help the American embassy without compromising general principles. According to a memo from Litvinov, Bullitt proposed to use Reed's royalties to pay the ruble expenditures of his embassy. As an alternative, Commissar of Finance Grigory Grinko generously offered to disburse one million nonconvertible rubles to the American embassy for its expenditures in Moscow, and to end the debate. The issue went to the Politburo, which did not support either of these proposals. Bullitt then suggested that Russia buy American films in dollars, import them, sell them in rubles, and transfer the surplus to the embassy. Soiuzkino, the Soviet Film Agency, approved this plan, and Litvinov asked Stalin to support it. Again, Stalin refused to strike a special deal with the ambitious American.[6]

Following Russian tradition, the embassy rented a log cabin in the country—a dacha—for officials to spend weekends there. It had been previously rented by the Lithuanian embassy and had a tennis court and rose bushes. Bullitt added a stable and three decent horses and named the roses after American presidents. "There was always something very comforting about driving through those big wooden gates after a long hard day trying to understand the Russians."[7] It was a hard task indeed. After talking to American diplomats in Moscow about their construction projects, the British consul in Leningrad wrote in his diary that they "were railing against the Russians they have to work with. The real start of the work . . . has not been made—after four months."[8] When the building for the embassy on Mokhovaia Street in central Moscow was just about finished, Litvinov realized that it neighbored the anatomic theater of Moscow State University, which was also "a workshop for manufacturing human skeletons, and in the summer this workshop poisons the air for the whole block." Litvinov was sincerely concerned: "Having had several unresolved arguments with Bullitt, I find it extremely desirable to avoid new reasons for conflict"—this time, about the smell of dead human bodies.[9]

Entertaining Semyon Budyonny, another veteran of the Russo-Japanese War who had made his way into the leadership of the Red Army, Bullitt brought up polo. The Soviet cavalryman did not know about the game, but Bullitt and Thayer told Budyonny that polo was a key element of training the American cavalry. In no time Bullitt and Thayer found themselves teaching polo to the Red cavalry on a field outside Moscow; they were surprised by the excellent quality of the horses that Budyonny had gathered from all over Russia, even from Siberia. Throughout the summer Thayer coached two teams of Soviet cavalrymen, and Bullitt judged the matches while riding his chestnut stallion. But then, the horsemen were called up for maneuvers and their horses were exchanged for tanks.

Watching Hollywood movies and drinking French champagne, the American bachelors dived into the Soviet life with its skeleton workshops and peaceful dachas, cavalrymen and ballerinas, gossip and arrests. Agents of the secret police accompanied the Americans everywhere—on the streets of Moscow, in the fields around the dacha, and even on their hunting trips. Working in shifts, the agents were always the same, and the diplomats learned their names, features, and habits. Some agents seemed happy to accompany Thayer while he was hunting; others were afraid of the gunfire. The Commissariat for Foreign Affairs commissioned George Andreychin to coordinate Bullitt's mission's relationship with the Soviet authorities; he was also supposed to inform on Bullitt and his colleagues. But this Balkan Communist had a reason to be loyal to the American ambassador and not to his Soviet employers: he had spent his youth in America and he wanted to return there. In April 1934 Bullitt asked Roosevelt to help Andreychin, who had long ago violated bail in Chicago: "He saves our tempers and almost our lives two or three times a day. He is one of the loveliest human beings I have ever known—a sort of Jack Reed in Macedonian terms. Some day he should be the Soviet Ambassador in Washington." Indeed, Andreychin was in danger: "Trotsky was his intimate friend." Andreychin had already served years in Siberian camps, and there was little doubt that he would be arrested again. Bullitt asked Roosevelt to pardon him: "I can think of no other act which would cost us so little and win so much good will here for you and me."[10] But Roosevelt did not help Andreychin.

Bullitt had particular respect for writers and poets. In Moscow he befriended Jurgis Baltrusaitis, a Symbolist poet who wrote in Russian and Lithuanian and who served as the Lithuanian ambassador in Moscow (1922–1939). Baltrusaitis knew everything and everyone in Moscow, Bullitt wrote to Roosevelt; he was a great source for understanding both the Moscow cultural elite and the NKVD. Reporting to Roosevelt about journalist Roy Howard's visit to Moscow, Bullitt explained: "This is the first time within my knowledge that any prominent American has talked like an American to the Bolsheviks. The usual run of businessmen who come here think that they will get somewhere by licking the Bolshevik boots." But Howard's speech "was so perfect," Bullitt wrote to Roosevelt with his usual flattery, "that it might have been made by yourself."[11]

Despite some initial successes, Russia betrayed Bullitt, and he complained: "Moscow has turned out to be just as disagreeable as I anticipated." Writing to the president, Bullitt expressed his desire to go back to Washington: "I am a bit homesick. It is a new sensation for me, and it arises from a very happy thing.... In this past year you and Mrs. Roosevelt and Miss LeHand have made me feel that I was a member of the family, and the thing I miss so much is the afternoons and evenings with you in the White House."[12]

Margaret LeHand was Roosevelt's personal secretary for more than two decades—from 1920 when they were both young and vigorous until 1941 when he was half-paralyzed and she had suffered a stroke. She took part in Roosevelt's five election campaigns—once for governor, once for vice president, three times for president. Her duties were endless; having started working as Roosevelt's secretary, later her role more closely resembled that of his chief of staff, with whom he discussed appointments, political tactics, and gossip.[13] LeHand emanated energy, running up staircases instead of using elevators, and performed somersaults at the parties. Living in the White House, she accompanied Roosevelt on his travels, including sailing on the military vessels that he was particularly fond of. Seven years younger than Bullitt and sixteen years younger than Roosevelt, she bound them together.

Bullitt's and LeHand's affair began just before his appointment as ambassador to the Soviet Union. Roosevelt knew about it, and the State Department was informed as well. After Bullitt's departure, the affair continued from a distance. Bullitt used to call her from Moscow; when he came to Washington, he took her out.[14] From time to time, Roosevelt, Bullitt, and LeHand dined together, and these dinners continued even after their relationship became strained. During one such dinner at the White House in February 1940, Roosevelt fainted suddenly. He had had a mild heart attack, which was kept a secret from the public.[15]

Although Bullitt purged his archive before leaving it to the Sterling Library at Yale, his transatlantic correspondence with LeHand preserved some intimate details of their relationship. On September 21, 1933, Bullitt returned LeHand her pearl earrings, "which turned up on the floor of the car" after a ride in the country; he returned these earrings with an official letter signed by "Special Assistant to the Secretary of State."[16] Before his departure to Moscow, they spent a happy week together. She sent candid letters to Moscow on official White House letterhead. "You really are an angel and I miss you so much" (January 14, 1934). "Silly, isn't it, to mind being without you for a few days when there have been so many, but I *do* mind" (December 30, 1934). "My love to you—much more of it than I like to confess" (January 17, 1934). "I hope Moscow is three feet deep in snow and that you are virtually (not virtuously) frozen!" (March 12, 1934). Bullitt had left Washington without saying goodbye to her. "I really am furious. Will you please use my other silly, stupid letter to light your cigarette" (Bullitt complied with the request, that letter vanished). "I hate Russia. I hate the Mr. Stalins of this world, and—and I did like you so much," she wrote (March 12, 1934). While Bullitt was in Moscow, Russia was on LeHand's mind. When the conservatives in Congress and the Supreme Court blocked a package of labor reforms, she wrote to Bullitt, "strikes are threatening everywhere and the government powerless to help. Should we send for Stalin!???"[17] In another letter she asked how his Russian lessons were going and said that she had bought a Russian dictionary for herself, although she probably did not use it. She was jealous and aware of gossip: "at the Ritz at lunchtime three ladies at the table back of me were discussing a certain ambassador very loosely to my perfect fury.... I suspect the ladies will descend upon Moscow this summer, and I hope you will be in Hawaii or some place."[18]

In July 1934 Roosevelt planned a visit to Hawaii; it was the first presidential visit to the archipelago. Bullitt wanted to join him and prepared to take the Trans-Siberian Railway, which he had long wanted to do. Sailing from Vladivostok to Hawaii on an American vessel would send a strong message to Japan; a meeting on Hawaii between the American president and his ambassador to the Soviet Union would be a symbolic gesture that Bullitt believed could bring peace to the Far East. But Roosevelt did not approve of Bullitt's visit to Hawaii. As he explained to Bullitt, he was "ganged" by the officials of the State Department who convinced him that if he invited his ambassador to Russia he would also have to invite his envoys to Japan and

China, and such a conference would create "a stir... at a time when they want to avoid just that." Bullitt was "really terribly sorry" that this trip was off; "I had counted on it absolutely," he wrote to LeHand.[19] This was the first sign that his friendship with the president was cooling down; it was also an indication that Roosevelt did not support, or maybe did not understand, his game with the Soviets and the Japanese. Cancelling Bullitt's trip, Roosevelt sounded apologetic: he believed that they "could have had our little party in Hawaii without bringing on a World War," and he yielded "with much reluctance," he wrote. LeHand, as always, went to Hawaii with Roosevelt. About Bullitt's cancelled trip, she wrote on May 18: "I am terribly sorry, and wish there were something I could do."[20]

There is little doubt that LeHand helped Bullitt get precious information from the top levels of the administration, and he probably tried to use her to influence Roosevelt. But the president was also a master of such games. Bullitt and LeHand did not try to hide their relationship, and Roosevelt's entourage believed they were engaged and would soon be married. Even the Soviet guests of the White House knew about LeHand's connection to Bullitt. In May 1934 Evgenii Rubinin, an official from the Soviet Commissariat for Foreign Affairs, visited Washington; introduced to LeHand, he soon heard that she had intimate relations with Bullitt and that their wedding was planned for the summer, and he passed this gossip on to Litvinov.[21] The president viewed the relationship with respect: LeHand had devoted many decades of her life to him and had the right to have her own family. Some memoirists, however, say that the president was jealous and this was a reason for his cooling toward Bullitt.[22] In any case, the wedding did not take place, although the friendship between Bill and Margaret lasted for years. There was a rumor that she had come to Moscow and found out that Bullitt had been having too much fun with Russian ballerinas. In fact, although LeHand did plan a trip, she did not go to Moscow. But it was indeed a ballerina that made LeHand cancel her trip.

The Bolshoi Theater dancers frequented the American embassy in Moscow. The diplomats knew, of course, that the ballerinas had special motives for their visits; but the temptation to host them was strong. With his love of the navy, Roosevelt advised Bullitt to run the embassy like a ship: "you will be... cut off from civilization and I think you should organize your expedition as if you were setting out on a ship which was to touch no port for a year."[23] Among other things, this meant that there should be no women at the embassy. Generally, the diplomatic service was organized very differently from the military: the ambassadors and their staff lived in their missions with their wives. However, the twice-divorced Bullitt tried to keep the embassy all male. Bullitt wrote, "There is absolutely nothing for a woman to do here ... there is an intense intellectual ferment here ... but ordinary social life does not exist." Therefore, he argued, American women would be unhappy in Moscow unless they were of "an exceptional, intellectual type."[24] Despite his initial intention to recruit only the bachelors, some members of Bullitt's staff were married, and some had local wives or permanent girlfriends. One evening in 1934, Bullitt looked around the dinner table and noticed that every single wife was foreign born.[25] The next morning he telegraphed the State Department and insisted that diplomats with foreign wives not be hired in the future; he also tried to force the wives out of Moscow. This policy caused new tensions. Married to a Norwegian who mostly stayed with her parents while he was in Moscow, Kennan felt lonely. He complained in his diary: "The struggle of the spring has taken the heart of me. To be a diplomat is bitter enough, to be a married one is still bitterer."[26] Agreeing that it was a security risk, Roosevelt instructed Bullitt to monitor the behavior of those women who had already been in the embassy. With time, this policy was softened; Wiley stayed in the mission with his Polish wife.

When two junior secretaries at the embassy married Russian women, it was interpreted as a security risk, and the diplomats were transferred to other countries. Their wives, however, were not allowed to leave the USSR. The husbands wrote desperate letters to the State Department and even to Eleanor Roosevelt. Another employee, Elbridge Durbrou, lived with his Russian girlfriend, Vera, for four years. Then, in 1937, Vera suddenly disappeared; everyone in the embassy knew that she had been arrested. Durbrou had to be transferred to another embassy, but he returned in 1945 and found out that Vera had spent three years in the camps. Later Durbrou wrote, perhaps unfairly, that in comparison with Stalin, Hitler looked like a "little kindergarten kid."[27] In 1940 the former cypher clerk at the American embassy in Moscow, Tyler Kent, was arrested as a spy in the American embassy in London. When the FBI investigators asked Bullitt about Kent's work in Moscow, he said that he suspected Kent of spying after working with him for three months; Bullitt did not denounce him then but transferred him to another mission. It turned out that Kent's Moscow lover, the English-speaking Tatiana, had recruited him to spy for the Soviets; still, after multiple investigations, the FBI could not decide whether Kent was a Nazi or a Communist sympathizer. In his memoirs,

Charles Thayer wrote that "the romantic attachments and resulting complications of the bachelors soon outmatched any indiscretion that wives might have committed." Writing in 1959, Thayer noted that the policy of recruiting personnel to the American embassy in Moscow was later revised with the opposite principle in mind: "preferably no bachelors."[28]

The ambassador loved unusual entertainment. In the 1920s, according to Vice President Henry Wallace, Bullitt threw stunning parties in Paris, at which butlers served guests in the nude; Bullitt probably spread this gossip himself.[29] His patron in the State Department, Walton Moore, saw the ambassador slightly differently: "Your preference is for conversation with men who are thinking about world affairs. You prefer what my colored cook calls 'snag' parties. Is this a correct diagnosis?" he wrote to Bullitt.[30] Despite the security concerns and the presence of the ambassador's daughter, "snag parties" continued at the embassy. John Wiley joked that NEP (the abbreviation for the Bolsheviks' relatively liberal "New Economic Policy" of the mid-1920s) actually stood for "New Erotic Policy." American diplomats' relationships with their Russian girlfriends were unambiguous, and conversations at the embassy were similarly frank. The State Department complained to Ambassador Bullitt that, according to confidential information, his employees drank too much and were "pawing women"; Bullitt's superiors were also unhappy that the ambassador had ignored Madame Litvinov while turning over his wine cellar to the Bolshoi's dancers.[31] Charles Bohlen, who had a reputation of a playboy even before his arrival in Moscow, wrote that "there were usually two or three ballerinas running around the embassy." They came over for lunch or dinner and then stayed until dawn, talking and drinking. Then a bachelor, Bohlen wrote, "I have never had more fun or interest in my whole life. . . . This embassy . . . is like no other embassy in the world."[32] Ballerinas from the Bolshoi seemed to have a special right to have relations with members of the diplomatic corps, Bohlen wrote in his memoirs. Further, he said that one of Andreychin's main functions was supplying the girls to eminent foreign guests.[33] Following in Bullitt's footsteps, Bohlen would become the US ambassador to the Soviet Union (1953–1957) and then France (1962–1968)—one of the "boys" whom Bullitt launched to the top just as he did it for the Stalin ballerinas.

For a while, the ambassador chose Irina Charnotskaya as his favorite ballerina. Having danced at the Bolshoi since 1927, she was at the peak of her career when he knew her. According to Bohlen, Charnotskaya truly believed in the Communist doctrine and spent many hours convincing her American friends of the glory of the Soviet Union.[34] Thayer wrote in his diary that Charnotskaya took "a trio consisting of B[ullitt], B[ohlen] and myself by storm.... We simply cannot keep our hands off her. She has become an acquisition of the embassy." She slept in a vacant room, which the three "carefully lock[ed]" and then fought "violently" for the key. Historian Frank Costigliola, who first published this evidence from Thayer's papers, noted not only a heterosexual attraction of the three diplomats toward an exotic woman but also a homoerotic fascination within the "trio."[35] Bullitt wrote later, "Aside from ballet girls, and a few other NKVD agents, who are ordered to establish contacts with the diplomatic corps, all Russians know that it is not healthy to speak too often to foreigners, and, if they do, they disappear. The NKVD has succeeded in making fear the dominant emotion in Russian life."[36] In 1940 FBI director J. Edgar Hoover reported to Roosevelt that American diplomats' relationships with Russian girls resulted in "amazing" leaks. According to Hoover, the women used a simple technique: they pretended that they did not speak English and let the diplomats indulge in political debates in their presence. Hoover went further in his suspicions; he wrote that some male employees engaged "in sexual perversion in the Code Room of the Embassy."[37] Whether or not these stories were true, they combined erotic fantasies with Orientalist ideas about Russia as a space of risky pleasures. Soviet agents continuously played on these treacherous rumors, and Bullitt and his friends were all too happy to rely on the agents' help.

With time Bullitt developed a more serious relationship with Olga Lepeshinskaya, who was little more than eighteen years old and had just begun to perform at the Bolshoi. Much younger than Charnotskaya, Liolia (as she was called both in the theater and at the embassy) quickly achieved tremendous success: she won a number of state prizes and became known as "Stalin's favorite ballerina." Later, she was thrice married, to a film director and two generals. One of those generals, a high-level officer in the NKVD, was imprisoned in 1951 but soon released; there were rumors that Lepeshinskaya paid a visit to Lavrentiy Beria to get her husband out of jail.

Charnotskaya and Lepeshinskaya had much in common. Both became stars in a profession in which success depends as much on talent as on discipline and training. As prima ballerinas of the Bolshoi, they walked a thin line between art and prostitution. Later, during the war, they both performed near the front lines to provide entertainment for Soviet soldiers. After the war, both held high administrative positions in the world of Soviet theater, which could be earned only through high-level contacts. Their early dealings with Bullitt and other American diplomats, which were supervised by the Soviet authorities, also contributed to their success.

In August 1934 Bullitt vacationed in Odessa and had "a bully time." He wrote to George Andreychin that he liked everything there; he called the hotel "one of the pleasantest hostelries that I know in the world." Andreychin helped him organize his trip, and Bullitt was grateful. It is obvious from their letters that they were very close; Bullitt called Andreychin "my boy." Andreychin wrote to Bullitt, "your letter made me very happy: first, because it tells me that you are enjoying yourself, and second, that you have not forgotten me. I am missing you terribly. Especially now, when Liolia [Lepeshinskaya] is back here and wants to know a million intimate things of which I am ignorant." Then, Andreychin's letter sounds alarming: "A young woman arrived few days ago from America. She knows Marguerite LeHand (she showed me her letters and telegrams). Miss LeHand had been planning to come to Moscow and the damned New Yorker spoilt it all."[38] From this letter we understand what happened in the summer of 1934 between the ambassador and the president's personal secretary: gossip about Bullitt's dalliances with ballerinas led LeHand to cancel her visit to Moscow and cancelled their wedding.

Writing about the "damned New Yorker," Andreychin was referring to Grace Davidson, a journalist who wished to write a book about Bolshevik Moscow. It was not her first visit to Moscow; she had an ongoing affair with Boris Steiger, a socialite and secret agent who was well known among the foreigners in Moscow. LeHand wrote Bullitt on June 4, 1934: "Miss Grace Davidson of the Boston Post, who writes particularly well, will get to Moscow about August 30th. She is, I think, quite devoted to Mr. Steiger, who means nothing to me. She is almost indecently fond of me, and has asked me to give her a letter to the Ambassador. . . . She knows most of the officials, I think."[39] Upon her arrival Bullitt met Davidson for a luncheon, and he wrote about their meeting to LeHand. He knew that she learned too much from Steiger, but he could not neutralize the gossip. After talking to his secretary Roosevelt wrote Bullitt an ironic letter dated June 3, 1935: "I have been much interested in hearing from Missy [LeHand] the story of Grace Davidson. You must be glad to have her on her way back to America."[40] Bullitt thus learned that the gossip about him had reached the president. From his correspondence with LeHand, we can garner that Bullitt apologized, complained about his health, and even went to Vienna to see a doctor.

Bullitt's subordinates in the embassy remembered Grace Davidson well. Charles Thayer described her as someone who had come to Russia "for emancipation after reading the books about free love in Russia."[41] Her lover, Boris Steiger, was an interpreter and an expert in fine arts, though everyone in the embassy knew he was, as Irene Wiley put it, "the GPU agent whose job was to watch the Diplomatic Corpse."[42] Davidson also knew it, and LeHand learned it as well. While Davidson was in Moscow, her father died, and she had to go back to the United States. LeHand commented: "That is an amazing story about Grace. . . . I feel awfully sorry for her because she certainly loved him [Steiger] deeply. She undoubtedly assumed too much. However, he should have sent a few less cables urging her to return."[43] After meeting Davidson again in Washington, LeHand sent Bullitt a letter that was as warm as always, though this time with a twinge of bitter irony: "I had a whale of a session with your girlfriend Grace Davidson. How shocked you must have been when she told you Steiger's *real* job! . . . She is writing a book and wrote a long letter to the Soviet embassy here in Washington. . . . What a humiliating experience the whole affair must have been. . . . I think at the moment G[race] D[avidson] is a little unbalanced—her whole story was bitter."[44] The letter ends with assurances of love and hope that they will meet again soon; LeHand was able to put on a good face even in difficult times, a skill learned during her many years with Roosevelt.

The atmosphere in Moscow and the entire Soviet Union changed on December 1, 1934, when the leader of the Leningrad Communists, Sergei Kirov, was murdered in his office, allegedly by a jealous husband. Bullitt was away, and John and Irene Wiley were hosting a reception that night in Spaso House. She was talking to Radek, when a man entered the ballroom and whispered something to him; Radek's face turned white, as if he were about to faint, and he left the party. Within fifteen minutes, all the Russian guests had left. The hosts did not know the reason until one of the guests, the ubiquitous Boris Steiger, came back and told them that Kirov had been murdered, and that there would be consequences. Irene Wiley noted one of these consequences: before that night, she and her husband saw Russians constantly and freely; after it, their meetings were "rigidly controlled and restricted."[45]

Referring to the swift and surprisingly complete version of the events that he received from the Lithuanian ambassador, Jurgis Baltrusaitis, Bullitt wrote that the assassination of Stalin's possible successor, Kirov, would intensify the state terror: "The arrest and exiling of innocent human beings in all quarters of the Soviet Union continues apace." His closest friends in Moscow, including Andreychin, now were in jail and probably being tortured. "I can, of course, do nothing to save anyone," Bullitt wrote. "It is extraordinarily difficult to preserve a sweet and loving exterior under the circumstances."[46]

Still, preserving such an exterior was his duty as a diplomat. Pushing back against the terror that had shrouded the country, the ambassador decided to organize a large reception to celebrate the coming of spring in 1935. From Washington he sent a telegram to Irene Wiley, the first lady of the embassy, asking her to arrange a party and telling her, "the sky is the limit." A creative artist stuck in the midst of terror, Irene was thrilled. "I have always wanted to design and stage a ballet, but this was far more exciting."[47] Her partner in this venture was Charles Thayer, whom Bullitt asked to create a party "that would compete with anything Moscow had yet experienced, before or after the Revolution." Wiley decided that the Spring Festival would be arranged in white, green, and gold, and that it would feature a small collective farm in the corner. The flowers were not a problem this time—white tulips were delivered from Finland. But they could not find green trees in Moscow; Irene found firs and pines "too sad and wintry." They uprooted a dozen birch trees, put them into Bullitt's bathtub, which was illuminated by his sun lamp, and the buds opened on the day of the party. Serious preparations went into building a collective farm in the American embassy. Wiley and Thayer wanted to have some white sheep present, but the stink was overwhelming, so they went to the Moscow Zoo and discovered that mountain goats smelled better; a half dozen of them were put on a platform at the head of the buffet table. Following the advice of Alexander Tairov, the famous theater director, they found big fishing nets, soaked them in gold powder and glue, and stretched them along the marble walls of the huge ballroom. They filled the nets with hundreds of zebra flinches, which fluttered and sang merrily behind the gold mesh. The ambassador covered all of the expenses personally. The embassy had been already known in the Moscow diplomatic corps as "Bill Bullitt's circus." This time, it lived up to its name.

In February 1935 the embassy officially revealed that Bullitt was sick with "streptococcal angina" and was being treated in Vienna. But he was, in fact, in good shape; visiting Berlin, he fascinated the American ambassador in Germany, William Dodd: "Bullitt still impressed me as quite proud of himself, and rather more boyish than one could expect for a man of his years."[48] He arrived in Moscow on April 13, 1935, and let everyone know he was sick; he complained about his health even to Deputy Commissar of Foreign Affairs

Krestinsky.[49] However, the Spring Festival took place as scheduled, on April 23, 1935.

The guests arrived at midnight. Ambassador Bullitt and Councilor Wiley, wearing white ties, tails, and gloves, awaited the guests under the chandelier in the huge hall; a finch flew around them. Commissar Litvinov and his English wife, Ivy, were among the first guests to arrive; she immediately took one of the "collective farm" baby goats, holding it in her arms throughout the evening. At the start of the ball, five hundred guests watched in awe as projected images surrounded them. Flowers appeared on the walls, a constellation of stars complete with a bright moon turned up on the high-domed ceiling, and multicolored spotlights shone down on the guests from the balcony. Alexander Tairov, a brilliant theater director with a Cubist bent, had designed the show. The guests danced among the columns where the son of the lord of the mansion had killed his father seventeen years before. In the dining room there were pens with baby goats, sheep, and bear cubs. Cages with roosters hung on the walls; they were supposed to crow at three in the morning. The ball was "Russian style," playwright Mikhail Bulgakov's wife remarked in her diary with irony.[50] The male guests' costumes attracted her attention most of all. All the diplomats, except the military attachés, wore tailcoats. The leading Bolsheviks looked different from the foreign diplomats: Bukharin was dressed in an old-fashioned frock coat, Radek wore a hiking outfit, and Bubnov was in a khaki suit. A socialite and mole, baron Steiger was dressed, of course, in a tailcoat. Bulgakov did not have a tailcoat, so he came in a black suit; his wife, Elena, was in a black ball gown with pale pink flowers.

Thrilled by the success of his party, the ambassador reported to the president: "It was an astonishingly successful party, thoroughly dignified yet gay. Everyone happy and no one drunk. In fact . . . it was the best party in Moscow since the revolution. We got a thousand tulips from Helsingfors and forced a lot of birch trees into premature leafage and arranged one end of the dining room as a collective farm with peasant accordion players, dancers, and all sorts of baby things, such as birds, goats, and a couple of infant bears about the size of cats. We also had pleasant lighting effects done by the best theater here and a bit of cabaret."[51] Although he suffered from the "internal streptococci" and told everyone he went to bed about 7.30 every night, the Spring Ball was an exception. The "Turkish ambassador and about twenty others remained until breakfast at eight," and as Bullitt wrote to Roosevelt, "I survived the night with the assistance of a few doses of strychnine."[52]

Despite the purges and terror, there was everyone at this American ball who was anyone in Moscow, except Stalin.[53] The future victims drank, danced, and flirted together with their executioners, many of whom would later also perish. The intellectual Bolsheviks (Bukharin, Bubnov, and Radek were among the guests) would lose their power and lives in a few months. The high-ranking military commanders (Tukhachevsky, Egorov, Budyonny) had already become pawns in the game between the Soviet and German intelligence services; most of them would be executed over the next few years. Litvinov's whole team was also there; he would survive the purges, but his Commissariat for Foreign Affairs would be purged in 1939. Andreychin was not around; he had already been arrested. The towering figures of the Soviet theater—Meyerhold, Tairov, Nemirovich-Danchenko, and Bulgakov—were at the Spring Festival; they all expected to be arrested and tortured at any moment. For some, the wait would be short; for others, painfully long. The Americans wanted to have some honest fun; it was a smart gesture to emulate a collective farm, the core symbol of the Soviet disaster, in the main hall of the Spaso House. As if they had a foresight, the finches escaped from the nets and flew around the embassy in a "terrifying panic."

Even Roosevelt and LeHand heard about the success of this party. "We have had lots of excitement over your Ball," LeHand wrote to Bullitt.[54] This ball is a focal point of Thayer's and Wiley's memoirs of Moscow, and from them we know many interesting details. Thayer had already had a painful experience organizing American parties in Moscow. The previous reception had featured an animal trainer with seals from the circus; they juggled obediently until the trainer got drunk, at which point the seals went for a dip in the salad bowl. The animals for this ball were rented from the Moscow Zoo, and they behaved themselves, with some exceptions. The roosters underperformed, as if on a real collective farm. On Thayer's command, the cages were uncovered, but only one rooster out of twelve began to crow, albeit loudly. Another rooster escaped and landed in a dish of duck-liver pate that had been delivered from Strasbourg.[55] However, it was the bears that most entertained the guests; they did not need a trainer to give a memorable show. Wiley remembers only one baby bear: "To achieve a real effect of spring, I thought we should have at least one wild newborn animal. The director of the Moscow Zoo produced the most charming baby bear," and he ran around the room while the guests fed him milk from a baby bottle. At some point in the night, Radek, who was known for his sharp wit, transferred the nipple from the bear's bottle to a bottle of champagne. The cub took several swallows of Cordon

Rouge before he noticed he'd been fooled. Meanwhile, the devious Radek disappeared, and General Egorov, the head of the Red Army's General Staff who was supposed to lead his men to victory over Japan, picked up the crying bear to console him. As the general rocked the bear, it vomited profusely on his medaled uniform. Thayer soon appeared at the scene of the crime. Half a dozen poorly trained waiters were fussing with Egorov, as he bellowed: "Tell your ambassador that Soviet generals are not accustomed to being treated like clowns!" The general left the embassy "cursing and shouting, 'This is the last time I will ever walk through this door'"; Wiley felt better when the general returned an hour later, "gay as a lark, in a new uniform." A veteran of the First World War, Egorov received the highest Soviet military rank of a marshal; then he was arrested and executed for espionage in 1939.

Throughout the night, the commander of the Red Cavalry, Semyon Budyonny, danced the Cossack *trepak*, "with his center of gravity almost touching the floor, his arms folded on his chest, and his legs working like locomotive pistons."[56] Exotically mustached, Budyonny also became a marshal (there were only five marshals in the entire Red Army in 1935) and would survive the purges. A Czech jazz band, which was performing at the time in Moscow, was hired along with gypsy dancers to entertain the guests. A Georgian restaurant served food on the second floor, with *shashlyk* (kebabs) cooked on an open fire and ethnic music playing in the background. The event ended at ten in the morning with a wild Caucasian dance, the *lezginka*, which General Mikhail Tukhachevsky performed with Liolia Lepeshinskaya.[57] Madame Litvinov watched the sun rise with a baby goat in her arms. Another Moscow beauty, Elena Bulgakova, had already left by then; as she wrote down next morning, "we wanted to leave at three but the Americans did not allow us to.... At about six we got into their embassy Cadillac and drove home. I brought home a huge bouquet of tulips from Bohlen."[58]

Bullitt's stay in Moscow and his friendship with Bulgakov were coterminous with Bulgakov's work on the third, pivotal draft of *The Master and Margarita,* his magisterial novel. His wife's diary makes it clear that Bulgakov based his Satan Ball, a central chapter in the novel, on the Spring Festival at the US embassy. According to this diary, Bulgakov drafted the scene of the Satan Ball after he and his wife came home from the Spring Festival at Spaso. The action he depicted was charged with a decidedly non-Soviet eroticism; situated halfway between *The Great Gatsby* and much later fantasies such as *Eyes Wide Shut,* the scene is explicitly American: "Margarita screamed and shut her eyes for several seconds. The ball burst upon her in an explosion of light, sound and smell.... Scarlet-breasted parrots.... Some naked Negroes.... A low wall of white tulips. . . . Champaign bubbled in three ornamental basins.... The naked woman mounting the staircase between the tail-coated and white-tied men . . . a spectrum of colored bodies that ranged from white through olive, copper and coffee to quite black."[59]

In this novel, Woland is a foreign "consultant" who visits the corrupt, frightened Moscow of the mid-1930s. Mighty, mischievous, and able to perform magic, Woland is a modern devil. Several assistants accompany him; helping with miracles, they entertain Woland and explore Russia. Although their mission is not entirely clear, one of their purposes is to observe "Muscovites en masse" and to evaluate the psychological change in the populace. "The Muscovites have changed considerably—outwardly, I mean, as too has the city itself.... But naturally I am ... interested in the much more important question: have the Muscovites changed inwardly?" Woland asks his entourage. "A vital question, indeed, sir," they confirm with one voice. "I'm not really a magician at all," Woland says in an attempt to clarify his objectives and methods: "I simply wanted to see some Muscovites en masse and the easiest way to do so was in a theater." He chooses a Moscow theater named in an American way, "Variety," and stages experiments that combine his magical powers with scholarly logic. Like a psychologist, he stages uncertainty, nudity, and violence, and he comments on their dramatic results. The Muscovites' responses were adequate, perhaps universal, Woland concludes. "They're people like any others. . . . They're over-fond of money, but then they always were. . . . They're thoughtless . . . but they sometimes feel compassion too." Woland continues, "They're ordinary people, in fact, they remind me very much of their predecessors, except that the housing shortage has soured them."[60]

These were the central issues of the time, and they variously engaged Freud and Trotsky, Bullitt and Bulgakov. To what extent can the power of the state transform men, women, and their relations? Did Bolshevism change human nature, and what remained unaltered? At Bullitt's dinners in Moscow, the Americans and their Russian friends and girlfriends had much to say about these questions. Bulgakov also took part in these debates; conservative in his customs, ironic in his writings and no Soviet sympathizer, he was probably closer to Bullitt than many others. They had many other topics to discuss as well. In *The Master and Margarita*, Bulgakov depicts a Russian author who is trying to rewrite the narrative of the Gospel. Insane for all practical purposes, he revises the stories of Christ, Judah, and Pontius Pilate. His approach to canonical issues is clearly subversive though subtly Soviet. The Master and his manuscript would both have perished if Woland had not invited his girlfriend, Margarita, to preside over the Satan Ball as its chief witch. Naked and exhausted, Margarita greets the myriads of guests, who are mostly ghosts coming from distant times and lands. She watches the miraculous transformation of a random Moscow apartment into a palace of luxury and vice. In his gratitude, Woland takes the Master and Margarita to his land, though it is unclear whether that is heaven, hell, or some place on earth.

One guest, however, came to this fictional ball from the historical Moscow. Baron Maigel, whom Woland convicts and shoots at the end of his ball in *The Master and Margarita,* is a satirical portrait of Baron Boris Steiger. "With a welcoming smile to his guest," Woland introduces Maigel as "a guide to the sites of the capital for foreign visitors." Woland declares that Maigel with his "unquenchable curiosity" and "conversational gifts" will meet an "unhappy end" in real life. To save Maigel "from the agonized suspense of waiting," Woland shoots him, and with this act of ritual sacrifice ends his ball.[61]

In real life, Steiger would fall victim to the purges a little later. He was arrested on April 17, 1937, in a Moscow restaurant, during dinner with the new American ambassador to Moscow, Joseph Davies. The child of Baltic barons, Steiger was an official employee of the Commissariat for Foreign Affairs and a secret agent of the Commissariat for Internal Affairs. Everyone in Moscow high society knew about his role as an informant. Thayer spoke of him as "a cultured man with an excellent sense of humor and a fund of stories," which he loved to tell in flawless French. He had obvious connections in the Kremlin but spent "most of his time" in the foreign embassies in Moscow; Irene Wiley wrote that he "had become a great friend of ours."[62] Steiger did considerable damage to Bullitt: he told his occasional lover, Grace Davidson, about Bullitt's relationship with Moscow ballerinas, and Davidson passed along this information to LeHand and Roosevelt. A few years later, in a letter to Roosevelt from Paris, Bullitt vengefully spoke of them both—Davidson was back in the United States, and Steiger was imprisoned in Liubianka, the notorious NKVD prison in Moscow. "If you do not know what the Liubianka is, ask your friend Grace Davidson. Her love, Steiger, is now interred there. You will certainly remember the gentleman she adored so because he used to knock her on the floor and jump on her stomach. For a New England girl, that was exciting."[63]

At the time of the Spring Festival, Bullitt and Bulgakov were good friends. Earlier, in December 1933, Elena Bulgakova noted in her diary that the

American ambassador had arrived in Moscow. Reading about this event in a Soviet newspaper, she was probably concerned about the American royalties for Bulgakov's play, *The Days of the Turbins* (1926), which had been produced at Yale (the premier was in March 1934). The translator of this play, Eugene Lyons, was their friend in Moscow; he could tell the Bulgakovs that Ambassador Bullitt loved theater, was a graduate of Yale, and could help them receive their royalties. Indeed, Bullitt attended a performance of *The Days of the Turbins* at the Moscow Art Theater soon after his arrival. The play, which was forbidden in 1929, was unbanned in 1932, allegedly after Stalin personally intervened. Through Intourist, the Soviet state travel agency, Bullitt requested a manuscript of the play, which he kept in his desk. Thayer recalled that his first encounter with Bullitt after his arrival was connected to *The Turbins*. Thayer, who had just started to learn Russian, was unemployed and wanted a job in the American embassy. The ambassador was then living in the Metropole Hotel, and Thayer managed to push his way past the doorman and introduced himself. Bullitt asked him to read a page from the manuscript on his desk. It was *The Days of the Turbins*.[64] Thayer could not yet read Russian, but he knew the play and paraphrased the plot. His cheating did not escape the ambassador, but Bullitt appreciated the skills of the young man who eventually became his interpreter and a career diplomat.

Bulgakov and Bullitt met on September 6, 1934, at a performance of *The Turbins*. Bullitt told the playwright that "he had seen the play four times, and he went out of his way to praise it." Bullitt could sympathize with the Turbins, who witnessed the way that the First World War and then the Russian Revolution destroyed the aristocratic order of which they were a part. Realistic, reasonably critical, and conservative in comparison to some other experiments in Soviet theater, the play was closer to *It's Not Done* than to *The Great Gatsby* or *The Master and Margarita*. With pride, Elena Bulgakova wrote down that Bullitt knew the play very well: "He followed along with an English translation of the script. He said the first few times he had to glance down at the text fairly often, but now he rarely had to."[65] Bulgakova's diary documents many occasions on which she and her husband attended receptions at the embassy, and the American diplomats paid visits to their small apartment in central Moscow. At first, this acquaintance seemed unusual to the Bulgakovs' friends: "The curiosity was killing them—friendship with Americans!" On April 11, 1935, the Bulgakovs received the Americans in their apartment, where "caviar, salmon, homemade pate, radishes, fresh cucumbers, fried mushrooms, vodka, and white wine" were served. On April 19, they had lunch with the embassy's secretary, Charles Bohlen. On April 23 the Spring Festival was held at the embassy; though hundreds of dignitaries attended, the Bulgakovs were treated as if they were a royal couple: "Bohlen and Faymonville went down to help us in the lobby. Bullitt instructed Mrs. Wiley to entertain us," and Mrs. Wiley was the first lady of the embassy.

On April 29 the Bulgakovs hosted Bohlen, Thayer, Irene Wiley, and several other Americans. "Mrs. Wylie invited us to go to Turkey with her," Bulgakova wrote in her diary. The next day, the Bulgakovs were at the embassy again. "Bullitt brought many people over to meet us, including the French ambassador and his wife and the Turkish ambassador, a very fat and jolly fellow." The Bulgakovs spent the next evening, the third in a row, with the US diplomats. "Wiley had about thirty guests. . . . All our friends were there, Bullitt's secretaries"; the indispensable Steiger was also there. The Bulgakovs gossiped with Thayer, the secretary of the embassy, and Faymonville, the military attaché, about the private life of their colleague, Bohlen. Bohlen courteously flirted with Elena Bulgakova, sending her flowers and enjoying spending time with her. In his memoirs Bohlen wrote about Bulgakov in detail. The diplomat knew about Bulgakov's play *The Fatal Eggs*, which was forbidden by Soviet censors, about Stalin's telephone call to Bulgakov, and finally, about Bulgakov's struggle to obtain an exit visa.[66]

Bulgakov and Bullitt—one a doctor who became a writer, the other a writer who became an ambassador—had much to talk about. They shared interests in Istanbul and Paris, literature and politics, the universal nature of man and the limits of his transformation by the state. One was more successful in literature, the other in politics, but both were elegant, ambitious, and aristocratic. Both were born in 1891.[67] Bulgakov, known for inventing funny and strange names for his fictional stories, probably noticed the similarity of their names (one of Bulgakov's pseudonyms was M. Bull); as Freud and Bullitt wrote, similar names cause "unconscious identification." Both men were proud of their ability to understand the present and predict the future.

At times, Bulgakov and Bullitt saw each other almost every day; when Bullitt was away, Bulgakov and his wife socialized with his assistants, particularly Bohlen and Kennan. They conversed in French, and if there was any difficulty communicating they could rely on Bullitt's interpreters. With time, Elena's entries about these contacts became more reserved, even monotonous. On February 16, 1936, she penned, "Bullitt was very courteous, as always"; on February 18, "The Americans are very nice"; and on March 28, "we were at Bullitt's. All the Americans, including him, were even sweeter than usual."

Two weeks later she wrote: "As always, Americans are extremely nice to us. Bullitt begged us to stay longer."[68] The ambassador, himself a novelist and playwright, introduced Bulgakov to European ambassadors and lauded his work. Cultural connections were a part of his duties. He could also help Bulgakov by demonstrating this writer's international prestige to the Soviet authorities. However, Bulgakov needed more immediate help.

While Bulgakov was writing about the Master who was writing about Christ, he was so sick that he was afraid of leaving home; doctors saw his ailment as a neurosis and treated it with massages and hypnosis.[69] He was in the middle of a long, painful conflict with the censors and cultural authorities. All this time, the Bulgakovs were trying to leave the USSR on medical grounds. They discussed their emigration plans with American diplomats, and probably with their European colleagues as well. On April 11, 1935, when the Bulgakovs hosted Bohlen and Thayer, Elena wrote down: Mikhail "said that we applied for passports for foreign travel. . . . The Americans responded positively and said it was time to go."[70] The Bulgakovs submitted their application for emigration papers in June 1935. In August, they were denied an exit visa and were left in despair. The word "refusnik" was coined much later, but it was a refusnik who wrote *The Master and Margarita*.

On October 16, 1935, the Bulgakovs traveled to the countryside with Thayer. Two days later, they dined with the ambassador: "Bullitt came, and we talked for a long time about the *Turbins*, which he loved." Bullitt then asked Bulgakov about his most recent play, which had been censored. The play, entitled *The Life of Monsieur de Moliere*, tells the story of a humiliated but brilliant playwright who finds himself in mortal combat with a supreme power. After much trouble, *Moliere* was shown in Moscow four months later, and Thayer and his colleagues attended the dress rehearsal. On February 16, 1936, the Bulgakovs attended a reception at Spaso House to greet Bullitt who had just returned from America: there was the diplomatic corps and a few Russians, among them Budyonny. Three days later, Bulgakov again visited Bullitt, who showed the guests a film about an English person who "stayed in America because he was fascinated with the Americans and their way of life." On February 21, Bullitt came to see *Moliere* and, according to Elena, "during the tea break . . . Bullitt spoke unusually highly of the play and of Mikhail in general, referring to him as a master." Shortly thereafter, *Moliere* was banned from the stage. On March 14, the ambassador once again invited the Bulgakovs to dine with him. "We decided not to go, as we did not want to hear all his questions and expressions of sympathy." Two weeks later, however, the Bulgakovs visited

Bullitt again. "The Americans, including the ambassador, ... were even nicer than ever." On April 12, they attended Sergei Prokofiev's concert in the embassy. "As always, the Americans are surprisingly nice to us. Bullitt urged us to stay longer, to listen more to Prokofiev, but we left about 3am by the car of the Embassy that Kennan offered us."[71] Kennan visited them for a dinner later the same week. On October 7, Kennan "wanted to pick us up by car about 11pm. I did not go," wrote Elena. However, Mikhail did go to the embassy. In November, Bulgakov went at least two more times to the receptions at the embassy.

The demonic protagonist of Bulgakov's novel *The Master and Margarita* is a bald foreigner with philosophical interests, magic skills, and rheumatic pains. A witness of Christ's passions, Kant's interlocutor, and now a foreign consultant to the Soviet authorities and explorer of the internal change among the Muscovites, Woland has the human features of Bullitt. Woland's face was "tilted to the right side, with the right-hand corner of the mouth pulled downward; the skin darkened by the timeless sunshine." The figure is complex and tragic, but also ironic. "Deep furrows marked his forehead parallel to his eyebrows," and Woland's eyes reflected his self-contradictory nature: "In the depths of the right eye was a golden spark that could pierce any soul to its core; the left eye was as empty and black ... as the mouth of a bottomless well."[72] And even Woland's entourage, which accompanies their demonic boss in all his mystical adventures, resembles the staff of the American embassy: for example, the tall, ironic, and clumsy Kennan is depicted as Koroviev. Although the Bulgakovs socialized with the ambassador's entire retinue, their relationship with Bullitt was particularly close. After Bullitt's departure, Bulgakov never returned to the embassy. In April 1937, he was invited to a costume ball, this time organized by the daughter of the new ambassador, Joe Davies. Bulgakov did not go, saying that he did not have a proper costume.

Moscow changed Bullitt, and he eagerly demonstrated this transformation to his subordinates in Moscow and to his superiors in Washington. In July 1935 he gave a speech in Virginia. Comparing Bolshevik Russia with Nazi Germany, Bullitt's undiplomatic rhetoric was at least a decade ahead of Kennan's "Long Telegram" and Hannah Arendt's *Origins of Totalitarianism*. "The noblest words that can issue from the mouth of man have been prostituted and the noblest sentiments of the heart of man have been played upon by propaganda to conceal the simple truth: that those dictatorships are tyrannies imposing their dogmas on an enslaved people," said Bullitt.[73] His disenchantment with Stalinism became a mass phenomenon about fifteen years later, as documented in *The God that Failed* (1949), a collective repentance of Western fellow travelers of Soviet communism who had observed it from a safe distance. What was different with Bullitt, Kennan, and a few other Americans in Moscow was the tragic ability to see both the facts and the people on the ground.

12

DISENCHANTMENT

O nce, the staff of the embassy found a microphone in Bullitt's office at Spaso House, but it was not wired to anything. Thayer, Kennan, and Durbrow spent nights in the attic of the ambassador's office, in shifts, a revolver in one hand and a flashlight in the other. Nobody appeared; those who installed the microphone knew about the ambush. The diplomats built a trap in the corridor that led to Bullitt's office: hitting the cable, the agent would trigger an electric alarm. In response, all the electricity in the embassy was cut. After some insistence and laboring, the electric supply resumed, but Thayer found out that his trap had vanished along with the microphone. Later on, fighting wiretaps became a routine in the embassy. The Soviet secret service continued bugging the embassy even after Joe Davies, a much friendlier ambassador, replaced Bullitt. During his tenure, a microphone was found in his bedroom just between his and his wife's pillows.[1] This was all new for the Americans; before Bullitt's mission to Moscow, the US embassies around the world did not have to contend with wiretaps and other security threats that have since become commonplace.

Thayer always carried a revolver in his pocket. He learned Russian and interpreted for Bullitt, willingly traveling across the Soviet Union. He preferred Tbilisi to Moscow, but he loved the whole empire. Thayer noted the surprising coexistence of xenophobia and hospitality among Muscovites. "Russian hospitality is a curious thing. Perhaps because for so long there has been little stability in their political and economic lives, with the police, Czar-ist and Bolshevik, confiscating and arresting at pleasure, they've come to look on possessions as rather transitory things, and when they have a bit of good luck they try to share it as quickly as possible with their friends. . . . What is more, they expect any temporarily affluent friend to do exactly the same thing with them."[2] This was, in fact, what the Soviet government expected from its new friends at Spaso House.

The Soviet government needed road-building equipment, trucks, rails, locomotives, weapons, and much more. In an effort to pay for this massive import, the government sold gold to Germany, timber to Sweden, and furs and collectible art to the United States. Litvinov played on the rivalry between France and Germany, trying to obtain credit from both countries. Hoping to get state-backed loans, the Soviet Union refused to purchase American goods and products for cash. However, no American loans or credits could be given to a country that did not pay its war debts, which Russia had not done. Involved in the grand geopolitics and petty accounting debates, Bullitt thought that Litvinov was obstructing his access to Stalin, and he tried to circumvent the commissar. Stalin thought that Bullitt was standing between him and Roosevelt, making it difficult to get loans and credits.

From Moscow, the Comintern funded the Communist Party of the USA, which engaged in propaganda and espionage campaigns. From the start of diplomatic relations, the Roosevelt administration viewed Soviet propaganda in America as an unacceptable interference in internal affairs. In July 1935 Bullitt warned the State Department about the forthcoming Third Congress of the Comintern in Moscow. Led by Bullitt's frequent guest, Karl Radek, the Comintern was determined to expand its activities in America. The State Department decided to limit its response, sending a note of protest. For its part Moscow accused Bullitt of provoking a diplomatic crisis. Walter Duranty, the Moscow reporter for the *New York Times*, brought to the embassy the rumor that Bullitt was interested in this crisis because it would have given him an opportunity to return to Washington and get a position in the admin-istration. Informing the State Department about this allegation, Bullitt added that Duranty's articles were so completely pro-Soviet he suspected Duranty was on the Bolshevik payroll.[3] Featuring many American guests, the Third Congress of the Comintern called for revolution in the United States and elsewhere in the world. When Bullitt protested, the Commissariat for Foreign Affairs explained that the Comintern was a nongovernmental organization: it just invited American trade unions to collaborate with the Soviet Union.

Bullitt was determined to convince the State Department that this interference in American affairs grossly violated the agreements on the basis of which the United States had established diplomatic relations with the Soviets.

Growing tensions in Europe were proving Bullitt's old prophecies true. In April 1935 he wrote to the State Department that he had been convinced since the Treaty of Versailles that the resurgence of a nationalist movement in Germany was inevitable and that a revisionist Germany would absorb Austria. "The statesmen and diplomatists in Europe are in such a neurotic state of mind that everything is possible," he wrote to Roosevelt.[4] In June the president sent him to Warsaw to attend the funeral of Polish leader Joseph Piłsudski. There, Bullitt, at his own initiative, spoke with Hermann Goering. "When he was 250 pounds lighter he must have been a blond beauty of the most unpleasant sort. He is really the most unpleasant representative of the nation that I have ever laid eyes on. . . . He made me feel that the Germans will achieve nothing but a series of national disasters until they cease to take the *Nibelungenlied* seriously," Bullitt wrote to Roosevelt. The president responded ironically: "What a grand picture that is of that Goering person! If you get a figure like his I will order a special uniform for you and send you to all official funerals."[5] Interestingly, in Bullitt's reports about German leaders he used a kind of homophobic vocabulary that he never used in his reports about the Soviet leaders. When the Nazis named their military academy after the recently murdered Ernst Roehm, Bullitt reported, "In view of the revelations about Roehm, the English equivalent would be the renaming of Sandhurst 'Oscar Wilde Institute.'"[6]

The letters that Bullitt wrote to Roosevelt fill dozens of boxes in his archive at Yale. He wrote them from many different places—Moscow, Washington, Paris, and the capitals of the Near East. In the spirit of dispatches that the aristocratic ambassadors of the eighteenth century wrote to their monarchs, Bullitt both informed the sovereign and entertained him. These letters offered gossip about high society, psychological observations, and allegations about the intimate lives of spoiled Europeans, including the Bolsheviks and the Nazis. They also demonstrated the uniqueness of Bullitt's sources of information, the breadth of his connections, and the depth of his intuition. He had a close, almost familial relationship with the president, and in their correspondence Roosevelt often addressed him "Bill Buddha." In public service, promotion depends on personal relations more than in many other domains. An experienced master of these relations, Bullitt fell into a trap: the more he demonstrated his competence and manipulative skills, the more fear and resistance he aroused in his superiors, particularly in Roosevelt. Trying to make up for the wasted decades of his career, he could not afford to relax and swim with the current, which is the secret of many successful officials in any country.

Bullitt's restlessness was motivated not only by careerism but also by the forthcoming tragedy that he saw more clearly than many others did. He had resigned from the diplomatic service at the end of the First World War and returned to it when the danger of a new, even bigger war was already in the air. Nevertheless, he never stopped playing his practical jokes. On March 4, 1936, the State Department received an unusual report from Moscow, argu- ably the strangest dispatch its official mailbox has ever seen: "I believe that what follows is an accurate picture of life in Russia in 1936, but a regard for truth compels me to admit that the remainder of this dispatch was written not by myself but another American envoy." Citing the Honorable Neil S. Brown of Tennessee, the American ambassador to Russia from 1850 to 1853, Bullitt informed the authorities about the current situation. "This is a hard climate, and an American finds many things to try his patience, and but few that are capable of winning his affections," wrote Brown. "One of the most disagreeable features that he has to encounter is the secrecy with which every- thing is done. He can rarely obtain accurate information.... His own move- ments are closely observed by eyes that he never sees.... Everything is sur- rounded with ceremony, and nothing is attainable but after the most provoking delays." Speaking about the reign of Nicholas I, the ambassador wrote about harsh police tactics, censorship, and spies. "No nation has more need for foreigners, and none is so jealous of them." Bullitt was astonished to find these feelings, which were so close to his own, articulated in a dispatch written by a distant predecessor. "This is the best school in which to Ameri- canize our countryman," Brown wrote about the Russia of 1850.[7]

Watching the waves of terror rolling through Moscow, Bullitt was horrified by the senseless acts of mass violence. Thayer wrote that by 1937, "every two or three days we read in the papers the name of some acquaintance who had been convicted of espionage or had confessed to sabotage or had been denounced as a traitor."[8] From prison Andreychin managed to pass along a message to Bullitt, asking his old friend "for God's sake to do nothing trying to save him," otherwise he, Andreychin, "would certainly be shot."[9] Bullitt relayed the message to Roosevelt.

Andreychin managed to serve out his term—ten years for espionage and Trotskyism—in the northern camps of Ukhta and Vorkuta. In January 1938 he was brought to Moscow and spent two more years in prison there. With the outbreak of war, Andreychin, who held Soviet, American, and Bulgarian citizenships, was released. He was able to find employment in the Soviet Information Bureau in Kuibyshev, where many Soviet offices and foreign embassies had been relocated. There, Andreychin again met the staff of the American embassy. On December 28, 1941, Edward Page, the second secretary of the embassy who had worked with Bullitt in Moscow years before, talked to Andreychin and wrote a detailed memorandum about their conversation. He sent a copy of this "top secret" memo to Bullitt. This paper was never published, and I will present it here almost completely.

Page reported that Andreychin had just arrived in Kuibyshev after serving a six-year term in a northern camp. With irony, he noted that Andreychin was "completely rehabilitated (whatever that may mean)." He received American support, including the five hundred dollars that Charlie Chaplin sent him through Bullitt, and he was grateful. This money, Page explained, would see Andreychin and his family through the winter. Page was more excited when Andreychin shared with him "some exceedingly interesting explanations with regard to the mysteries of the Soviet Union from 1936 to 1939." According to Page, the former Soviet ambassador to the United States, Alexander Troyanovsky, who was then also in Kuibyshev, told Andreychin this:

> Back in 1934 the Soviet government had been needlessly difficult with Bullitt, but various factors had been responsible. First, Stalin had let Litvinoff down on his commitments to Roosevelt. Second, Bullitt as a result thereof had himself been hard-boiled personally with Litvinoff. Third, they suspected Bullitt of trying to bring them to blows with the Japs for which they knew they were not prepared.
>
> They, therefore, decided to get rid of Bullitt, apparently with the idea of making him the scapegoat for the bad turn in Soviet-American relations. They believed him to be a politician who was attempting to use his successes in Soviet-American relations to obtain the Presidency or at least the post of Secretary of State. They also believed they could discredit him in the eyes of the president simply by sabotaging his mission and spared no efforts in order to bring about this result.

Troyanovsky also told Andreychin that he had taken part in these efforts. He went on to say that Bullitt had "proselytes" whom he had "hypnotized" into sharing his anti-Soviet views (he mentioned Henderson, Kennan, and

Thayer). However, Troyanovsky was impressed by Bullitt's appointment to the Near East—a mission he considered to be "much more important than it appeared." Releasing Andreychin from his northern imprisonment, Troyanovsky obviously wanted to reestablish contact with Bullitt: "the mistake made by the Soviet Government in underestimating and antagonizing Bullitt must now be redeemed at any cost. . . . Soviet-American relations are all-important to Russia and every means must be used to improve them," Troyanovsky said. Sending Andreychin to the American embassy, he also suggested that he write a letter to Bullitt, renew their friendship, and "use his influence to soften Bullitt's feelings toward the Soviet Union." At the end of this conversation, Troyanovsky told Andreychin, "I have ways and means of knowing all that they do" at the American embassy.[10]

While Bullitt was accusing Litvinov of interfering with his cordial relations with Stalin, the Commissariat for Foreign Affairs waged a campaign of personal revenge. Troyanovsky and Litvinov did ultimately best Bullitt in Moscow. Roosevelt came to believe that Bullitt was responsible for the deterioration of American-Soviet relations, and this was one of the reasons that he replaced Bullitt with his political opposite, Joseph Davies. But in 1941, with the war going badly for the Soviets and Moscow desperately in need of American aid, Troyanovsky and his colleagues decided to try something new. In the hopes of getting in touch with Bullitt, who had been appointed the president's special representative in the Middle East, they orchestrated Andreychin's visit to the American embassy.

Troyanovsky worked for the new and powerful Soviet Information Bureau, which ran domestic and international propaganda. Its chief, Solomon Lozovsky, was deputy commissar for foreign affairs responsible for the Far East, which meant mostly Japan. Lozovsky was an experienced, and unusually entrepreneurial, Soviet official. In Kuibyshev in 1942, he created the Jewish Anti-Fascist Committee, which raised huge sums of money for the Soviet military effort in the United States and Europe (as the secretary of this committee, he was arrested and executed in 1952). Having saved Andreychin from the Gulag in 1941, the Soviet Information Bureau hired him to do for them in Kuibyshev what he had done earlier in Moscow, that is, maintain contacts with the foreign diplomats and lobby for Soviet interests. Troyanovsky not only asked Andreychin to tell Page that Soviet-American relations were more important than ever; he hinted that "every means must be made to improve them." More specifically, Troyanovksy said that the Soviet government had been mistaken in "underestimating and antagonizing Bullitt," and that he sought to remedy this mistake at any cost. He and other Soviet officials still believed that Bullitt was headed to the top of the American government. Seeking contacts with the Roosevelt administration and the American public that would go beyond the official channels, Troyanovsky and Lozovsky counted on Bullitt. Possibly, Lozovsky was already thinking about his Jewish Anti-Fascist initiative and wanted Bullitt's help with it. Grasping the situation, Page forwarded a copy of his classified memo to Bullitt.

However, the experienced Andreychin did not want to help the regime, which had brought him many years of senseless suffering. His letters to Bullitt were full of complaints about his loneliness in Russia, yearnings for American friends, and hopes that America would win the war with Japan. Passing his letters to Bullitt through American diplomats, Andreychin could be sincere. He was "happy as a lark" to receive a message from Bullitt; this message inspired him to create "hopes and plans" that were all about America. These handwritten letters from the broken man whom Bullitt used to call "my boy" were touching; but Bullitt still could do nothing to help him. "Twenty years spent in Russia have taught me that friendship, love and all human relations in general need certain conditions *sine qua non* for thriving," Andreychin wrote. His only friends were Americans, with an exception of one man who remained in the Gulag. "I still live on the interest of the spiritual values which I accumulated in my years in America." In Russia, he felt "not only a very lonely man but an outsider, a person to be shunned." However, his friendship with Bullitt put him in a much more favorable situation than millions of his Soviet peers who died or suffered in the camps. He lived in Kuibyshev with his wife and daughters. He had a job, and the American embassy helped him. Still, he was in despair: "I shall never feel safe as long as I remain here," he wrote.[11]

In spite of the war between Japan and the United States and the coalition between Stalin and Roosevelt, diplomatic relations between the USSR and Japan remained intact until the very end of the war. Deflecting the Japanese threat that Stalin had long feared was a strategic victory for Soviet diplomacy in the Far East. First led by Maxim Litvinov and later by Solomon Lozovsky, the Soviet diplomats outmaneuvered their American counterparts, Cordell Hull and Sumner Welles, at tremendous cost to the United States. Stalin was neither grateful nor consistent: Lozovsky was executed during the last wave of terror but Litvinov survived all these waves. Working with Lozovsky in the Soviet Information Bureau, Andreychin also survived the war, though not for very long. In 1946 he was sent to his native country, Bulgaria, to run the chancellery of its pro-Soviet government. In 1949 he was arrested again—this time under suspicion of being a British and American spy. He was brought back to the Soviet Union and shot. In 1989 Andreychin was again rehabilitated, "whatever that may mean," as Page would say.

Bullitt's final message from Moscow was an unusually harsh, unrestrained letter to the secretary of state, which he sent on April 20, 1936. He had already received an appointment to Paris and was able to speak frankly. Summing up years of conversations with Kennan and other Russian experts, the letter contained the basic elements of the American politics of the future Cold War. The Soviet Union, wrote Bullitt, was "unique among the great powers. It is not only a state but also the headquarters of an international faith." To understand the Soviet Union, it is necessary to understand its geographical position, vast resources, and "racial composition." But what was "the most vital," he wrote, was to understand the substance of the "Communist faith," because it defined both the "peculiar internal institutions" of the USSR and its "extraordinary attitude" toward other states. The mystical content of this religion, explained Bullitt, was the belief that once communism was established everywhere on earth, vices such as greed or cruelty would be eradicated. But while the Communist paradise was being built, the state could and should lie, hate, and confiscate. Then, with the fulfillment of communism, the state would withdraw; evil, poverty, and war no longer exist, and a millennial grace would reign on earth. This is how Bullitt retold "the gospels according to Marx, Lenin and Stalin."[12]

The Soviet political system was a "godless theocracy," Bullitt reported to Hull. He saw it as a faith that ran counter to the Greek and Roman traditions and to the teachings of the Christian Church. "Moreover, they run counter to all that anthropologists and psychologists have been able to learn about the nature of man." Even though he knew that many were disenchanted and even more were oppressed or murdered, Bullitt did not deny that millions of Soviet citizens—including their dictator and his loyal associates—did believe in the Communist religion. Bullitt emphasized the sincerity of this faith: many Bolsheviks were willing to sacrifice not only others but also themselves.

By the mid-1930s the idea that communism or Marxism was a new type of world religion had already been explored. In Russia and later in France, exiled philosopher Nikolai Berdyaev had been advocating this idea for decades. Waldemar Gurian, a Jew from St. Petersburg who converted to Catholicism and worked in Germany, turned this idea into the main thesis of his political philosophy, which he articulated in writings published in the early 1930s.

Bullitt did not know this literature. Based in his experience with the Soviet Union, he improvised a theory that gained prominence much later, during the Cold War. Developing his argument about communism as a world religion, Bullitt compared it to Islam. Both religions, he thought, contained many absurd regulations, but these absurdities only made them stronger. Thanks to this strength, the Muslims, wrote Bullitt, were once at the walls of Vienna. Like Islam, communism also promised universal salvation by the sword. In the 1930s, "the communist Caliph" was Stalin, Bullitt wrote to Hull in the same report: "he is the embodiment of the holy spirit of communism."

Like the Muslims at the gates of Vienna, as Bullitt imagined them, the Communists were ready to forgive any sin—deception, robbery, even mass murder—if it was committed in the name of their faith. Like Islam, militant communism was an international affair; the aims of the Communist International were exploitation, deception, and violence for the sake of its God, Bullitt wrote. The Soviet Union threatened not only American freedoms; it also threatened American lives. Bullitt stated, "There is no doubt whatsoever that all orthodox communist parties in all countries, including the United States, believe in mass murder." Their threat was real because the Soviet Union was a country endowed with vast territory and huge natural resources—more self-sufficient, Bullitt wrote, than any other nation. Although the "chief weakness of the Soviet State today is, indeed, the inefficiency of its bureaucracy," the country had the capacity for tremendous economic growth. However, according to Bullitt, the standard of living in the Soviet Union was still very low—lower than anywhere else in Europe, including the Balkans. Preserving its monopoly on foreign trade, the Soviet Union was not interested in developing the international economy. On the contrary, Stalin's regime would prefer to sow chaos in capitalist countries in hopes that a world revolution would be born.

In this report Bullitt laid the discursive foundations of what would become the American political logic of the Cold War period, which became mainstream only twenty years later. "Russia has always been a police state. It is a police state today." Order throughout the Soviet Union was maintained by the secret police, which eliminated anyone who complained. In the nineteenth century there was a saying, "Scratch a Russian and you will find a Tatar"; now it was right to say, "Scratch a communist and you will find a Russian." That is why our reports, he added, resemble the reports of Honorable Neil Brown, written in the 1850s; moreover, they look like reports written by British ambassadors to Moscow during the reign of Ivan the Terrible. "To speak of the Russians as 'Asiatics' is unfair to 'Asiatics'": Japan and China created great civilizations, Bullitt wrote, but Russia had never ceased to be barbaric, and Stalin was following in the footsteps of Ivan the Terrible and Peter the Great. However, Bullitt acknowledged the strength of the Soviet army, which in his opinion had nothing to fear but the Japanese. Nazi Germany "for many years" would not be ready to attack Poland and the Soviet Union, wrote the American ambassador in 1936; but this time, his prediction was clearly wrong.

Still, the Soviet Union had great potential, he observed: "the territory which the Communists hold today is a base uniquely adapted to their needs." The Soviet bureaucracy, he believed, had to be afraid only of itself. "The single real fear of the Communists is that their bureaucratic machine might break down under the strain of war. [The] dread of the Kremlin is so great that all Russian officials, except the highest, hesitate or refuse to make decisions.... The communist form of State requires a bureaucracy of exceptional ability." But the Russians, Bullitt wrote, "have always been and are bad bureaucrats."

From this observation Bullitt drew further findings that even many decades later sound shocking. His findings related to "the racial composition" of the Soviet bureaucracy. Since the Russians remained poor bureaucrats and the socialist state required an efficient bureaucracy, the country was actually run by the Jews. "Extraordinary numbers of the Jews are employed in all the Commissariats." Bullitt provided the statistics: in the USSR, according to his calculations, there were sixty-one commissars and their deputies, and twenty of them were Jewish; yet there was only about one Jewish person for every sixty Soviet citizens of other ethnic backgrounds. "The upper bureaucracy in nearly all commissariats is Jewish." Bullitt named the leaders with whom he was dealing, and many of those were Jews: the People's Commissars for Foreign Affairs, Internal Affairs, Foreign Trade, Transportation. Only "the army was relatively free of Jews, but there are many in the Ordnance Department."

It was 1936. The Nazis were triumphing in Germany, Europe was pursuing a policy of appeasement, and terror reigned in the USSR. In Germany the Nazis had already banned Jews from many professions, including public service and medicine. Bullitt addressed the potential for a rise of anti-Semitism in the Soviet Union: "This astonishing number of Jews in the better paid positions [in the Soviet bureaucracy] has not yet produced overt anti-Semitism, but there are many bitter comments on the fact that about 80% of those who can arrange to pass their vacation at Sochi, the expensive and fashionable summer resort on the Black Sea, are Jews." Again discussing the future, Bullitt gave a valid prognosis this time: "The strain of a long war, therefore, might produce a wave of violent anti-Semitism, and increase the already notable inefficiency of the Commissariats."[13] This was exactly what happened in the Soviet Union about a decade later, when a public campaign of anti-Semitism was unleashed in Moscow and, until Stalin's death, many expected that mass pogroms would be carried out.[14]

Bullitt would continue to develop his geopolitical vision in Paris and Washington, but it really matured in Moscow. "We should use our influence quietly to oppose war in the Far East . . . because if there is a war, someone may win it." Any result of the war—either Communist China or the China dominated by Japan—was against American interests, he wrote. At the moment, the Communists did not expect a major revolution in Europe, but they hoped, he said, that a great war there would lead to a new chain of revolutions. By fomenting war in Spain, they expected revolution would spread to France or even Poland and Romania. They needed a European war, and they played on tensions between France and Germany as much as they could. Bullitt argued that American diplomats should do everything possible to preserve the balance of power in the Far East and delay a Franco-German war; that the Soviet Union should be treated not only as a trading partner but also as a dangerous rival; and that the American and European Communist Parties should be confronted as agents of the USSR. The main thing that the federal government had to take care of, he wrote, was to increase the purchasing power of ordinary Americans, so that the Communist religion would remain alien to them.[15]

Roosevelt listened to Bullitt, but he did not follow his advice. Despite Bullitt's insistence that someone from the "Russian experts" of the State Department should succeed him, the man Roosevelt sent to Moscow was Joseph Davies, who had made a substantial contribution to Roosevelt's reelection campaign. Like Bullitt, Davies took part in the Paris Peace Conference but later lived in Washington, where he played golf with Roosevelt. In Moscow, he showed extraordinary naiveté, ignored the "Russian experts" at the embassy, and demonstrated full confidence in the local authorities. Kennan said that Davies made such an impression on the embassy staff (which had been hired and trained by Bullitt) that they considered resigning collectively. But common sense prevailed, and Kennan, Bohlen, and others left Moscow one by one. Davies shaped Roosevelt's notion that the Soviet Union, like America, was building a modern and, in its own way, democratic society, and that Stalin, like Roosevelt, supported progressive policies. According to this theory, modernity, progress, and democracy operated differently in the Soviet Union than they did in America or Europe, and they had to be adjusted to operate in accord with the peculiarities of the Soviet people. Just as the New Deal would emulate elements of the Soviet economy such as state planning, the Soviet Union would import the necessary mechanisms for entrepreneurship and competitiveness from America.

At the invitation of the Kremlin, Davies observed the Moscow show trials of 1937 and saw how the tortured Bolshevik leaders confessed their incredible sins. Terrified, indignant, and fearing that his ulcer was about to burst, Kennan translated these confessions to Davies. During the breaks the ambassador gave interviews, explaining how fair and well-organized the court process was. At the trial Davies ate sandwiches that were delivered to the courtroom straight from the embassy freezer (he ate nothing else). Davies's wife, one of the richest women in America, built a large collection of icons, paintings, and jewelry while she was in Russia. These objects, which Boris Steiger helped her collect, came from the estates that had fallen victim to the revolution. The authorities let the Davieses take their collection back to America, and it is currently on display at a private museum in Washington, DC. We know some details about this business from Irene Wiley. Buying antiques for rubles made them extremely cheap, but Irene realized that every antique had been confiscated or stolen; "it represents sorrow and suffering, every such object tells a story of want and pain." After this insight, Irene saw every antique shop in Moscow as a graveyard, and she stopped collecting.[16]

Because of either greed or stupidity, Ambassador Davies strongly supported the Soviet government. He reassured Roosevelt and the world that the Soviet word was as good as the Bible's. Under his guidance the embassy produced a film, "Mission to Moscow," which praised the Soviets and Stalin. Davies served as ambassador until June 1938, when Stalin was preparing to enter into a dangerous alliance with Hitler. It was Bullitt from Paris—and not Davies from Moscow—who warned Washington about the preparations for the Molotov-Ribbentrop Pact. Again, Roosevelt was not terribly interested in Bullitt's analysis. In a conversation with one of his top officials, Harold Ickes, in March 1937, Roosevelt complained that week after week, Bill Bullitt and other experts were sending him conflicting messages. Distrustful of these dispatches, Roosevelt remarked that "when the international experts felt sure that war was coming, he was easy in his mind, but that when they all saw nothing but peace, then he began to worry."[17]

For Roosevelt, Davies's endorsement of the Soviet Union was more effective than Bullitt's condemnation. During the war, the president needed to sell an alliance with the Soviet Union to the American people: a military coalition with the Soviets would be more palatable if he could convince his people that Stalin was not a medieval tyrant but a creator of an alternative modernity. Admiring Stalin, Walter Duranty justified Soviet excesses with references to Dostoevsky: the *New York Times* correspondent also believed that the Russians loved to suffer and this perverted desire could, according to Duranty, explain collectivization. During the war, Bullitt wrote later, Soviet fellow travelers worked in the State Department, the Treasury, and even the Department of Defense.[18] Conversely, the few experts on Soviet affairs that existed in the United States—most of them former employees of Bullitt—lost their jobs in Washington precisely because they spoke and wrote the truth about the Soviet Union.

13

SAVING PARIS

In August 1936 Bullitt was finally appointed US ambassador to France. He loved the country, enjoyed speaking its language, and considered Paris his second home. He also liked the city's perfect contrast with Moscow. Bullitt had known great figures of French politics for a long time, and they knew him. His special combination of formal manners and creative energy attracted the French. He knew that during his service in Paris, European history would move with unusual speed, and the ambassadorship was his chance to change it for the better. What was happening in France was "tragically interesting," he wrote Roosevelt in December 1936.[1] The French expected financial and military support from the new American ambassador, who did not miss opportunities to emphasize his special relationship with Roosevelt. Using newly installed transatlantic cables, Bullitt was able to call Roosevelt directly; he also wrote him long telegrams and very long letters. He did not trust European communication lines, which he believed could be hacked by multiple interested parties, and organized a courier service that delivered ciphered mail from one American embassy in Europe to another.

Robert Murphy, counselor of embassy in Paris and later assistant secretary of state, wrote about his service with Bullitt with much enthusiasm, calling him "a brilliant man with a profound knowledge of Europe and its history. He was convinced that the European conflict would directly threaten the United States, so he felt his own role in the approaching tragedy was bound to be important. . . . He felt he had a tacit mandate from Roosevelt to act as his eyes and ears in Europe. . . . He had a great influence upon French policy." Murphy added that Bullitt's relationship to the president was "remarkably intimate." When Bullitt was in Paris, he and Roosevelt often talked at length by trans-Atlantic telephone and "threshed out matters of policy with no correspondence to record their discussions," Murphy wrote.[2] In his role as the key ambassador of the United States in Europe, Roosevelt's "eyes and ears in Europe," Bullitt also relied on his writing skills. A former journalist, he was able to communicate complex ideas via quick, witty formulae that could catch the attention of his busy reader.

One of the most influential members of the Roosevelt administration, Harold Ickes, saw Bullitt in May 1938 in Washington and then visited him in June in Paris. They talked about the future. Bullitt told Ickes that Italy would find Ethiopia a burden; Franco was bound to win in Spain; Hitler's timing had been perfect and he would have his way with Czechoslovakia, acting in a manner that neither Russia nor France could stop it; Japan would win battles in China but lose the war. Bullitt also told Ickes that the civilized world was undergoing one of its great upheavals, and he felt strongly that the United States should keep out of European embroilments. Overestimating the French, Bullitt thought the war would last for twenty years and totally destroy Paris. He hoped that the United States would remain free and strong and assume the burden of rebuilding whatever was left of Western civilization in the aftermath of the war.[3] For the moment, Bullitt's predictions were surprisingly correct. In July, however, Roosevelt told Ickes that he found Bullitt's reports to be "too pessimistic."[4]

In Paris, Bullitt and his daughter, Anna, occupied the official residence on Avenue d'Iéna, overlooking the Trocadero and Eiffel Tower. The home had a large dining room suitable for receptions, a small library, and an excellent wine cellar. High-ranking guests appreciated Bullitt's knowledge of French wines, which he liked to combine with exotic Russian snacks, usually caviar. Bullitt also kept his own apartment near the Champs Elysées, which was something like a studio with an extra room for his Chinese servant. Rumor had it that he used the space to entertain his high-society girlfriends. In 1936 Cissy Patterson visited her old friend in Paris.[5] In September 1939 the ever-jealous LeHand wrote Bullitt that she heard from a mutual friend in Paris that Bullitt had "secretly married" a certain countess. "I know I shall strangle that woman when I see her—war or no war!"[6]

At some point Bullitt rented a small chateau in Chantilly, near Paris. The mansion was close to a waterfall, the park was beautiful, and Bullitt enjoyed the river where he could paddle an American-style canoe. He kept a stable at Chantilly, and some of the best French races took place nearby. In Chantilly he felt "like a participant in the last days of Pompeii," he confessed in a letter to Roosevelt; on his part, the president wrote that Bullitt's next choice would probably be Versailles.[7] Ickes described Bullitt's home in Chantilly as a "perfectly charming old chateau, with ten thousand acres of wood with beautiful streams."[8] He enjoyed staying with Bullitt so much he was surprised to hear that, despite the charms of Paris, the ambassador wished to move back to the States and wanted a job in Washington. "When Bullitt comes to this country, he brings a large supply of fresh caviar and Champagne. I always enjoy talking with Bill Bullitt. He thinks that the chances of war in Europe this spring are 50/50," Ickes wrote in 1939.[9]

The ambassador had much success in Paris. Since the Paris Conference, Bullitt had befriended Prime Ministers Daladier, Blum, and Reynaud who changed places with surprising speed. Bullitt was closest with the Socialist leader Leon Blum, who became prime minister shortly before Bullitt arrived in Paris. Blum publicly announced that he planned to do for France what Roosevelt had done for America, and Bullitt did not miss the chance to inform Roosevelt about Blum's aspiration. Together, Bullitt and Blum happily agreed that France was "as definitely on the Left as the United States was on the Left in 1933." As for Blum's opponents, "the aristocracy and upper bourgeoisie are just as dumb here as their opposite numbers in the United States," Bullitt wrote.[10] For him, Blum personified his long-standing idea that a moderate, non-communist Left was the only viable counterweight to Soviet Bolshevism and German National Socialism.

But Blum was in a coalition with French Communists; answering to Moscow, they could "raise hell" in France at any time. France had signed a treaty of mutual assistance with the USSR, but Bullitt told the French that the Kremlin would ignore its obligations. The war in Spain was in the news, and the Spanish ambassador told Bullitt that the Republican air force consisted of Soviet fighter planes manned by Soviet pilots. However, Bullitt did not believe the Soviet air force could help Czechoslovakia. In a report to Roosevelt, he wrote that Czechoslovakia was "the next item on Hitler's menu" after Spain, and that France and Russia would breach their obligations and fail to act.[11] He also warned the State Department that, if Italy entered a military coalition with Germany, "the result would be tragic not only for France and England but for every country in the world including the United States."[12] Bullitt wanted Roosevelt to contact the pope in hopes of stopping Mussolini. He did not want to appease the Italian dictator: "to believe that the government of the United States will ever be able to cooperate with Mussolini is as dangerous to the future of America as would have been the belief that our government could cooperate with Al Capone."[13]

This was a good prediction, but Bullitt made poor ones as well. When the Nazis started their invasion of Belgium, Holland, and France, Bullitt sent a warning to Roosevelt saying that in order to escape defeat, the British could install the government led by the pro-Nazi Oswald Mosley. That would mean that the British navy would fight against the United States, and Bullitt advised Roosevelt to convince the British to transfer their navy to Canada to defend the dominion that might have been a refuge for the British Crown. There were other "hypotheses that we often discuss but never put on paper": Bullitt cherished whispering them into Roosevelt's ear.[14] He insisted that Roosevelt should send the Atlantic Fleet to the Mediterranean in order to warn Mussolini against opening hostilities; Roosevelt refused to follow this advice, which would probably have sent the United States into war at a very early moment. Roosevelt's ambassador at large, Norman Davis, wrote to the secretary of state: "While Bullitt is a very brilliant and able man in so many ways, . . . he has been quietly conveying the impression that he is the spokesman for the President in Europe. . . . We always seem to have some prima donna trying to play a personal role, which can be done only to the detriment of the United States."[15]

From Poland to France, the endangered nations of Europe needed America's help. But with President Roosevelt claiming neutrality, Bullitt had nothing to offer the French but rhetoric. "We ought to make it clear that the United States, like God, helps those who help themselves," Bullitt told the president.[16] He believed Germany would inevitably increase in strength. There was no legitimate reason to prevent Germany's economic development, which it derived from its increasing trade and influence in Romania, Poland, and the Balkans. What was needed, according to Bullitt, was the decoupling of Germany's economic dominance from its political power on the continent. "I do not believe that political domination must necessarily follow economic domination," he wrote. Bullitt saw Hitler's demands to revise the Treaty of Versailles as legitimate; he had predicted the treaty's detrimental impact two dozen years earlier. In his view Germany should have gotten a chance to develop Central Europe and the Balkans economically, but it should be politically limited by a new system of treaties that would limit armaments and produce "a general revival of a feeling of European unity." Bullitt knew his ideas were ambitious; they were also characteristically precocious. "It sounds like a large order. It is a large order," he wrote Roosevelt. The civil war in Spain forced people to "realize that there is such a thing as European civilization," built upon "very old civilized principles," Bullitt argued. "There is beginning to be a feeling that if the nations of Western Europe do not hang together, they will hang separately."[17]

Increasingly frustrated, Bullitt often drew in his dispatches a disturbing analogy between Roosevelt and Woodrow Wilson, which failed to convince Roosevelt because the president did not share Bullitt's critical attitude toward Wilson. Remembering the First World War, Bullitt hoped that America would avoid direct involvement in the new catastrophic war in Europe. Remembering Versailles, he hoped that if the war were to happen, America would win both the war and the peace, which for Bullitt meant an entirely new arrangement for Europe. In his letters to Roosevelt, he continuously emphasized that America shared responsibility for European peace, which for him meant European unity. It was up to the United States to turn German strength toward "constructive rather than destructive purposes." The secret was, again, in promoting "a general effort to make the giving of those concessions to Germany a part of a general plan of unification for Europe."[18]

Roosevelt's closest adviser on international affairs in Washington, Sumner Welles, played with the idea of an international peace conference in Europe, which would allow Roosevelt to meet with the European leaders. Dispatched to Europe in early 1940, Welles traveled for six weeks and suggested the possibility of American mediation to Hitler, Mussolini, Chamberlain, and Daladier. However, they all refused to accept this American help. Bullitt believed, of course, that he would cope with the problem better than Welles. When Welles was in Paris, Ambassador Bullitt was conspicuously absent. The State Department sent Kennan to guide Welles through Italy and Germany, but Welles was not interested in courting his expertise, and the two barely spoke.[19] According to Bullitt, Welles "eulogized Mussolini" in Paris and spread the idea that Hitler's army was undefeatable; Bullitt's friends were bewildered, and he conveyed their incredulity to Roosevelt.[20] Indeed, Welles once confided to a fellow New Dealer that he thought the Duce "was the greatest man that he ever met."[21] But even in Rome, his talks led to nothing. Welles complained that "the vitriolic tongue of Bill Bullitt" colored the coverage of his mission in the European newspapers.[22]

The idea of European unification was increasingly present in Bullitt's dispatches from Paris before the war. In 1936 Ambassador Bullitt said a European war "will mean such horrible suffering that it will end in general revolution, and that the only winners would be Stalin and company."[23] The way to promote peace, he advised Roosevelt, was to emphasize "some basis for understanding between the French and the Germans." While the Russians, British, and Italians were all opposed to French-German reconciliation, it was in the interest of the United States, along with Poland and the smaller states of Europe, to promote such a reconciliation. Bullitt and Blum agreed on this strategy in December 1936. Blum emphasized that American support would be crucial for any attempt at reconciliation with Germany, but Bullitt saw further. In his dispatches from Paris between 1937 and 1938, Bullitt advocated the idea that the only chance for peace was "some scheme which will be little short of the proposal for the unification of Europe." He defined this unification as a system of financial controls, limitations of armaments, and international trusts that would deliver raw materials from the former colonies. Supported by the United States, a united Europe would compensate Germany for the unfairness of the Treaty of Versailles and prevent the impending war by eliminating its driving forces.[24] Bullitt warned that Soviet Russia and fascist Italy would do everything to kill such a proposal. He was not sure about the British position, and urged Roosevelt to influence the British diplomats so that they would be more favorable to his project of pan-European, anti-Soviet reconciliation. He was opposed, however, to his old friend and incoming British ambassador to the United States Philip Kerr's plan, which proposed appeasing Hitler by letting him dominate Central and Eastern Europe all the way to the Soviet border. Bullitt informed Roosevelt that his French friends were united against Kerr's proposal, but it would only strengthen Hitler and lead to an early war. Again, Bullitt was right; Kerr abandoned his plan after Germany occupied Czechoslovakia.

Bullitt's influence in France was unusual for a foreigner. He attended the meetings of the French cabinet so frequently that the press named him a minister without portfolio. Some accused Bullitt of sympathizing with Hitler, which was a poorly drawn conclusion from his well-publicized hatred of Stalin. "The democracies should refuse to choose between either of alternatives—communism and fascism," Bullitt wrote in 1936.[25] He was probably right:

under the circumstances, it was impossible and unnecessary for European powers to decide between two dictators who were determined to divide the continent. But the policy implications of this stance were unclear. The situation changed erratically during the fateful months that culminated in the Munich agreement and the Molotov-Ribbentrop Pact. It is possible that more activist and flexible American diplomacy could have pulled the Nazis into negotiations and prevented the German-Soviet Molotov-Ribbentrop Pact of 1939. At this point, however, Roosevelt was unprepared for such a strategy, and the two "princes of darkness," Stalin and Hitler, outmaneuvered him in Europe. The Japanese attack on Pearl Harbor was the price the United States would later pay for this failure.

Bullitt's counterpart in Berlin, Ambassador William Dodd, dealt with Nazi leaders in a tougher, more straightforward way. A brilliant historian, Dodd sent the State Department gloomy but accurate reports of the dismal developments in Germany. His dispatches influenced Roosevelt, and Bullitt grew jealous. He told Roosevelt that Dodd's open hostility to the Nazi regime was inappropriate for his position as a diplomat, ignoring the fact that his tone in Moscow had been no less challenging than Dodd's position in Berlin. Bullitt suggested that Roosevelt might want to replace Dodd with his friend Hugh Wilson, a career diplomat, and Roosevelt followed this advice in 1938. The tragedy of history was that both of them were right, Dodd about Hitler and Bullitt about Stalin. The irony of history, however, was that Dodd's daughter had become a Soviet spy. Living with her father in the ambassadorial residence in Berlin, twenty-five-year-old southern belle Martha Dodd fell in love with Boris Vinogradov, secretary of the Soviet embassy who also happened to be an officer in the NKVD. Vinogradov recruited Martha, and she provided him and several other Soviet agents with documents from her father's desk. Their romance lasted until Vinogradov's withdrawal to Russia, where his colleagues executed him in 1938. Martha returned to America and continued to spy for the Soviets. She married the New York millionaire Alfred Stern, recruited him, and in 1956 they both fled from American prosecution, finding asylum in Moscow and later in Havana. Bullitt visited Ambassador Dodd and his daughter every time he was in Berlin, but he probably did not suspect Martha's espionage; still, his distrust of his colleague's diplomacy proved well founded.

Bullitt also offered the president advice on domestic affairs. The dismal experience of the Soviet Union did not dissuade him from supporting economic equality and redistribution. In the 1930s he was a loyal New Dealer:

driving the country "toward a fairer distribution of the national income," Bullitt wrote, was the only way of saving it from class warfare and the "eventual crash of all that we care about in America."[26] For him, Roosevelt's new appointments to the State Department had to meet two "absolute requirements": they had to be New Dealers, and they also had to know the difference between Budapest and Bucharest.[27]

Promoting the French-German rapprochement on the cusp of the Munich agreement, Bullitt warned Roosevelt in May 1937 that as long as Hitler was interested in a friendly understanding with Great Britain he would abstain from annexing Austria. However, the moment Hitler found out that "the British have been playing him for a sucker, I think he will act—probably via a revolt of the Nazi[s] within Austria."[28] In November 1937 Bullitt visited Goering in Berlin. In his report Bullitt compared the Nazi leader with "the hind end of an elephant," but nevertheless paid close attention to the instructive details in Goering's words. Goering told Bullitt that Germany was determined to correct the errors of the Versailles treaty by annexing Austria and the Czech Sudetenland. But he also said that the National Socialists had no intention of occupying or annexing Ukraine. From Bullitt, Roosevelt and the State Department learned of the Nazis' plans four months prior to the annexation of Austria and ten months before the Munich agreement. Even Sumner Welles, a longtime opponent of Bullitt in the State Department, appreciated his insights.[29] It was in Welles's best interest to circulate Bullitt's dispatch to the American embassies in Europe and Asia; even so, American and European diplomats later repeatedly referred to Hitler's actions in 1938 as "unexpected."

In September 1938 Prime Minister Daladier told Bullitt that Hitler would accept nothing except the "absolute humiliation of every nation on earth." The chance for peace was one in a thousand, Daladier said. Still, he believed that Germany would eventually lose the war and France would win it. The Bolsheviks were the only ones who stood to gain anything, Daladier told Bullitt, as they could then install Communist regimes throughout Europe. "Cossacks will rule Europe," Napoleon had said on the island of St. Helena. Bullitt agreed with Daladier: Napoleon's saying was about to come true.[30]

The talks in Munich were "an immense diplomatic defeat for France and England," Bullitt wrote, and his sympathies belonged entirely to France. Horrified by the results of Munich, Bullitt sent a telegram to Roosevelt immediately after he learned about them from Daladier. "The war would be long and terrible, but whatever the cost in the end France would win," Bullitt wrote to the State Department.[31] Later, he told a friend that before Munich, the United

States would have had no trouble coming to an agreement with Russia. After Munich, Russia began negotiations with Berlin and raised its price.[32] On October 13, 1938, Bullitt briefed Roosevelt in Washington about the outcome of the Munich agreement. Drawing on the French leaders' impressions of Hitler, Bullitt convinced Roosevelt that the Nazi leader was a maniac and that meaningful negotiations with him were impossible, a view Roosevelt neglected to apply to other dictators, such as Stalin and Mussolini. Bullitt also told Roosevelt about the supremacy of Germany's air force, a permanent theme in their subsequent correspondence.[33]

In Paris in the summer of 1938, Bullitt hosted the sons of his old friend and rival, Joseph Kennedy, then the American ambassador in London. The Kennedy brothers planned an extensive European tour, and for some reason they were particularly interested in traveling to Russia. In Bullitt's letter to John Kennedy, the ambassador proposed a three-week journey for the boys to Berlin, Warsaw, Kaunas, Tallinn, and finally Moscow. John and Robert Kennedy arrived in Paris in June and stayed as the guests of the ambassador until the Munich crisis, at which point they were forced to change their plans. War in Europe could start at any moment. In a timely fashion, the *New Yorker* published a profile of Bullitt. Worthy of Woland, the wording was not entirely flattering: "Headstrong, spoiled, spectacular, something of a nabob, and a good showman."[34]

In Paris, Bullitt cultivated a friendship with two relatively young Frenchmen, financier Jean Monnet and politician Guy La Chambre, and both relationships produced extraordinary results. Monnet first met Bullitt at the Paris Peace Conference and then worked in the League of Nations; soon, he returned to the family business, the cognac trade. Then he moved on to international finance and helped to stabilize the Polish and French currencies. In the mid-1930s Monnet lived and worked in China, helping Chiang Kai-shek finance his railways. This international experience helped him become a founding father of the European Union, but not until much later in his career.

In 1929 Monnet met the artist Silvia Giannini. The financier was almost twenty years older than she was, but that did not spoil their love. Giannini was married, and her husband would not grant her a divorce. They carried on an affair for five years and found a happy resolution when Monnet came to Moscow in August 1934. It was then that Bullitt and Monnet developed a fantastic plan, which they carried out three months later. In November Monnet returned to Moscow from Shanghai, and Silvia arrived there from Switzerland. In the capital of the victorious proletariat, they devoted two days to the most incredible wedding. Silvia took Soviet citizenship, divorced Giannini in his absence, and married Monnet. The French ambassador in Moscow, Charles Alphand, took part in organizing the event along with Bullitt, and one might imagine that Andreychin was also helpful. This is how on November 13, 1934, the future creator of the European Union was married in Moscow.[35] A personality as effective in international affairs as he was secretive in his personal life, Monnet later traveled to Washington to help realize Bullitt's idea to supply the French with American airplanes even though America was still neutral and could not legally do so. Bullitt recommended him to Roosevelt, and Monnet thus started to network with leading American politicians. Eventually, he managed to accomplish what others could not: he united Europe, and American support was crucial for the task.[36]

Over the course of his service in France, Bullitt ceaselessly heard, spoke, and wrote about airplanes. His friend Guy La Chambre became the French minister of aviation in spring 1938. In conversations with La Chambre and French pilots, Bullitt came to understand the relationship between technology and politics, which gave a new boost to his vision for a united Europe. Aviation, he wrote, was a "new element" that changed the rules of European security: an airplane could cross European borders and destroy different states in just an hour. "The modern bombing plane has confronted Europe with an alternative of unification and destruction." Both the lessons of the First World War and the development of new technologies, especially aviation, "made Europe an absurdity," Bullitt wrote. The old Europe of mosaic borders, nostalgic empires, and revisionist nation-states would be no more. "These dinky little European states can not live in an airplane civilization.... Today they have an alternative of submerging their national hatreds and national prides sufficiently to unify the continent or of destroying themselves completely and handing Europe over to the Bolsheviks."[37] When the French knew that German bombers could destroy Paris in twenty-four hours and the Germans knew the French could destroy the Ruhr the same day, war seemed impossible.

The real situation on the ground and in the skies was quite different. La Chambre told Bullitt that France and Germany had enough bombers to destroy each other's capitals, but Germany had a much bigger fleet of fighters to protect itself. Moreover, its advantage was increasing every month. In those crucial years, Germany was manufacturing more planes per month than France and England combined. On August 9, 1938, Bullitt gave a dinner to honor Charles Lindbergh, the American celebrity aviator with vaguely pro-Nazi sympathies. In the presence of La Chambre, Lindbergh produced wildly exaggerated numbers of Germany's annual production of military airplanes, which in his estimate outnumbered French, British, and Soviet forces combined. Bullitt reported these numbers to Roosevelt with the obvious purpose of getting American military support for France and England, a purpose that they finally, though belatedly, realized in 1940.[38]

La Chambre sought massive deliveries of American airplanes, but Roosevelt had already signed the Neutrality Act, which prohibited the sale of weapons to warring parties in Europe. Bullitt was constantly writing Roosevelt that France could only protect itself if America supplied it with airplanes. With his usual creativity, Bullitt suggested a way the president might bypass the Neutrality Act. If the American planes were built in Canada, paid for by the French, and only assembled with the help of American patents, equipment, and components, they could be sold legally. The assembled aircraft would be delivered from Canada directly to France. Elaborated together with La Chambre, the operation was run by Monnet, whom Bullitt said he trusted "as a brother."[39] In October 1938 Roosevelt received Monnet and approved the idea of using Canadian factories to circumvent the Neutrality Act. In January 1939 the president ordered his cabinet to realize this unusual plan, even though some members attempted to sabotage the cause. Bullitt, who flew in to Washington for the occasion, insisted that France would receive not only the obsolete Curtiss fighter but also the latest plane, the still-classified Douglas bomber. On January 16, 1939, Roosevelt ordered a demonstration of the Douglas for two French experts, whom Monnet had flown in for that purpose. Tragically, the plane crashed during the test flight; the American pilot was killed, and the French colonel on board was badly hurt.[40]

Bullitt pushed for revisions to the Neutrality Act, calling its advocates in Congress "the Hitler allies." He told Roosevelt that if the act remained in force, France and Britain would lose the coming war, and America would have to fight Hitler in the Western hemisphere. If, however, America supplied its European allies with weapons, there was a chance that France and England could win without the help of American soldiers. Unfortunately, most of the American airplanes arrived in France too late to help in the fight, though some were in place when Germany attacked France. Piloted by the French, the American Curtiss planes were "definitely superior" to the German Messerschmitts, Bullitt proudly reported.[41] Later, in September 1939, Bullitt lobbied for making Monnet the representative of both the French and British governments for purchases in the United States.[42] It was the start of Monnet's stellar career, which eventually materialized Bullitt's project of the postwar integration of Europe on the base of the American support. As one historian formulated the secret of Monnet's success, it rested on his "special role as flow regulator along the American aid pipeline."[43]

Despite all the troubles and pleasures of prewar Paris, Bullitt remained seriously concerned with Soviet events. Along with other diplomats he received plenty of information about purges, arrests, and executions in the Soviet Union. Apart from greedy sympathizers like Joseph Davies, American and European envoys in Moscow had no illusions about these events. However, their superiors in Washington, London, or Paris found it difficult and even dangerous to acknowledge what was going on. Bullitt developed his own theory of Soviet terror that was as forward-looking as his other geopolitical ideas. He did not think Stalin was crazy at all; for Bullitt, he was the perfect tyrant—a ruthless but rational dictator. According to Bullitt, Stalin's only domestic goal was to remain in power at any cost, and his only international goal was to expand his influence as far as he could, until he met credible resistance. There was so much discontent brewing in the Soviet Union that Stalin decided to eliminate any possible opposition leaders. The worse things became in Soviet agriculture, industry, and military development, the greater the internal suppression of political discontent.

In March 1939 Bullitt sent to Roosevelt a detailed and hugely important report about a top Nazi meeting. Otto von Habsburg, the last crown prince of Austria-Hungary, gave Bullitt his account of the meeting, painting a clear picture of Hitler's intentions. After the invasion of Czechoslovakia, the prince said, Poland would follow. In 1940 and 1941 Germany planned to settle its accounts with France and England, which would probably mean the German occupation of their possessions in South America. Using these colonies as a base, Germany then planned to attack the United States and exterminate its "Jewish democracy." Writing personally to Roosevelt, Bullitt expressed full confidence in the authenticity of the document.[44] In August 1939 Nazi Germany and the Soviet Union signed a non-aggression pact. The vocabulary of American diplomacy was soon enriched by the concept of the "totalitarian state," which was used to refer to both Russia and Germany. From Paris Bullitt watched how his old friend and skillful opponent, Maxim Litvinov, lost his chair in the commissariat to one of the vicious fathers of the Soviet terror, Viacheslav Molotov. The Molotov-Ribbentrop Pact had brought about the realization of Bullitt's most fearsome predictions. His friend Anthony Biddle was then the American ambassador to Poland; together, they awaited the new division of Poland between the two predatory states. America remained neutral, so when the Germans intercepted correspondence between Bullitt and Biddle they used it to accuse the American diplomats of anti-German sentiment. After the occupation of Warsaw, Biddle remained the American ambassador to the Polish government-in-exile; residing in Paris, he continued to work with Bullitt on Polish problems. Both men were particularly interested in the mysterious fate of thousands of Polish officers who disappeared after the Soviet invasion of eastern Poland. In 1943 Biddle informed the American government about the full scale of the Soviet massacre in a location that became known as Katyn.

In the meantime Roosevelt was still enjoying Bullitt's jokes. In 1939 he told Ickes about a telephone conversation in which Bullitt had said, "Mr. President, of course the English foreign office is listening to our conversation and we will have to be careful about what we say. You and I know that they are a bunch of pusillanimous, double-crossing, tricky people. . . . And undoubtedly the French foreign office is listening too. . . . You know that bunch too, they are just as bad as the English." Roosevelt replied, "Well, Bill, I agree with everything you have said." He was evidently delighted with this episode.[45]

In Paris Bullitt met Walter Krivitsky, one of the first and perhaps most important in the long chain of NKVD "defectors," former Russian intelligence agents who fled to the West and provided detailed information about Stalin's methods, perpetrators, and victims. Krivitsky first joined the Bolsheviks in 1917 and enjoyed an excellent career that culminated, twenty years later, in a covert posting in The Hague. A polyglot Galician Jew posing as an antiques dealer, Krivitsky coordinated Soviet intelligence throughout Western Europe. When purges of the Soviet army and NKVD began, Krivitsky and his colleagues were in danger; some were recalled to Moscow and never returned. In September 1937 Krivitsky's friend and colleague Ignace Reiss refused to return to the USSR. He was soon killed in a Swiss village, leaving behind an open letter to Stalin that appeared in European newspapers. Having learned from Reiss's mistake, Krivitsky did not hide in a remote canton but instead asked the French government and the American ambassador in France for help. Bullitt helped Krivitsky receive police protection and publish his story in the Paris newspapers; he also issued him an American visa and bought him a ticket to New York. Upon his arrival in the United States, Krivitsky got into trouble with immigration authorities, and Bullitt once again interfered. Krivitsky's book, *In Stalin's Secret Service,* caused a sensation in 1939. The signing of the Nazi-Soviet pact confirmed Krivitsky's predictions. He testified in

Congress and then worked with the British Secret Service; it was because of his help that MI5 eventually broke the spy ring of the "Cambridge Five." In February 1941 Krivitsky was found dead in a Washington hotel. American police believed the cause of death was suicide, but few doubted that Krivitsky was killed by Soviet agents.

Based on the information he obtained from Krivitsky, Bullitt initiated an investigation against Alger Hiss, a State Department official close to Undersecretary Welles. When Bullitt informed the State Department and wrote to Roosevelt that Hiss was a Soviet spy, he pointed to evidence from Daladier and the French counter-intelligence. The State Department did not respond to this information, and Hiss continued his career. In 1944 Hiss was responsible for the institutional development of the future United Nations. Later, he was one of the key participants in the Yalta Conference, where he was officially responsible for the Middle and Far East but also prepared crucial documents on Poland that met the Soviet demands. In 1948 Whittaker Chambers, a former Soviet spy and the editor of *Time* magazine, exposed Hiss in his testimony to the House Committee on Un-American Activities. When Hiss was finally put on trial in the winter of 1949, the proceedings boosted public awareness about Soviet espionage and helped the careers of Congressman Richard Nixon and Senator Joseph McCarthy. In 1952 Bullitt testified to Congress about the Hiss case; he was sure that Hiss was a spy. Convicted for perjury, Hiss served about four years in prison but died in his home. Since then, most experts believe that Hiss was a Soviet agent in the State Department throughout the fateful years from 1939 until 1947. Bullitt had been right again. The damage that Hiss's activities inflicted upon Europe, America, and the United Nations has still not been entirely appreciated; many related documents remain classified.

In 1950 the leading liberal historian Arthur Schlesinger Jr. published an essay in *Look* magazine titled "What Made Them Turn Red," which characterized John Reed, Bullitt, and Hiss as members of the same political family. Enraged, Bullitt wrote a letter to *Look* accusing Schlesinger of "an attempt to whitewash various Soviet agents by use of my good name." Bullitt insisted that both of his postings in Russia were part of his lifelong strategy to reduce the Soviet threat. Again, he appealed to the memory of Reed: "In 1921, I learned the truth about the last months of John Reed in the Soviet Union and his complete disillusionment. Reed was my friend. His widow became my wife. My alleged 'glowing faith in the Soviet Union' is an invention of your author, Arthur Schlesinger Jr."[46]

Bullitt also supported the defection of Victor Kravchenko, the Soviet Army captain who served in Washington for the procurement of war materials under Lend-Lease. In conversation with David Dallin, the Belarusian Menshevik who became the American economist (and coauthor, with Boris Nikolaevsky, of the remarkable book *Forced Labor in Soviet Russia*, published in 1947), Kravchenko spoke of his intention to remain in the United States. Dallin introduced Kravchenko to Bullitt who brought the defector to his childhood friend Francis Biddle, attorney general of the United States. In 1944 Kravchenko asked for political asylum. Soviet authorities demanded his extradition, and former ambassador Joseph Davies asked Roosevelt to agree to their request. However, the FBI was interested in Kravchenko, Roosevelt stayed firm, and Kravchenko remained in America. His 1946 book, *I Chose Freedom*, told the world about Soviet collectivization, terror, and the Gulag. Interestingly, Eugene Lyons, the left-wing journalist who in the mid-1930s in Moscow was Bullitt's friend and Bulgakov's translator, helped Kravchenko write his book in English. In 1949 the French Communist Party accused Kravchenko of defamation but lost the case in court. Forced to live in the United States under an assumed name, Kravchenko was found dead in his Manhattan apartment in 1966; as usual, the police deemed it a suicide.

At 2:50 in the morning of September 1, 1939, Bullitt woke Roosevelt up with a telephone call. Ringing from Paris he informed the president that German planes had bombed Warsaw and several German divisions had crossed the Polish border. "It started," said Roosevelt. "God help us!" His secretary LeHand wrote Bullitt: "Everything is so horrible—apparently Hitler meant what he said about this 'bloody' war. It still seems like a nightmare from which I will soon awaken."[47]

Bullitt knew the war would become a world war. Seven days later, he wrote a letter to Roosevelt asking to be recalled from his post and given a place in the cabinet. He suggested Anthony Biddle to replace him in the Parisian embassy: "Tony is just as eager to get to work in Paris as I am to get to work in the United States, and I can promise you with my customary modesty that from my experience here, I know now more about how to get ready for war than anyone except yourself," Bullitt wrote to Roosevelt. To start, Bullitt proposed "colossal purchases" of the best American aircraft—"at least ten thousand planes and fifteen thousand engines—none of which exist." Without their superiority in the air, Bullitt wrote, France and Great Britain would lose the war. "The only road to salvation lies through a quadrupled production of planes in the United States."[48] In organizing this production Bullitt saw his new role. "I honestly believe that I may be able to be of much more use in America during the next two years."[49] He wanted to be secretary of war, or possibly secretary of the navy. But Roosevelt appointed two Republicans to positions, shaping a coalition cabinet. Bullitt remained in Paris asking Roosevelt, again and again, to send aircraft to France. In December 1939 Bullitt relayed to Washington the words of Daladier, who said the Germans would advance through Holland and Belgium. Their famous maneuver to bypass the Maginot Line was not actually such a surprise.

In November 1939 the Soviet Union attacked Finland. Over oysters with top diplomats in the League of Nations, Bullitt decided to launch an initiative to exclude the USSR from the league. Even the Finnish minister of foreign affairs did not believe the proposal would get the majority of votes in the league, but Bullitt urged him to present the proposal and convinced the French to support it. On December 14, 1939, the league expelled the Soviet Union. In March 1940 Bullitt took part in a scandalous exchange with Joseph Kennedy, the American ambassador in London. After a meeting at the White House, Kennedy told reporters that Germany would soon win the war, while France and the United Kingdom would "go to hell." Bullitt accused Kennedy of disloyalty to the president and advised him to "shut up." In February 1940 Ickes saw Bullitt in Washington. "To my surprise, Bullitt does not want to go back to Paris. He would like a big job here. . . . So I said that I will tell the President that he [should] make Bullitt Secretary of War. This would suit Bill," Ickes wrote in his diary.[50] A liberal and an ambitious New Dealer, Ickes liked Bullitt: "Bill is one of the most intelligent and talented people whom I know," he wrote.[51] He did suggest Bullitt for the position, but once more an appointment failed to materialize.

Bullitt was always in a rush, and Roosevelt was always late. The president was neither a philosopher nor a prophet, but the child and leader of his democratic age, and he was bound by many forces. Primary among them were Congress, public opinion, and lingering memories of the First World War. In May 1940 Nazi troops attacked France. Only after German tanks and bombs bypassed French fortifications, which Washington considered to be state-of-the-art defenses, did Roosevelt realize Bullitt was right: the defeat of the European allies would mean the domination of "totalitarian states" over Europe, a war in the Atlantic and a threat of German invasion of America. The American army was not prepared for war, but the navy had an excellent fleet, largely based in Hawaii. This fleet should have protected America from German cruisers. But what if, after conquering France and England, the Nazis took possession of European fleets and led their newly combined armada across the Atlantic? In May 1940 Roosevelt asked Bullitt to convince the French government to move its fleet from the Mediterranean Sea to Africa and the West Indies to ensure the Germans could not capture it. Bullitt was also instructed to start similar conversations with the British. In fact, after France surrendered, the French sailors sank several ships, while some fled to England and Egypt, and the British navy destroyed others. However, Bullitt successfully negotiated with the French government the evacuation of its gold reserves to America.

Ironically, Bullitt did not bring up the possibility of a Japanese attack on the United States, though the Far East was his favorite area to prophesize about. Even in December 1937 he wrote Roosevelt from Paris to say that a Japanese attack on the Soviet Union was likely, and that the prospect of a Japanese attack on the United States was nonsense. He advised the president to draw Japan into an arms race in the Pacific, thereby draining its resources and making it less likely to attack China; but of course China had already been attacked and would be attacked many times more.[52]

Almost daily, Bullitt's embassy cabled the State Department about bombings in central Paris. On June 3, 1940, Bullitt was attending a luncheon at the French Ministry of Aviation when a bomb fell through the ceiling less than ten feet from his head. The bomb failed to explode and Bullitt was unharmed. On another occasion the ambassador was drinking sherry with guests when an air raid began; according to an embassy cable it involved 155 bombers. Bullitt and his guests left the embassy to inspect the damage nearby and then returned to their glasses.[53] The embassy had a wine cellar that, though "not in the least bombproof," was used during the attacks; Bullitt decorated it with Turkish and Bokharan rugs, so it was "the last word in Oriental style and comfort." As he wrote to the president, "Our motto is: 'We don't mind being killed, but we won't be annoyed.'" During the bombings Bullitt wrote fascinating letters to Roosevelt, skillfully mixing requests and gossip. Most modest among his requests to the president was the shipment of twelve machine guns to help defend the embassy, and this was granted. During the war Bullitt often became impatient in conversation with his bosses. "You cannot tolerate today the incompetence of any individual[s] or organizations which [are] preventing supplies from reaching dying French men, women and children," he wrote to the secretary of state.[54]

The Germans were approaching Paris faster than anyone had expected. Secretary of State Hull asked Bullitt to help his friend Prime Minister Paul

Reynaud to evacuate the government, the navy, and the remains of the army to North Africa. The staff of all foreign embassies left the city. On June 9, 1940, Roosevelt ordered Bullitt to leave the city and follow the French government, wherever it went.

Bullitt refused to leave Paris, telling Roosevelt of his decision in the most dramatic letter of his career. "This may be the last letter that I shall have a chance to send you before the communications are cut. . . . No American ambassador in Paris has ever run away from anything, and I think that is the best tradition that we have. . . . I shall do my best to save as many lives as possible and to keep the flag flying," he wrote. Indeed, American ambassadors had remained in Paris during the French Revolution, the Prussian occupation of 1870, and the German offensive of 1914.[55]

Comparing the German offensive with the Franco-Prussian War, the French government expected the Communist uprising to begin before the Germans even entered Paris. It was poor foresight, but Bullitt bought this logic and passed it along to Roosevelt on April 30. "The moment the French government leaves Paris the Communists of the industrial suburbs will seize the city, and will be permitted to murder, loot and burn for several days before the Germans come in," he telegrammed the president. "After the first shock and disorder, a stern, cruel but orderly German regime will be installed." The United States was still a neutral country, but Bullitt expected he would nevertheless be arrested or forcibly isolated by the invading army. The German regime "will in one way or another prevent me from having contacts with anyone," he wrote. Still, he briefed Roosevelt about the potential escape routes through Italy, Finland, and even Siberia. He still hoped to get a position in Roosevelt's administration. "If the calm of death descends on Paris I should like to be in very active life trying to prepare the USA for Hitler's attack on the Americas that I consider absolutely certain." Bullitt's fantasy was that while he was busy fighting for law and order in the Parisian underground, Roosevelt would proclaim him a hero, make him secretary of state, and demand the Germans release him out of respect for the office. "I think the wisest course for you would be simply to announce my appointment, and inform the German government that you desire my return to the United States to be facilitated." Finally, he composed something like a provisionary farewell: "In case I should get blown up before I see you again, . . . I thank you from the bottom of my heart for your friendship."[56]

The president and the State Department responded with a series of cables ordering Bullitt to evacuate the embassy. He refused, and after deliberations, on June 11, 1940, Roosevelt telegraphed Bullitt to offer his support wherever he was. Roosevelt's words betray his unease: "No authority can be given to you to act as a representative of the French government or local government, but, again, being on the spot, you will, as a red-blooded American, do what you can to save human life." Responding to this extraordinary permission, Bullitt wrote that he had never run away from danger: "If I should leave Paris now I would be no longer myself."[57] Antony Biddle, Bullitt's friend and ambassador to Poland, followed the French government as acting envoy of the United States.

On June 12, two days before the German entry into the capital, the French government asked Bullitt to become acting mayor of Paris, as they put it. The government had left Paris in a panic, declaring it an "open city," but Bullitt insisted that the police and fire departments should remain. That same day, he attended a service at Notre Dame; people saw him weeping as he prayed. There was no Communist uprising, but while German troops were entering Paris they were shot at in the proletarian district of Saint-Denis. The commander of the 10th Army, General von Küchler, who had recently leveled Rotterdam, ordered his artillery and aviation units to bomb the city. Bullitt was able to contact his colleague in Berlin, Ambassador Hugh Wilson, who insisted the Germans respect the "open city" status. Paris was not shelled.

On June 14, 1940, a column of German troops entered a deserted Paris. They chose Hotel Crillon for their headquarters; decades earlier, it had housed the American delegation during the Paris Peace Conference. Bullitt sent two of his attachés there in full military uniform. They presented themselves at the entrance to the Crillon and were directed to von Küchler's office. Having been treated to the best cognac the hotel had, the attachés called Bullitt and connected him to Küchler. They arranged a meeting, at which they discussed the safety of the embassy and property of Americans in Paris; there were still twenty-five hundred American citizens in the city. Küchler invited Bullitt and his two attachés to the German military parade, which was held the same day at Place de la Concorde. The Americans did not accept this honor. The embassy issued hundreds of certificates guaranteeing the safety of the homes and businesses belonging to Americans in Paris, and the Germans respected these certificates.

On June 16, the incredibly swift Jean Monnet produced a startling proposal for French-British union, which would entail joint defense, foreign, and financial policies. Having negotiated the details of the project, De Gaulle and (after some hesitation) Churchill signed on to the idea. "The two governments declare that France and Great Britain shall no longer be two nations but one."

Marshal Pétain buried the plan, arguing that, given the circumstances, a union with Great Britain would be like marrying a corpse.[58] Two days after leaving Paris, the Reynaud government fell and Pétain became prime minister. After some intrigue, he prevented the French cabinet and Senate from departing to the residences that had been prepared for the government-in-exile in Morocco. Instead, the government moved to Vichy.

Bullitt's role in these events was often discussed in counterfactual terms. Secretary of State Hull thought that, if Bullitt had only left with the government to Bordeaux, he could have prevented the debacle of Vichy. De Gaulle wrote the same thing in his memoirs, suggesting that, if Bullitt had been in Bordeaux at the critical moment when the Reynaud government fell, he could have done more for France than what he did in Paris. Robert Murphy, a career diplomat and adviser to the US embassy, argued that Bullitt saved Paris by influencing Reynaud's decision to declare Paris an "open city" and evacuate the army while leaving the police and fire brigades in place. Kennan also considered Bullitt's decision to stay in Paris as his "great service": in persuading the Parisian police to remain in the city, Bullitt helped the city survive. Paris would have been doomed if Bullitt had not dissuaded the French Cabinet from pursuing its original plan to fight the Nazis street by street, house by house.

Bullitt left Paris for Vichy two weeks later, on June 30, for meetings with Pétain and his ministers. "Their physical and moral defeat has been so absolute that they have accepted completely for France the fate of becoming a province of Nazi Germany," he wrote to the secretary of state. The British would soon suffer the same fate, President Lebrun told him, and then it would be the turn of the United States. "It seems that you wish to become Germany's favorite province," Bullitt told Admiral Darlan. "The simple people of the country are as fine as they have ever been. The upper classes have failed completely," he wrote Hull about the failure of France.[59]

One American, Charles Glass, recalled seeing Bullitt in Vichy. Impeccably dressed, Bullitt emerged from a black limousine and "looked so dashing and neat, just like the hero in the million-dollar picture, compared with all those who ogled him," Glass wrote.[60] The American ambassador attended a meeting of the National Assembly on July 10, when it gathered in a theater to confirm that the government should not go to North Africa to fight against the Nazis but should instead stay in Vichy and cooperate with the Germans. "The death of the French Republic was drab, undignified, and painful," Bullitt wrote. France had become a "new fascist state," and Bullitt proposed severing diplomatic relations. "The last scene of the tragedy . . . was well placed in a theater."[61] On July 15, 1940, Bullitt traveled to Lisbon and from there flew home to the States.

Upon his return Bullitt found himself in the same dubious position that had become familiar to him since his resignation in 1918. With good reason, he considered himself a war hero, the man who saved Paris. But his enemies knew he was an official who did not execute orders from his superiors. In August 1940, Bullitt gave a speech to the Philosophical Society in Philadelphia —the same venue where another ambassador, Thomas Jefferson, had delivered his famous speech telling America about the French Revolution. Playing a little historical game, Bullitt sent a draft of his speech to Roosevelt and signed the cover letter "Thomas Jefferson," addressing Roosevelt as "George Washington."[62]

America was in danger, finding itself in the same situation that France had been in a year ago, he said. Dictators were always convinced that democracies would respond much too late, Bullitt argued. For the United States, the defeat of the British fleet would have the same effect as the bypassing of the Maginot Line had for France. If America did not go to war, war would come to America. According to Bullitt's calculations, if Germany conquered Great Britain the total strength of their combined navies would be five times larger than the American fleet. In Philadelphia, Bullitt called for the mobilization of the industrial sector for the war effort and demanded military conscription. "Bullitt's speech was simply terrific spoken in a kind of white passion.... There is naturally an isolationist outcry of 'warmonger, near-traitor! etc.,'" Isaiah Berlin said of his address.[63]

Roosevelt and Sumner Welles approved the speech, and it made a splash. Bullitt, however, felt betrayed. Roosevelt had promised to give a follow-up speech that would further develop Bullitt's arguments, but the president did no such thing. The isolationists in Congress were stronger than ever. Still, in September, Roosevelt decided to send fifty old warships to England in exchange for the use of naval bases in three British colonies, a modest scheme that would grow into the colossal Land-Lease deal a few years later. Signed in September 1940 and prepared largely by Bullitt, this destroyers-for-bases deal was a milestone in the US policy.[64]

In November Bullitt resigned, and Roosevelt accepted his resignation in January 1941. The president offered him the place of the ambassador in London, a strategic position for the moment. Again, "Bill Buddha" wanted more.

14

FRONTS OF WAR

A s the world was rushing toward a new war, conflicts worsened within the State Department. European and Russian experts found themselves at odds with the Latin American specialists who dominated the department. The Nazis were the enemy, but the Soviets were the problem. European experts at State saw the Soviet Union as a serious and potentially dangerous challenge, a murderous regime with unpredictable foreign policy objectives. Experts on the Americas saw the USSR as a distant but friendly country, viewing "Uncle Joe" (as the Americans called Stalin) as just another friendly dictator and potential ally. For a while Secretary of State Cordell Hull, a generalist, balanced the two groups. Still, he did not trust the Russian experts because what they said just did not make sense. In 1938 Hull summoned Kennan to find out what had happened to the American Communists who had emigrated to the Soviet Union. Thousands of American citizens from Minnesota, New York, and Chicago had left the country to help build socialism in the USSR, where they disappeared without a trace. Kennan, who had seen some of these people in Moscow, knew perfectly well where they ended up: in the Soviet prisons, forced labor camps, and mass graves. But he could not explain that to the bewildered secretary of state. Hull would not believe that any group, even the Russian Communists, could act so irrationally as to eliminate their own supporters. To his despair Kennan saw that producing the facts was destroying Hull's trust in him and his fellow experts.[1] British diplomats who knew Russia well also felt isolated. Reader Bullard, the UK consul in Leningrad, wrote in his diary that he would have liked to devise a special punishment for people who induced others to move to Soviet Russia.[2]

The East European Division of the State Department was closed down when a distant cousin of Roosevelt's, Sumner Welles, became deputy secretary of state. Robert F. Kelly, the head of the division, was a knowledgeable analyst of Soviet affairs who trained Kennan and Bohlen in Riga before Bullitt opened the embassy in Moscow. Most of his experts had previously worked at the American embassy in Moscow, where they had firsthand experience of Soviet socialism. Their anti-Stalinist reports were very different from Ambassador Davies's enthusiastic dispatches.

It was 1937, the peak of terror in the Soviet Union and a crucial moment in European politics. Bullitt protested Welles's appointment. Taking it personally, he interpreted it as a step forward in Welles's fight against his friend Walton Moore, who oversaw the European affairs; but he also knew of the ideological differences between these two influential figures and their groups, which would define American foreign policy for years to come.[3] An expert in Latin America, Welles purged Moore's friends, the "Russian experts" and other free-minded intellectuals in the State Department. Bullitt suspected Welles of sympathizing with European dictators such as Mussolini.[4] Welles also supported Roosevelt's idea that the Soviet Union was a progressive state, and that personal friendship with Stalin would mitigate any difficulties with the Soviets. Kennan later wrote that the closure of the East European Division was the result of Soviet influence at the highest reaches of the government. With bitter irony Kennan expressed his surprise that Senator McCarthy did not reveal those who closed the East European Division. In his usually balanced memoirs, Kennan did not name these internal enemies whom he declared Soviet spies.

For the rest of their lives Bullitt's and Kennan's firsthand experience of "Russia's degradation" under Stalin defined their political ideas and personal choices; in the 1940s, this experience made them different from their colleagues in Washington. Kennan wrote that, in Moscow, these "hammer-blow impressions, each more outrageous and heartrending than the other" had such an impact on his judgment that he felt at odds with official thinking in Washington "for at least a decade thereafter."[5] When Isaiah Berlin, an Oxford philosopher seconded to the British embassy in Washington, befriended Charles Bohlen, he found out that Bohlen was "still pretty touchy about Russia, like everyone who has sat there, particularly with Bullitt."[6] Cosmopolitan, competent, and endowed with the tragic sense of history, Bullitt and his fellow Russian experts did not fit into the new framework of international relations. While many American generals and admirals felt at home in the expanses of Europe, Africa, and the Pacific, many American diplomats continued to see the world as shaped by the Monroe Doctrine and the Good Neighbor Policy.

In May 1940, immediately after the German invasion of the Netherlands, Harry Hopkins became Roosevelt's personal representative for European affairs. An experienced administrator, he had created the system of social support that was central to the New Deal, but he had no international experience whatsoever. Theoretically, Hopkins sympathized with socialist ideas and liked the Soviet Union. Bullitt wrote later, in 1948, about Hopkins's "infinite ignorance in foreign affairs." Hopkins based his decisions on wishful thinking—"a sheer ostrich infantilism," as Bullitt wrote, which was "the most fatal vice in international affairs." Still, these optimistic wishes were what American democracy needed at that moment. "All Americans wanted to believe that the Soviet Union was what Harry Hopkins said it was," Bullitt wrote in *Life* magazine. His message was clear: in wartime politics, Hopkins had won the position Bullitt believed was his own.[7]

In October 1940 Ickes again suggested to Roosevelt that he should make Bullitt his secretary of state. "I cannot do that. He talked too much, and is too quick on the trigger," said the president.[8] Indeed, the differences between Bullitt, who thought Stalin and Hitler were "the twin princes of darkness," and Hopkins, Welles, and Davies were serious and increasing. In April 1941, Bullitt published an extended essay, "What Next?" in *Life* magazine. It is a remarkable document of the forgotten political world that briefly emerged in the period between the Molotov-Ribbentrop Pact and the Nazi attack on the Soviet Union. France was defeated, the United States was neutral, the Soviet Union was Hitler's ally, and Great Britain alone fought against the triumphal Germany. "Hitler will not stop. He can only be stopped," Bullitt wrote. If Great Britain should be conquered, he warned, the United States would be in danger of immediate attack by the combined forces of the German and British navy. Hitler would first strike in South America, taking the continent country by country. "If Europe, Asia, Africa, and South America as far north as the Equator should be in the hands of the dictators, we would be completely encircled," and nine-tenths of mankind would be mobilized against America. Bullitt's conclusion was that America had to realize war was imminent; the nation had to mobilize everything possible—its navy, industry, and people—for the sake of victory. America's military efforts were terribly delayed, though "no government in the world was so fully informed with regard to relations between Stalin and Hitler as the American government." According to Bullitt, American diplomats—not the spies—warned of the forthcoming pact between Soviet Russia and Nazi Germany as early as the end of 1934; they also warned about the later attack on the Soviet Union.[9]

When the German-Soviet war started in the summer of 1941, Bullitt published another essay in *Life* magazine, urging Roosevelt to send aid to Stalin, but to do it only on the condition of Stalin's "formal, written, public pledges" to respect prewar boundaries and to commit to "the formation of the confederation of the European states."[10] These conditions were very different from the American wartime policy of unconditional support of the Soviet Union. It was true that Bullitt knew infinitely more about the enemies and allies than Hopkins. But Roosevelt's strategy of giving all and any possible support to the Soviet Union did lead to victory in the Second World War. Securing the gigantic transfer of arms and equipment to the USSR through Lend-Lease, Hopkins's shuttle diplomacy helped the United States, the Soviet Union, and Great Britain win the war. The same strategy also led to the Yalta Conference, Soviet control over Eastern and Central Europe, the bloody revolution in China, and the Cold War.

Things were changing fast, and now Bullitt could not keep up with the intuitive Roosevelt. On July 1, 1941, a week after the start of the German-Soviet war, Bullitt told the president that although the policy of supporting anyone fighting against Hitler was sound, he did not think the Soviet Union would be able to withstand the attack. And if the Nazis were able to procure vast Soviet resources, they would catch up with America in oil, steel, and other materials. America needed to develop its military industry faster than the Germans could develop their military industry on Soviet territory, Bullitt argued.[11] Always personal, he blamed Roosevelt's opposing opinion on the manipulation of Sumner Welles, his old enemy in the State Department. But the main cause of Roosevelt's increasing estrangement ran deeper. Bullitt's political principles and experience in Moscow put him at odds with Roosevelt's pragmatic policies. "When our government began in 1941 to treat the Soviet Union as a 'peace-loving democracy' instead of a predatory totalitarian tyranny, it made one of the most disastrous errors in the history of the United States," Bullitt wrote later. Bullitt and Roosevelt "were at opposite poles in their views of Stalin," Orville Bullitt, his brother and historiographer, stated.[12]

In June 1941 Roosevelt's secretary of twenty years, Margaret LeHand, had a stroke, and the president was left without her service. From the surviving letters it is clear that she was still in love with Bullitt, but his feelings for her turned into friendship. If Roosevelt connected her premature illness with her unhappy engagement, that could be another reason for his disappointment in Bullitt. Margaret was left partially paralyzed and lived with a full-time nurse in Somerville, Massachusetts. In several letters Bullitt asked her to join him on his Ashfield farm. Dictating her letters to the nurse, Margaret refused. She died three years later.

According to Ickes, Bullitt lunched with Roosevelt in early June 1941 and insisted that the United States should enter the war. "Bill said that if Roosevelt waited too long, he would go down in history as the man who by his failure to act had destroyed American civilization as we know it." Ickes agreed with Bullitt that the president was "too sure in his sense of timing." After the German attack on the Soviet Union, Ickes telephoned Bullitt to ask him what he thought would happen next. Bullitt was pessimistic. The Russian army was composed of peasant soldiers who could not fight a mechanized war, he said. During the rapid retreat of the Red Army from the Western borders of the Soviet Union, Bullitt even believed that some Soviet generals were on Hitler's payroll.[13]

Roosevelt did not want to involve Bullitt in talks that concerned American relations with Britain and the Soviet Union, but they continued their lunches and correspondence. Laying out his wartime philosophy in his letters to Roosevelt, Bullitt saw the Second World War as "an immense opportunity" for the States because it could make America the "dominant political power" in the world. The Allies ought to be supported to the extent that they were useful, he argued, and suggested several conditions for Lend-Lease that he wanted Stalin to accept. The USSR had to agree to guarantee the eastern boundary of Europe as it existed in August 1939, before the double invasion of Germany and the Soviet Union. The Soviets also had to agree to a postwar confederation of European states and promise to make no demands on China. In their correspondence, Roosevelt agreed with Bullitt, but he also believed Stalin was willing to help him. "If I give him everything I possibly can and ask nothing from him to return, *noblesse oblige*, he won't try to annex anything." In response, Bullitt reminded Roosevelt that "when he talked of *noblesse oblige* he was not speaking of the Duke of Norfolk but of a Caucasian bandit whose only thought when he got something for nothing was that the other fellow was the ass."[14] The situation was more complex. Roosevelt's real fear was that Bullitt's carrot-and-stick policy would force Stalin to strike a separate deal between Nazi Germany and Soviet Russia, a sort of new Brest-Litovsk that would strengthen the Nazis. Bullitt responded that a separate pact between Russia and Germany was impossible because Stalin would never again trust Hitler, who betrayed their previous pact. It was a crucial point, and there was no way to verify it.

In November 1941, Roosevelt offered Bullitt a new and challenging mission. The president wanted a clear picture of what was happening in North Africa and the Middle East. The British troops were fighting the Nazis close to the holy sites and oil fields of Arabia and Palestine, but it was unclear where American interests should lie in the region. Bullitt's mission to Northern Africa would be a deeply personal endeavor. The president "wanted the sort of report that would make him feel as though he had been there himself.... He stated that he wished this trip to be made for him and for him alone," Bullitt wrote after another lunch at the White House. The two men also discussed Sumner Welles; Roosevelt "flatly" said that Welles would do everything to knife Bullitt in the back, and he promised to prevent any such behavior.[15] Bullitt agreed to the mission with a view that, upon his return, he could organize "appropriate action to carry out" his recommendations in Washington. He was still angling for a top position in the Roosevelt administration.

In November 1941 Bullitt was appointed personal representative of the president of the United States in the Near East with the rank of ambassador. "Reposing special faith and confidence" in Bullitt, Roosevelt asked him to go to Northern Africa and then to India, Burma, and the Dutch East Indies.[16] In a telegram to Churchill, Roosevelt asked him to assist "my old friend Bill Bullitt" with his new mission. On his way to Egypt, Bullitt learned of the Japanese attack on Pearl Harbor. The British governor of Trinidad told him the news and did not hide his joy that America would join the Allied powers. Bullitt's response was quite different; he later wrote that the blindness of American democracy made the Japanese attack so unexpected and disastrous: "All democracies find it hard to face unpleasant facts and prefer to cling to happy illusions until they are hit on the head as we were at Pearl Harbor. But if democracies do not act in time ... they are obliged finally to resort to the most costly form of defense—war."[17] With America now at war, Bullitt set about surveying the situation in Iraq, Iran, Syria, Lebanon, Palestine, and Egypt. He warned that Hitler could send several divisions from the Russian front to Turkey to secure Middle Eastern oil and recommended that the United States send reinforcements to Egypt, where some American troops were already stationed. General Marshall confirmed Bullitt's concerns, and Roosevelt seemed pleased with the report. Bullitt traveled in the region for about a month, and he was clearly in a rush to return to Washington. The trip was as successful as it could be, and Roosevelt wanted him to return for a follow-up. But Bullitt refused: he was waiting for a position in the wartime administration.

Still striving to take part in the war, in June 1942 Bullitt became a special assistant to the secretary of the navy, a position that was not so different from the one he had left more than twenty years earlier. In this modest role, he flew to Europe to see Churchill and de Gaulle, and discussed a possible invasion in Africa with General Eisenhower. Bullitt recommended that Jean Monnet head the civil administration of the occupied areas. He counted the German submarine arsenal and advised Roosevelt to liberate Edouard Herriot, the former French prime minister imprisoned by the Vichy regime. He wrote drafts of propaganda booklets that the Americans were disseminating among troops landing in Africa. But Roosevelt kept him away from more important diplomatic talks, and Bullitt was not involved in the Anglo-American meetings in Casablanca and Cairo.

In November 1942 Roosevelt asked Bullitt for advice about organizing civil administrations in American-occupied territories in Europe. Bullitt unexpectedly used the opportunity to tell the president how to wage war and build peace. In a series of letters Bullitt outlined his vision of postwar Europe, focusing on the Soviet threat. These letters foreshadowed Cold War rhetoric, summed up Bullitt's Soviet experience, and applied what he had learned in Moscow to the new realities of the Second World War. The third and most important of these letters, from January 29, 1943, suggested that Roosevelt start new conversations with Stalin about "an integrated, democratic Europe." Again, Bullitt's political thinking about the future of the Pacific, North Africa, or even France led to new, grand-scale speculations about Russia. "The Russians are an immensely endowed people, physically strong, intellectually gifted, emotionally rich. The Ukrainians are even more gifted than the Russians. They were overcome by the Russians by force of numbers. The Russians win their battles both in the field and in bed. No race on earth, not even the German, has shown such burgeoning energy."[18]

We may all admire the courage of the Soviet soldiers, Bullitt explained, but Stalin had not changed. The wishful thinkers argued that in the course of war Stalin had become a Russian nationalist; but Russian nationalism had never been peaceful, Bullitt explained. "The extraordinary valor with which the peoples of the Soviet Union have fought against the Nazis has rendered the Russians so popular in both the United States and Great Britain that all possible virtues are being attributed to the Soviet government." For Bullitt, it was nothing more than "a warm sentimental wave of enthusiasm" and "wishful thinking." The Soviet Union was still a totalitarian dictatorship with no freedom of speech, press, or religion; fear of the secret services was universal. America was in a practical alliance with the Soviets, but it was also committed to democracy in Europe. America fought the war to prevent Nazi domination of Europe and could not allow the victory to result in Soviet domination on the continent. After the defeat of Germany, Bullitt forecasted, the Soviet state would begin to show its aggressive nature, and the United States would have to confront this just as it had previously confronted the Nazis. According to his prediction, Stalin would try to annex Russia's neighboring states using his favorite method of staging revolutions across Europe. Bullitt came up with an almost accurate list of fifteen European states that would fall under Soviet domination without American intervention, but he was particularly concerned about Poland. As long as the Soviet Union remained dependent on American aid, however, the president could protect Europe from postwar Soviet aggression. Bullitt wanted Roosevelt to urge Stalin to make war on Japan and respect the prewar boundaries in Europe. Bullitt also wanted Roosevelt "to get Churchill to work for an integrated Europe." Bullitt believed that as long as the world was in war, Roosevelt was in a position to get these public commitments from Stalin and Churchill. He also proposed an "immediate order to Hull to reorganize the Department of State" (*For the President*, 585). As a military strategy, Bullitt proposed landing US troops in Greece and Turkey instead of northern France. Having fought their way through the Balkans and Romania, the soldiers would rid Hungary, Austria, and Poland of Germans, and then they would arrive in the Baltic to finalize US control over Central and Eastern Europe. Having taken Europe from the south, American troops would contain the USSR within its prewar borders. Had Stalin not accepted this strategy, Bullitt recommended focusing on Japan and delaying the landing in Europe (590).

These letters to Roosevelt unveiled Bullitt's idea of a united Europe—a project he had been presenting to Roosevelt continuously since 1937, when he saw in this project "the only chance, . . . the slim one" to save peace. Then he hoped that the "sweeping proposal" would come from Blum, and it would be "some scheme that would be little short of the proposal for the unification of Europe."[19] Later, during the war, Bullitt argued that after the defeat of Germany, Italy, and Japan, it would be necessary to ensure that Europe turned into a single, powerful, and integrated state. Only a united Europe could take part in ruling the world on a level playing field with the United States, Great Britain, the USSR, and China. Moreover, only a united Europe could stop the spread of communism, which would grow stronger after Soviet victory over Hitler. It was a pioneering but clear program of European unification. "An integrated democratic Europe, pacific but armed, is a vital element for the creation of world peace. How can such a Europe be achieved?" (585). Bullitt sought the disarmament of Germany and Italy and the destruction of their military industries. He also envisioned that a democratic Europe would eventually include those two states as equals and facilitate their reconstruction. He acknowledged that the Soviet Union could not be disarmed, and precisely for that reason, united Europe had to be strong and powerful. Bullitt wrote that "an Anglo-Saxon armed dictatorship over all the earth" was a bad idea; instead, he forecasted a confrontation between continental Europe, integrated into one state, and the Soviet Union (585). He believed that in such a world, the United States and Great Britain would serve as outside arbiters; in case of trouble, they would provide economic and military help to the newly unified Europe. This balance of power would be in the interest of Great Britain and the United States, he wrote, as it would stabilize relations between integrated Europe and the Soviet Union.

Referencing the League of Nations' failure to keep the peace after the First World War, Bullitt proposed to start working on European integration while the war was still going on. It was necessary to get the Allies to sign on to the idea of a united Europe while the USSR and Great Britain were still thoroughly dependent on America. After the war ended, the Soviet Union would do everything to prevent the unification of Europe, Bullitt wrote. The position of England with regard to the European project was not clear, and he suggested that Roosevelt should discuss the idea with Churchill.

In the midst of the war, Bullitt proposed getting the Allies to publicly consent, in exchange for continued American aid, to building a united Europe that would include both winners and losers of the war. American allies had to provide guarantees that "the states of Europe are not to be over-run and are not to be placed in tutelage in British and Soviet spheres of influence." If either or both the United Kingdom and the USSR failed to give such public assurances, Bullitt recommended pivoting American military planning from Europe to Asia. Only the "explicit engagements" of both allies would give America "the decisive voice in the settlement in Europe" after the war (592). As a diplomatic strategy, Bullitt advised Roosevelt to get verbal consent for building a united Europe first from Churchill and then from Stalin. He suggested starting these talks sooner rather than later, because the defeat of Germany would diminish America's most persuasive bargaining chip, military aid. Moreover, he advised the whole State Department to focus on pursuing this entirely new task of postwar settlement.

A united Europe was a radical idea well beyond the horizon of American policy-makers. For Bullitt, however, it was an essential part of the postwar world. Both the Soviet Union and Great Britain had to "agree explicitly" to the "American" project for Europe, which was, for Bullitt, a crucial step toward worldwide coordination of peace efforts. "Europe is to be organized as a democratic unit which will take its place along with the United States, Great Britain, the Soviet Union and China as one of the great guarantors of world peace," Bullitt wrote to Roosevelt (585).

The president did not respond to this semi-official letter from the assistant to the secretary of the navy; he probably replied in a personal conversation, and his response was negative. Moreover, it seems that this particular letter from January 29, 1943—a letter that contained an alternative strategy of American landing in Europe, a project of united Europe, a list of countries that were under threat of the Soviet interference or annexation, and an advice to reorganize the Department of State—forever distanced Bullitt and Roosevelt, even more than their political disagreement about Stalin or their personal conflict about Welles. To the president, focused on the routine of global war, Bullitt's ideas sounded haughty and untimely, even utopian. Having promised Stalin that he would open the second front in Europe and then delaying the landing in France, Roosevelt sought to maintain the combat capability of Soviet and British troops with generous American supplies. Stalin had his own ways to express his discontent with the delay of the second front. Despite receiving vast amounts of American military aid, Stalin did not allow US pilots to use Soviet airfields in the Far East because of the Soviet neutrality toward Japan. American pilots shot down by Japanese forces who managed to escape to Soviet territory were kept in forced labor camps. Stalin's behavior was unworthy of an ally, but Roosevelt tolerated it because he did not wish to ignite the slightest conflict with Stalin. Bullitt's recommendations on the two most significant issues of the moment—relations with key allies and the strategic direction of the American offensive—were completely opposed to Roosevelt's plans. In early 1943 Bullitt's foresight was unsurpassed, unexpected, and probably incomprehensible. Roosevelt had asked him for a proposal regarding civil administration on the occupied territories; what he got was a treatise on the open future.

At the end of the war James Forrestal, who would soon become secretary of the navy, played golf with Joseph Kennedy, ambassador to Great Britain and father of a future president. According to Forrestal's account of the outing, Kennedy said that, after the German invasion of Poland, France and Britain would not have declared war against Germany if the United States had not encouraged them to do so. It was Bullitt who pulled Roosevelt into the war against the Germans, convincing him that Hitler was an enemy of Western democracy. If America had not entered the war, Kennedy said, the Nazis would have seized the USSR, and Great Britain would have remained neutral. In response, Forrestal asked what Kennedy thought the Germans would do after they conquered Russia? We do not know Kennedy's answer—they were playing golf, after all.[20]

In May 1944, five weeks before D-day, Bullitt applied to enroll in the army. In an official response John McCloy, assistant to the secretary of war, asked Bullitt to withdraw his application. As Bullitt wrote their conversation, McCloy said, "my knowledge of the French situation was so great and my influence on the French so large that no matter the rank I might have I would, within a month, actually be running relations with France." McCloy also told Bullitt that the president wanted to personally handle all matters of policy toward France, without receiving advice from anyone. Bullitt replied that he simply wanted to fight and that he would agree to any military role, even as a chauffeur. McCloy told him it would not work; even as a chauffeur, Bullitt would soon be "running the entire show." Roosevelt said that he "knew all about France," and McCloy told Bullitt that the president forbade Secretary of War Henry Stimson from making any decision with regard to France without his consent. As a result, the desk in the Oval Office was "filled with directives concerning French" that awaited Roosevelt's consent "at the crucial moment before the invasion." An additional problem for France, according to McCloy, was the fact that Roosevelt was opposed to everything that came from de Gaulle and Jean Monnet. "The truth was," McCloy told Bullitt, "the President hated de Gaulle personally." Isaiah Berlin, who had British sources, also noted that Roosevelt's administration did not believe that de Gaulle represented France and did not "want to mortgage the future by supporting him."[21] McCloy promised to talk with Roosevelt about Bullitt once again, but he also told Bullitt that Roosevelt "was gradually disintegrating as did all men who held great power for too long."[22] McCloy knew what he was talking about: over the course of his career, McCloy served five American presidents.

Roosevelt was ready to make concessions, and he did so with Stalin in Yalta in February 1945. At the Yalta Conference, Roosevelt produced a draft for a new international organization, which inherited many features of the League of Nations. Roosevelt was as physically weak in Yalta as Wilson had been in Paris. Bullitt had warned both presidents, Wilson and Roosevelt, and he was right both times: after defeating the enemy, America had to use its might to win the peace. In Yalta, Roosevelt continued to pursue friendship with Stalin, but just a month later he accused Stalin of disrespecting their joint decisions on Poland and Germany.

In the meantime Bullitt made another extraordinary decision. In a letter to his old friend Charles de Gaulle, he offered his services to the French army. On May 25, 1944, General de Gaulle replied from Algeria: "Come now! Good and dear American friend! Our ranks are open to you. You will return with us into wounded Paris."[23] Bullitt became a commandant (major) in the French army and served in the headquarters of General Jean de Lattre de Tassigny, one of the best of the French commanders. Together with de Lattre, Bullitt landed in the south of France in August 1944, fought in the Vosges through the autumn, and liberated Alsace in January 1945. He accompanied de Lattre to the front, interpreted for him, and was responsible for disseminating propaganda behind enemy lines. De Lattre was known as a great strategist, but he also went into the front line "constantly" and always brought Bullitt along, as he reported to his brother—"so that I have a chance to be in the scrap both at the planning end and the execution." It was Bullitt's moment of redemption. In a revealing letter from the front, he compared his 1944 experience in France with his 1919 experience in Russia: "Nothing since 1919 has given me so much satisfaction as the job I am doing now, and I haven't felt so well in twenty years."[24] As an ambassador of a great power who became an officer in the army of his host country, Bullitt had no predecessors and, to date, no followers.

He enjoyed his service for France, a country he loved second after his own. The discipline in de Lattre's army was harsh and the conditions difficult, but the chef was excellent, and Bullitt was responsible for the wine cellar. There was no shower, and he could wash only during his rare visits to American troops. But Bullitt admired de Lattre, who was "taut, intense, intuitive"—all high praise in Bullitt's vocabulary.[25] Accompanying de Lattre, Bullitt was in the middle of the battles at Toulon and Marseille and took part in many village and mountain attacks: "saw a lot of the real thing at distances of a few yards," he wrote in a letter. He used this word—"real"—as the key to his new experience: "I have been able to be of some real service at various times," he wrote to his brother. In December 1944 they were stuck in the Vosges, and de Lattre lamented the low morale of his army: "The general impression is that the nation has neglected, has abandoned us."[26] Bullitt was then "Chef de la Section d'Action sur le Morale de l'Ennemi," responsible for the propaganda among the Nazi troops; but he was clearly important for the morale of the French soldiers. On January 5, 1945, de Lattre formed the Second Shock Battalion, which had Bullitt's initials, WB, and the Philadelphia Liberty Bell on its tricolor flag. The battalion song included a couplet about Bullitt:

> *Commandant William Bullitt*
> *Is the godfather of the battalion,*
> *He is the man who understands our journey,*
> *His big heart we thank,*
> *When we shout: forward, forward!*[27]

In October 1944 Bullitt went to Paris to open the gates of the embassy he had left four years ago, a dramatic gesture. In a French uniform, he mounted the balcony to survey the Place de la Concorde, and Parisians burst into applause. Bullit joked that they probably mistook him for General Eisenhower, who was just as bald.[28] But the war was still going on, and on December 18, 1944, he wrote to his brother, again predicting the future: "The Boches are still fighting like tigers and will have to be beaten in field after field and that will not be a short job, but I think that six or eight months ought to cover it—unless there is some sort of catastrophe."[29] In January, Bullitt was seriously injured in a car accident in Alsace. He damaged his left leg, hip, and ribs, and this injury was to plague him for the rest of his life. He was sent to an American hospital in Paris. His old friend and longtime secretary, Carmel Offie, who was now deputy political adviser at Allied Force Headquarters in Italy, visited him; Bullitt asked for books on foreign affairs and history. Later Bullitt returned to the front and remained with General de Lattre until the end of the war. On the day the French entered Baden-Baden, de Lattre publicly spoke of appointing Bullitt as governor of the city; apparently it was a joke. On July 14, 1945, the French army held a victory parade in Paris, reviewed by General de Gaulle. At the head of the parade that marched up the Champs-Elysées were the cars of de Lattre along with his best officers, Bullitt among them. Bullitt returned to the United States later in July, decorated with high French honors—the Croix de Guerre with palm and the Legion of Honor.

He returned to his apple farm in Massachusetts. From there, walking with a cane, experiencing back pain and fighting progressing symptoms of leukemia, the former ambassador and commandant observed world politics, read history books, and wrote for glossy magazines. His judgment of Roosevelt's legacy was harsh. When Roosevelt died in April 1945, Bullitt wrote that he had left American foreign policy "in bankruptcy," and that the new president, Harry S. Truman, "was a little man" who could not live up to his "time of greatness."[30] Having no international experience, Truman selected his advisers by balancing their conflicting interests. His Russia hands were Charles Bohlen, who became one of the most influential Soviet experts in Washington, and Joseph Davies, Bullitt's successor in Moscow and Stalin's fellow traveler. There was no role for Bullitt in the new White House.

15

HOMOSEXUALS

Bullitt's friend, President Roosevelt, may have betrayed him, but Bullitt directed much of the blame toward an enemy, the diplomat Sumner Welles. Welles was handsome, smart, and lucky. Married to a rich heiress eight years his elder, he was so close to Roosevelt that the presidential couple sometimes stayed in the Welleses' luxury home in Washington. Having served in several Latin American countries, in 1937, Welles was named undersecretary of state, which only sharpened his rivalry with veteran Secretary of State Cordell Hull. In his efforts to stop the war, Roosevelt dispatched Welles to Europe with a secret mission in February 1940, which failed completely. When America entered the war, Roosevelt ordered Welles to assemble a team of experts to define American political objectives in the conflict. Roosevelt's idea was to correct Wilson's mistakes by preparing a plan for future peace that would be better than the Treaty of Versailles and by creating an international organization that would be better than the League of Nations. Clearly, triumphal America would be a member, host, and leader of this new organization.

Sometimes Welles found himself in the center of strange scandals. He drank a lot, which was normal in those days, but apparently could not contain his sexual desires while intoxicated. Just after returning from his unsuccessful "peace mission" to Europe, Welles took part in the official funeral in Alabama of the former Speaker of the House, William B. Bankhead, and on September 16, 1940, was returning on the presidential train that was full of congressmen, officials, and journalists. In the evening he drank with Vice President Wallace and another high official, and then went to his compartment. Around six in the morning he called the conductor, an elderly black man, and offered him twenty dollars for oral sex. The conductor refused. Then Welles found another conductor and made the same request, with the same result. The two conductors contacted the secret service, which reported the incident. The file went to the FBI and from there to Roosevelt's desk, where it remained until April 13, 1941.[1]

That day Bullitt visited Roosevelt at the White House to talk about preparing public opinion for the imminent war with Hitler. Changing the subject, they proceeded to discuss mutual friends. Referencing the late Walton Moore, the counselor of the State Department to whom Bullitt reported as ambassador, Bullitt told the president about Welles's train adventure. Bullitt said that on his deathbed, Moore left him the documents about Welles that he received from railway officials and asked Bullitt to make these documents public. In his conversation with the president, Bullitt suggested that Welles was a threat to national security: his reasoning was that if a high-ranking official could commit such acts he could be blackmailed, and enemies could get important secrets that could cost American lives. The morality of the State Department was at risk if a man like Welles was at its helm, Bullitt argued. Roosevelt replied that he knew about the situation and had given Welles a permanent guard who was ordered to prevent him from repeating the incident. In response, Bullitt mentioned a recent speech of Roosevelt's and said that if the president sent troops on a new crusade in the name of American values, Welles could not possibly be among the leaders of that crusade. Roosevelt pointed to the door and told his secretary that Bullitt will burn in hell for his gossip.

Two years passed. In the spring 1943, Litvinov, who was then the Soviet ambassador to Washington, demanded that the State Department remove its Russian experts, who he believed were poisoning the Soviet-American friendship. These were Loy Henderson, Elbridge Durbrou, and Charles Bohlen (Kennan had already moved away from Washington). All of them had been Bullitt's men in the past. At that moment Roosevelt feared that Stalin could make a separate peace with Hitler, and Undersecretary of State Welles chose to appease Litvinov. As a result Henderson was sent to Iraq, and Bohlen was promoted to advise Harry Hopkins, whom Bullitt believed to be a Stalin appeaser.[2]

Having lost the support of the State Department, Bullitt unleashed a campaign of revenge. Together with the expelled Russian experts, Bullitt accused Welles of misinforming Roosevelt about Stalin and of making unsuccessful attempts to appease Hitler. At this point Bullitt saw Welles's strategy of creating the United Nations as being in immediate opposition to Bullitt's project for a united Europe. While his project of European unification was a radically new idea, Welles's design of the United Nations was, according to Bullitt, a revival of the League of Nations with all its fatal problems. Bullitt wrote that by its charter, the United Nations was made powerless to act against an aggression of "any bandit Great Power" that had veto power in the Security Council.[3] It was the same argument he had used against the League of Nations in 1919; and unfortunately, this argument was, and still remains, valid.

In this fight Secretary of State Cordell Hull was on Bullitt's side. Welles was Hull's rival, and without Bullitt's intervention Hull would probably have had to work with Welles for years to come. But at this point, Welles's misadventures leaked to the newspapers. Roosevelt suspected Bullitt of passing the documents over to his old friend Cissy Patterson, who then owned the *Washington Times*. Even worse, Roosevelt suspected that Bullitt bribed the conductors to testify against Welles. As Bullitt told McCloy in 1944, Roosevelt "believed the outrageous lie that I [Bullitt] had bought the affidavits in Welles' case for $50,000 and [gave] them to Cissi Patterson."[4] The accusation was probably slander, indeed. Facing the leaks, Hull threatened Roosevelt with resignation if he did not dismiss Welles.

Welles's resignation was finally announced in September 1943, exactly as he was preparing for an international conference in Moscow. Stalin and Molotov lost the pleasure of being briefed about the whims of Welles. Hull later told Roosevelt he should have been grateful to Bullitt for the elimination of Welles: "the exposure of his behavior would blow the Administration into the air," Hull said.[5]

Amazingly but expectedly, in the same months of 1943, another diplomat found himself in a similar situation, and this time it was Bullitt's friend. Carmel Offie, a longtime secretary of Bullitt's, was trying to strike up a relationship with a man walking in a park near the White House, but the man turned out to be a federal agent who brought him to a police station. Powerful friends, most probably Hull, saved Offie from persecution, but his career was ruined.[6] Bullitt and Offie could only praise God that Roosevelt's America was not Stalin's Russia: they knew that if a similar intrigue occurred in Moscow (as the one that befell Dmitrii Florinsky, their friend from the Commissariat of Foreign Affairs), Offie would have been tortured, forced to produce evidence against his boss, and perished along with him. Whether the campaigns against Welles and Offie were coincidental, or Offie's arrest was Welles's revenge on Bullitt, one of the ideological weapons of the Cold War had been cemented in these cases: the accusation of homosexuality became an established method of political discreditation.

Later, in 1953, the FBI Director J. Edgar Hoover informed the White House not only that Offie was a homosexual but, moreover, that he was a "mistress" of Bullitt. According to this report the FBI investigated Offie because "a reliable informant" advised the Bureau in July 1948 that Offie, who was then employed with the CIA, "was a homosexual and ha[d] participated in sexual activities with two individuals." Moreover, Offie "was a recipient of a substantial monetary gift from Bullitt," and Hoover's "reliable source of information advised that he understood the payments by Bullitt to Offie were similar to payments bestowed upon mistresses." The case was closed in June 1951 because Offie left the CIA. Two years later, Hoover wrote his memo to prevent Offie's appointment in the federal government.[7]

Despite the FBI's informant who misinterpreted Bullitt's long-standing and intimate partnership with Offie, Bullitt was probably heterosexual. However, his awareness of homosexuality was unusual for the time. A few years earlier he had accused his wife, Louise Bryant, of being a lesbian, in order to get custody of their daughter. To some extent Bullitt's awareness of these issues was rooted in his familiarity with psychoanalysis. The book he coauthored with Freud was written during the crisis of Bullitt's marriage and contained a detailed discussion of "psychological androgyny" that can be characteristic, Freud and Bullitt argued, to people of both sexes. "To be born bisexual is as normal as to be born with two eyes."[8] Usually people do not completely realize the psychological androgyny in their sexual activities; instead, this androgyny finds an outlet in political and cultural endeavors. Thus, according to this biography of Woodrow Wilson, the feminine core of his personality, which he never realized in sexual relations, drove both his successes and failures in politics. Having mastered these ideas in a scholarly collaboration with Freud, Bullitt could have applied them to his private affairs.

On both sides of the Iron Curtain, the peak of the Cold War was accompanied by paranoia, about which Freud would have had much to say. Well before his collaboration with Bullitt, Freud had articulated his explanation of paranoia as displaced, non-realized homosexuality. Joseph McCarthy saw homosexuality as an identifying feature of spies, as did Nikita Khrushchev, who addressed his 1962 battle cry, "You the damned pederasts," to the Soviet artists who practiced the non-figurative art. In America, many victims of McCarthy's accusatory campaign were homosexuals. Alger Hiss, one of the darkest figures of American diplomacy and a coauthor of the Yalta Treaty, was a Soviet agent and a homosexual. Journalist Whittaker Chambers, who outed Hiss, was also a homosexual and a former Soviet agent.

If McCarthy and his people needed a formal justification for the political harassment of homosexuals, they used the same rationale that Bullitt used against Welles: homosexuals should not hold positions of responsibility because they have something to hide, which makes them an easy target for blackmail. To some extent McCarthy's homophobia was a product of American provincial life, in which Cold War politicians cultivated isolationist fears. According to McCarthy's implicit logic, all depravity came from Europe, and homosexuality was an altogether alien, foreign invention. In fact, it usually turned out that the most cited reason for the cooperation of elite diplomats, financiers, and scientists with the Soviet regime was not blackmail but their ideological disagreement with the right turn of postwar America. But those on the Right, like McCarthy, did not wish to acknowledge this fact.

Homophobia was an important part of the campaign that McCarthy and his House Un-American Activities Committee (HUAC) launched against the State Department in 1950. Acting in coordination with the FBI but often competing with it, this committee outed homosexuals in various federal agencies, which led to the dismissal of dozens of people. The diagnostic "symptoms" of homosexuality, which the officials used in their secret but official correspondence, were laughable: a special kind of smile, a manner of speaking, a friendship between men, or a long stay abroad. The committee and related agencies considered anonymous tips and invited denunciations. As a final judgment they used fashionable psychological "tests," especially the Rorschach test and the lie detector. This sexual inquisition was carried out in different parts of the administration, including Military Intelligence and even the National Park Service. However, McCarthy had a special interest in the State Department. Of the twenty-five hundred letters McCarthy received during his 1950 campaign against the State Department, three-quarters denounced homosexuality among the employees. In a 1950 report Deputy Undersecretary of State John Peurifoy revealed a "homosexual underground" in the State Department. Responsible for internal security at State, Peurifoy explained that during the previous three years he had been able to identify and dismiss ninety-one employees, almost all of them for homosexuality. A German émigrée, Countess Waldeck, applauded the purge: "Somehow homosexuals always seemed to come by the dozen. . . . A homosexual ambassador or charge d'affaires or Undersecretary of State liked to staff his 'team' with his own people. . . . It goes without saying that Moscow has long recognized the potentialities of the Homosexual International."[9]

The most prominent victims of this campaign were two senior diplomats who had been members of Bullitt's embassy in Moscow—Charles Thayer and Charles Bohlen. Like most of Bullitt's appointees, they made rapid ascents through the State Department bureaucracy. Thayer worked for a time as the director of *Voice of America* and in 1952, was nominated to be the American consul-general in Munich. At the same time, Bohlen was nominated to be the US ambassador to Moscow. He was meant to replace Kennan, whom the Kremlin had declared a persona non grata because he publicly said that the Soviet Union felt like Nazi Germany, where he had been interned during the war. Conceding to the Soviets, President Eisenhower withdrew Kennan and nominated his close friend Bohlen. Together, Thayer and Bohlen had to get Senate approval; that's when the problems started. The Senate received denunciations that accused both men of being homosexual, though not of being lovers. The two diplomats were certainly close to one another: Bohlen was married to Thayer's sister. They had all met in Moscow. Avis Howard Thayer visited her brother while he was serving in Bullitt's embassy and shared an apartment with Bohlen. Avis Thayer and Charles Bohlen married and lived happily thereafter, though Bohlen continued to enjoy a reputation as a ladies' man.

Two diplomats became fast friends in Moscow, in the stuffy atmosphere of the embassy that was guarded from the outside and bugged from the inside. In a letter to Assistant Secretary of State R. Walton Moore, Bullitt spoke frankly about the unusual relationship between Bohlen and Thayer. They were "in an intimate friendship," wrote Bullitt in his confidential letter, even in "intense intimacy." This friendship proved to be "destructive" to Thayer who "fell completely under Bohlen's domination," while Bohlen was attached to Thayer "with an almost violent affection." This relationship had led to an information leak, Bullitt wrote to Moore, though he did not specify this leak. Under Bohlen's influence, Thayer drank too much, and while Bohlen became "sly and unreliable," Thayer completely fell apart. Bullitt characterized Bohlen as a man of rare intelligence, but a snob, an egoist, and a "most peculiar person." Bullitt concluded his letter by asking that Bohlen be promoted and removed from Moscow. He asked to replace Bohlen by Kennan, who was about to return to Moscow after a medical leave. Using intense language that was unusual for diplomatic correspondence, Bullitt did not say whether Bohlen and Thayer had a sexual relationship but opened up the possibility of such an interpretation.[10]

The recipient of this extraordinary letter, Robert Walton "Judge" Moore, was a long-term friend and supporter of Bullitt. An old bachelor, he revered Margaret LeHand and encouraged Bullitt's affair with her. One would think that writing to this experienced official and well-connected man, Bullitt should not have hinted about anything inappropriate. More likely, something else happened. Moore interpreted Bullitt's letter literally—as a warning about the unsuitable professional proximity between the two friends and relatives. In accordance with protocol, Moore kept Bullitt's letter in the files that contained his highly classified correspondence. With time these files became available to his successors. Moore died in February 1941 as the counselor of the State Department, which was the number two position in the department, though Undersecretary of State Sumner Welles had more power. After Moore's death, there was no counselor in the State Department until 1945, when Russian experts (first Ben Cohen, then Bohlen, Kennan, and Bohlen again) took the position and held it for many years. It is easy to suppose that, after Moore's death in February 1941, his documents were moved to the office of Undersecretary Welles. He made use of this letter in his vendetta against Bullitt, which lasted long after Welles's resignation in 1943. If Moore on his deathbed gave Bullitt the documents that compromised Welles, after Moore's death Welles inherited the documents that discredited Bullitt's friends.

McCarthy's HUAC worked with the FBI, which had abundant but inconsistent information. The agency knew of Offie's homosexuality and knew that for many years he had worked and lived in proximity to Bullitt, Bohlen, and Thayer. On the other hand, the FBI and the State Department had multiple denunciations of Bullitt and his "boys'" liaisons with Moscow ballerinas. Puzzled, the investigators stopped short of accusing Bullitt, choosing to focus instead on his former subordinates. McCarthy vehemently objected to Bohlen's appointment. "Moscow is the last place in the world to which he should be sent," said the senator. Bohlen and Thayer were both tested for their alleged homosexuality on a lie detector. Unfortunately for McCarthy, psychologists were unable to identify any sign of homosexuality. The FBI interviewed twenty officials who knew Bohlen, and his Washington neighbors as well; nobody confirmed Bohlen's homosexuality.

The Senate confirmed Bohlen as ambassador to Moscow. He was influential enough to defend himself, but he could not help his friend and brother-in-law. After much deliberation, Thayer was dismissed from the Foreign Service for immoral behavior. He begged that the description of the reason for his dismissal would refer to his behavior with women rather than men. Even though FBI investigators knew that Thayer, who had been married for years, had had a love affair and child with his secretary, this request was not met. Dismissed without a pension, Thayer spent the rest of his life, along with his family, on the island of Majorca in the Mediterranean. Like Bullitt, Kennan, Offie, and many others in this circle, Thayer was not wealthy, and it would be inexpensive to live out his days there. In fact, the common perception of this group of diplomats as wealthy, snobbish aristocrats was entirely misplaced; it was their enemies, people such as Sumner Welles and Joseph Davies, who were wealthy. In Majorca Thayer wrote wonderful memoirs and an unpublished novel. In his diary he wrote, remarkably: "under Stalin you went to Siberia, under Hitler to Dachau or Buchenwald but under McCarthy to Majorca, which counts as progress."[11]

The FBI questioned Bullitt about Bohlen and some other Moscow "boys." Bullitt told the agents that, in Moscow, Bohlen drank "excessively" and Thayer "horribly and dangerously"; Bullitt reprimanded them repeatedly but did not doubt their loyalty. However, Bohlen's later role in the Yalta and other negotiations with the Soviets revealed him as a "careerist," and the ambassador "personally opposed" such people: "Bullitt advised that he feels that a Foreign Service officer should stand for his country and the truth even if he loses his job for his action." Sadly, the FBI did not comment on this statement.[12]

At the confirmation hearings, Senate majority leader Robert Taft said that "everybody who went to embassy in Moscow in 1933 and 1934 were homosexuals, the whole mission." When Taft was asked to produce evidence, he played a tape that revealed something entirely different: in Moscow, Bullitt asked one man, "Have you got a girl?" and then said, "Anybody who did not have a girl there, well, you better watch that fellow."[13] The senators had to decide for themselves why Bullitt hired homosexuals if only to encourage them to have sex with Russian girls. These hearings brought another figure, Nicolas Nabokov, to the fore. Nabokov, a cousin of the writer and a well-known composer, had been working with Thayer at Voice of America. He loved chatting with diplomats, and later he became an important figure in cultural Cold War. In its investigation of Bohlen, the FBI produced a report that cast suspicion on Thayer, Offie, and Nabokov, who were all friends with Bohlen.

Although the only actual homosexual was Offie, the investigation led to the removal of all three from their jobs and made sure that they could no longer work for the government.

Liberal-minded observers were horrified by the debate over Bohlen's confirmation. Arthur Schlesinger wrote to a friend, "We have passed beyond the Kafka phase and are moving into Dostoyevsky."[14] Charles Thayer compared the FBI to "the Gestapo or the GPU." He held the lowest of opinions about his enemies in the bureau: "They are clerks with access to files, junior officers who can screw some secretary in the archives to get the files for them. And they are everywhere." But the liberal enemies of McCarthyism also had access to files. Acting very much like McCarthyites, these liberals accused McCarthy of being a homosexual in 1952. The old bachelor immediately married his secretary. Although many thought he might be gay, it is also likely that McCarthy acted out the psychological mechanism Freud depicted so well, in which projective paranoia causes the subject to blame the world for the features he suppresses in himself. In 1954 the Eisenhower administration finally managed to destroy the angry senator by leaking information about a relationship between his two male assistants. The Senate investigated these allegations; the hearings were broadcast on television, and McCarthy's reputation was undermined forever.

Drawing on evidence that was inevitably insufficient, McCarthy and his people were trying to draw an essentialist, legally binding line between homosexuality and friendship. Bitterly decrying McCarthyism, which had destroyed some of his friends and threatened others, Kennan said the whole debacle resembled the Moscow show trials. It was against this cynical machinery that Kennan, in his memoirs, formulated the idea that the "intellectual intimacy" between men was the strongest and most satisfying among the human relationships. Even though Kennan knew from his time in the Soviet Union that friendship might not withstand torture, he saw during the McCarthy era that it could weather gossip and defamation. An ode to "intellectual intimacy" between men became a hugely important aspect of his life story.

16

UNITING EUROPE

W ith the removal of Welles, Hull became responsible for work on the United Nations. He tried to shape the UN into a global body in which the Big Four would play a less decisive role. While Welles imagined the inter-American system playing a central role in the UN, Hull envisioned an executive council, a general assembly, an international court, and social and economic agencies. From his comfortable retirement, Welles attacked Hull for his failure to take particular Latin American interests into account. Continuing the old rivalry between Latin American and Russian experts in the State Department, Hull's closest adviser in planning the UN was Russian-born Leo Pasvolsky, who started his career as the secretary to the last ambassador of the Russian Empire in America and published many books on the politics and economy of the Soviet Union.[1]

In 1943 Bullitt ran for mayor of his native Philadelphia on the Democratic ticket. The race was hopeless: his rival was the acting mayor, the Republicans had controlled the city since 1884, and Roosevelt's support was unreliable. The rumor was that the president first approved Bullitt's nomination and then retracted it, saying, "Cut his throat." In his letter to LeHand, Bullitt attributed his failure to "a combination which appeared for the first time in American politics—although it is nothing new for Europe—an axis of communists and reactionary Republicans. There was no conceivable lie they didn't circulate."[2] The former ambassador had more ambitious goals. The archive has preserved

Bullitt's detailed plan to create a National Morale Service, which would conduct public opinion surveys, study moral questions, and operate domestically and in foreign countries to scientifically advise the president on matters of public morality.[3] However, Bullitt's victory over Welles signaled his own demise. Neither Truman nor Eisenhower requested his advice on international relations.

In the mid-1940s Bullitt returned to journalism and wrote a big series of articles for *Life* magazine. His first essay was entitled "The Tragedy of Versailles." To organize peace is more difficult than to organize war, he wrote. The way a war concludes is important: if the winner fails to build a sound postwar order, a new war is inevitable. Habitually criticizing Wilson and preparing to criticize Roosevelt, Bullitt stayed faithful to cosmopolitan anti-isolationism, which was still central to the Democratic Party. International relations require that all sides adhere to basic moral obligations, he argued. This is why one cannot negotiate with dictators: they always deceive. At the end of every big war, Bullitt said, there comes a time when the world is ready for change, and the duty of the victor is to lead this change. Acting in the name of peace, the victor should rely on his strength and accept the burden of responsibility; this is what Wilson failed to do, and Roosevelt, Bullitt suggested, would fail too. The "moment of great opportunity passes quickly. . . . We must use our power when we have it. . . . Good intentions are not enough. . . . We as a nation cannot resign from this earth. . . . We cannot escape history"— these were Bullitt's words on the eve of the new American victory.[4]

In his essays for *Life* magazine, Bullitt emphasized the unification of Europe as the main postwar challenge. Moreover, he claimed that a united Europe was actually Roosevelt's idea. It was the president who "was convinced that the Treaty of Versailles would lead to war in Europe unless France and Germany could be reconciled and persuaded to work together for the formation of a confederation of European States." This idea "was entirely sound," Bullitt wrote, and played such an important role in Roosevelt's thinking that he made detailed plans to visit European capitals to discuss his idea about a European confederation after the conclusion of the war. But the Great Depression and Hitler ended this plan.[5] Having focused his postwar political efforts on building a European union as opposed to Welles's project of creating the United Nations, Bullitt hoped that ascribing this idea to Roosevelt would give it more clout. In Bullitt's vision, "a European federation of democratic states" should have been "open to all states which were not puppets [of the USSR] and had democratic constitutions and enforced a Bill of Rights—democratic

German states included." It was the only way to incorporate the Germans as equal citizens of Europe, and to prevent them from becoming "serfs in an enslaved Europe" under Soviet rule. Publishing this proposal in 1948 in *Life*, Bullitt suggested that it had matured much earlier, in 1945 or perhaps even in 1941. Roosevelt and Truman were both betrayed by the "officials of the Department of State who were devotees and expounders of the evil nonsense that the Soviet Union was a 'peace-loving democracy.'" Praising the Marshall plan, Bullitt wrote that American money alone could not prevent the Communist conquest of Western Europe. "Unless the remaining independent states of Europe could be united militarily, economically, and politically in a democratic federation, they would fall one by one to Soviet assault." It was the task for the United States "to use all its power to persuade the Western European democracies to forget their old hatreds and rivalries and unite for self-protection."[6]

Once again, Bullitt proposed turning the creation of a European union into a condition of American postwar aid. He mourned the fact that Marshall and his team, which included Bullitt's former associates Kennan and Bohlen, could not make this happen. For his part, Kennan stated, he promoted the unification of Europe as the only feasible method of postwar settlement, beginning in 1942. For Kennan, only a united Europe could help Germany reintegrate into the rest of the world. However, the Russians were firmly opposed to this idea, Kennan wrote, and Roosevelt did not wish to discuss divisive problems during the war.[7]

Bullitt's former associates in Moscow helped initiate the Cold War, and now they were the leading voices in foreign politics. But even they saw Bullitt's views as too aggressive. His experience was too distant from that of most Americans, and he knew it. Nonetheless, he tried to convince ordinary readers of his ideas. "We as a nation cannot resign from this earth," he wrote in *Life*. "We cannot wash our hands of it. . . . We cannot escape history. Pontius Pilate washed his hands, and the world has never forgiven him."[8] In fact, he opposed political realism on the moral grounds that were very much in the spirit of Wilson. Both his anti-isolationist stance and the evangelic rhetoric continued the Wilsonian tradition.

Things were changing quickly. In February 1946 Isaiah Berlin visited the State Department and met Bullitt there; they discussed Turkey and American relations with the United Kingdom. Berlin wrote in a letter, "Bullitt is not in the government or trusted much by anyone now. Nevertheless, I think that what he says is truer today than it was a fortnight ago." Stalin's speech in the

Bolshoi Theater in Moscow changed public opinion in Washington: according to Berlin, this speech "shook them all surprisingly, and all the weathervanes, Lippmann etc. . . . are generally talking tough, or at least complaining that Russia once more destroyed their hopes."[9] The same February, Kennan sent his "Long Telegram" from Moscow, in which he expounded on the views he had developed in his discussions with Bullitt almost ten years earlier. "At bottom of Kremlin's neurotic view of world affairs is traditional and instinctive Russian sense of insecurity."[10]

A similar impulse drove Bullitt's book *The Great Globe Itself: A Preface to World Affairs*, which was also published in 1946. The book starts with a Freudian idea, from *Civilization and Its Discontents*, that humanity's progress in mastering nature has surged much ahead of its progress in mastering its own affairs. The nuclear bomb gave new life to this narrative. Focusing on the new geopolitical situation that followed the use of the nuclear bomb against Japan, Bullitt had no doubt that the Soviet Union would soon master the bomb as well. America should be afraid of no country but the Soviet Union, Bullitt wrote. In October 1949 he debated these ideas over lunch with Kennan, who recorded the conversation. Bullitt said that de Gaulle would have been prepared to "take real leadership in Europe in the direction of integration," which would have helped to resolve the German problem. He blamed Roosevelt's violent aversion to de Gaulle for America's failure to take advantage of this opportunity.[11] He also blamed Roosevelt for American indifference to the Polish question.

Again, the key to Bullitt's thinking was the analogy between the two world wars, the two wartime presidents, and the two peace treaties signed at Versailles and Yalta. The Roosevelt administration made a mistake, Bullitt argued in his book, when it did not oblige Stalin to respect European borders. In exchange for Lend-Lease aid, Roosevelt had to negotiate with Stalin the postwar "European confederation of democratic states," which would include Germany. Bullitt's conclusion was gloomy. We were at war, he said, to prevent Germany from dominating Europe and Japan from dominating Asia. Now, after all our sacrifice, we clearly see that both continents may be dominated by the Soviet Union. In *The Great Globe Itself*, Bullitt was sharply critical of the United Nations, the creation of his old enemy Welles. The UN could prevent the collision between the great powers no better than the League of Nations, and for the same reasons. Now publicly, he contrasted his project to create a united Europe to Welles's project of the United Nations. He had lost his career, but he would not let go of his ideas.

The historical analysis of the relationship between the peoples and authorities in Russia, which both Bullitt and Kennan touched on, is the most important aspect of *The Great Globe Itself*. For both men the continuity of the Russian political tradition was inevitable and unbreakable. Bullitt gave more weight to changing ideologies such as imperialism or socialism; even though his picture was less detailed than Kennan's, it was in many ways more nuanced. But he shared with Kennan many insights on the continuity of Russian expansion in Europe and Asia. Both Bullitt and Kennan saw historical continuities from Genghis Khan to the Romanovs to Stalin in their analysis of Russian authoritarian tendencies.

In his analysis of relations between Russia and the West, Bullitt referred to classic British geopolitical texts, including those by Halford Mackinder, another participant of the Paris Peace Conference and critic of Versailles. While Bullitt was on his way to talk to Lenin in 1919, Mackinder was traveling to talk to Lenin's archenemy, White general Anton Denikin, whom he eventually saved from the Bolsheviks by organizing his flight to England. Mackinder wrote, famously, "Who rules East Europe commands the Heartland; Who rules the Heartland commands the World Island; Who rules the World Island commands the World."[12] In 1945 Kennan translated these theoretical concerns into the practice of Cold War politics: "A basic conflict is thus arising over Europe between the interests of the Atlantic seapower, which demand the preservation of vigorous and independent political life on the European peninsula, and the interests of the jealous European land power, which . . . will never find a place, short of the Atlantic Ocean, where it can from its own standpoint safely stop."[13] In his review of *The Great Globe Itself*, Nikolay Timashev, a Russian émigré and law professor from New York, criticized Bullitt for ignoring the great tradition of resistance to the state, which inspired many generations of liberal, radical, and socialist activists in Russia. The author of *Great Retreat*, a remarkable book about Stalin's cultural politics, Timashev urged his readers to respect the tradition of cultural protest that led to the Russian Revolution and still opened ground for hope.

Both Kennan and Bohlen had outstanding diplomatic careers. After participating in the Tehran and Yalta conferences, where he was Roosevelt's personal assistant and Hopkins's interpreter, Bohlen served as ambassador to the Soviet Union and France, wrote speeches for Marshall, and until the Cuban missile crisis, helped several American presidents formulate policies toward the Soviet Union. After his "Long Telegram," Kennan became the head of the new policy planning staff at the State Department. An influential adviser to Secretary of State George Marshall, Kennan was the architect of "containment," a massive geopolitical project that fundamentally shaped the postwar order. In formulating his dual strategy of containing the Soviet Union and restoring Europe, Kennan reiterated Bullitt's old idea that support for the Non-Communist Left in Europe was the best counterweight to Bolshevism. Bullitt's former associates probably knew that their former boss and mentor had formulated the idea of the Non-Communist Left long before them, in 1918.[14] But Bullitt's attitudes toward the Soviet Union were more aggressive than those of Kennan. He was critical of Kennan's idea of containment; for his part, Kennan did not fully support Bullitt's idea of a united Europe. Kennan wrote about Bullitt's later years: "Unquestionably, he deserved better of the country than he received of it.... In the end of his life, Bullitt became extremely bitter and violent.... It was a sad, but not unnatural, ending for an unusually sanguine and unjustly frustrated man."[15]

At least for his work in France, Bullitt did receive recognition from those people whose opinion he appreciated the most—military officers. He received many French medals and orders and in June 1947 was awarded the American "Legion of Merit." General Jacob Devers, commander of US ground forces in Europe, decorated Bullitt with this order for his "outstanding service" with the French armed forces during the Second World War. It was a rare example of an American official receiving an American award for military service in the armed forces of another state. In an article published in *Life* on June 2, 1947, Bullitt wrote that the communists in France had been too successful, and that Europe might lose its fight with the Soviets. The communists had set up the largest party in France, which combined excellent organization with powerful propaganda. They fought very well during the war, Bullitt said, not for France but for the Soviet Union. They were dangerous: if the communists were to march on Paris, who would defend it? A quarter of the Paris police were members of the Communist Party, and another quarter sympathized with it, he wrote. Bullitt's numbers were exaggerated, but his recipe for fighting communism was realistic: support for non-communist left-wing parties and American aid. First a social democrat, then a New Dealer, and finally a neoconservative, Bullitt would have been a good representative of the American political class if his ideas had not been more radical and precocious than those of his peers.[16]

In March 1946 Bullitt lunched with the top officials in the American navy— Secretary of the Navy James Forrestal and Admiral William Leahy. Forrestal wrote in his diary that Bullitt was "most disturbed about the Russian situation." Bullitt wanted the president to create a working group to evaluate policy vis-à-vis Russia.[17] Since the start of the Cold War Bullitt's ideas had converged with those in leadership positions in Truman's administration, which probably made him feel even lonelier: the jobs he should have had were taken by those he had mentored.

Bohlen wrote Marshall's famous June 1947 speech announcing his plan to rebuild Europe. In the glossy pages of *Life*, Bullitt agreed that the Marshall Plan was necessary to prevent Europe from falling into the hands of Stalin. Nonetheless, Bullitt thought the amount of American money being directed to Europe would be insufficient; again, he argued that the Marshall Plan ought to be reinforced by a union of European states. Only a united Europe could resist Soviet expansionism. The United States had to convince European states to forget their old feuds and unite against the Soviets. As he had done in his letters to Roosevelt years before, Bullitt suggested that the formation of a European confederation be a key condition of American aid. Following Churchill, who used similar terms in his postwar speeches, Bullitt urged the governments of Great Britain, France, and the United States to focus on creating a European federation or perhaps a "United States of Europe." For Churchill, a European Union was a conservative, British-led bulwark against Soviet Russia. For Bullitt, a "United States of Europe" was a projection of his American patriotism: if only the rest of the world would look like America, the world would be a better place. But according to Bullitt, everyone at this point had to understand that Europe must "unite or disappear." The prospective federation should be open to all nations on the continent that had a democratic constitution, those who won the war and those who lost it. In this vision, the union of European states would be specifically directed against the Soviet threat. As early as 1936, during his tenure as ambassador to the Soviet Union, Bullitt wrote to the State Department: "The fundamental aim of the foreign policy of the Soviet Union is to keep Europe divided."[18] In 1943 and then again in 1947, he repeated that the United Europe—"pacific but armed"—should be an important and, moreover, necessary factor in deterring Russia: "the Soviet Union can not be disarmed. Since this is so, Europe cannot be made a military vacuum for the Soviet Union to flow into. . . . The balance of power which is in the interest of Great Britain and ourselves to seek is the balance of power between an integrated Europe (with Germany and Italy disarmed) and the Soviet Union."[19]

This wisdom was so unusual, however, that even his closest friends did not embrace it. Kennan, who had initially supported Bullitt's plan for European unification, was becoming increasingly opposed to the idea. In April 1944 he came to Washington and stayed with Bullitt; influenced by their conversations, Kennan wrote about the necessity of long-term—"patient, persistent and intelligent"—efforts to achieve "the maximum degree of federation in Europe." For Kennan, however, a European federation would need Soviet consent. If Moscow agreed, this federation would prevent confrontation over the forthcoming division of Germany. Should the Soviet Union disagree, "we will be right and they will be wrong, and we will have to find ways of persuading them to accept our view," Kennan wrote to Admiral Leahy.[20] But as the war wound down, Kennan was increasingly critical of the European idea.

Gradually, Kennan realized that the litmus test for Soviet goodwill was not Germany but Poland, and the fate of Poland made him all the more melancholic. As he watched the Soviets launch their offensive in Poland and refuse to support the Warsaw Uprising, Kennan understood their actions as having "tremendous importance for the future of Europe." He saw the Soviet desire to liquidate the Polish government, "with all its records and archives and memories," as stemming not from any particular strategic interests but of "the interests of certain groups within the Soviet Government" to suppress the memory of their "past mistakes." Clearly, Kennan meant the Soviet massacre at Katyn. In 1944 he could only suggest that the United States "bow our heads in silence before the tragedy of a people who have been our allies, whom we have saved from our enemies, and whom we cannot save from our friends." Seeing the Polish question as "the touchstone of Russia's relations with the West," Kennan was not optimistic about the prospects of a European federation. With the legitimate Polish government replaced by Soviet puppets, "there remain[ed] for the Anglo-Saxon powers the division of western Europe into spheres of influence," the core element of Kennan's future policy of containment.[21] In September 1947 Kennan talked to Berlin, and they both took part in negotiating the Marshall Plan in Paris. "The State Department did not really want a Customs Union to be set on foot in the immediate future, but wished that the participating countries should react favorably to the idea of some eventual union," Kennan said.[22] Although Kennan's thinking had diverged from that of Bullitt by the mid-1940s, his postwar analysis leaned heavily on Bullitt's earlier writings. Indeed, his message to European diplomats in Paris closely resembled Bullitt's message from twelve years before. Kennan told Berlin that "there was a new set of men in Washington, with simple, honest minds," and he recommended the same to British diplomats: "Subtlety on our [British] part must at all costs be avoided, and we should send simple, honest men to represent us," Berlin wrote.[23]

In the meantime Bullitt wrote about Communists' increasing power in France and Italy. Repeating what he had realized about thirty years earlier, he pointed out that military loss and economic hardship were the parents of communism. Only American aid could restrain Soviet influence in Europe. Unlike Keynes, Kennan, or Monnet, Bullitt justified this aid on political rather than economic grounds. "Unless we are ready to take the ultimate consequence of having Stalin's empire extend across Europe and Asia, from Atlantic to Pacific, we shall have to give adequate help." Moreover, he suggested revising the very foundations of this aid. "We shall give, not lend," he insisted. The aid would not and should not be returned. "We are fooling no one but ourselves by calling these billions 'loans and credits.'" In fact, they were gifts— "gifts from the American taxpayer" that were supposed to keep foreign "countries from falling prey, one by one, to Soviet imperialism." These gifts would have never been returned, but—precisely as gifts—would contribute to friendship more than loans. These gifts, of course, could have been called bribes. But Bullitt was not cynical about the American aid. "Man lives, in the deepest recesses of his being, by faith and hope." For the French and other Europeans, he thought, this faith and hope needed to focus on the "United states of Europe"—or Europe, "in the long run, will be united under Soviet tyranny."[24]

In Bullitt's mind the postwar project to unite Europe was a political response to the expansionist policy of the Soviet Union rather than an economic plan focused on international trade and customs fees. In the meantime the Marshall Plan was beginning to work, financing the restoration of many European countries, including Greece and Turkey, and stopping the spread of communism there. The Soviet Union refused to accept this assistance and pressured its new allies—Poland, Czechoslovakia, and Finland—to decline it.

At the end of his life, Bullitt was unemployed and uninvolved. Wealthy and mostly healthy, he turned his discontent into quarrels with old friends and disciples. His recollections of Roosevelt became ironic, even dismissive. Sarcastically, he wrote in *Life* that when Roosevelt came into the White House in 1933, he ran his foreign policy, "impelled by his life-long interest in our Navy and his passion for postage stamps." Repeating Wilson's mistakes, Roosevelt had first promised voters that he would avoid war, and then he used his political genius to enter it. Versailles made the Second World War inevitable; Yalta made the Cold War inescapable. Having won the war, the United States lost the peace, but the Soviet Union had won both. Such was the "tragicomedy of American foreign policy," according to Bullitt.[25]

In 1947 he went to China to visit his old friend Chiang Kai-shek. A civil war was raging there, with the Americans and the Soviets supporting opposing sides, the first proxy war of the nuclear era. In a long essay in *Life*, Bullitt warned his readers that a victory for Soviet-style communism in China was imminent. As Bullitt understood it, China was "caught in the sort of vicious circle that has become familiar to the Europeans since World War I."[26] For the Chinese government, inflation was the only way to cover the war costs. Inflation would hurt the middle class, creating a base for the Communist movement, which would completely destroy the middle class. Only American aid could prevent a Communist victory, Bullitt said; moreover, the task could be accomplished at a surprisingly low cost. Because of hyperinflation, the whole budget of the Chinese government was equal to the municipal expenditures of New York City, and American aid would make a palpable difference. Bullitt gave detailed advice on how he would spend American money in China. He would increase salaries, cut the army, punish corrupt officials, decentralize the government, reduce social inequality, and bring in foreigners to collect taxes and control elections. Whether his calculations were correct, the US government did not follow Bullitt's advice. The victory of the Chinese Communists led to enormous loss of life and wealth and resulted in a decade of terror.

Written during President Truman's election campaign, the Berlin crisis, and the start of the Cold War, Bullitt's essays in *Life* magazine personally attacked George Marshall, then the secretary of state, for engineering Chiang Kai-shek's military defeat by preventing American supplies from reaching China. His was a "dishonorable" policy in which "the blind [were] leading the blind." Bullitt also accused Truman of "making Berlin another Munich." Even Truman could not "be so ignorant" as to believe his own statements, Bullitt wrote in 1948. "Vital interests of the American people throughout the world have been endangered by incompetent leadership.... We face today a struggle not for security but for survival."[27]

In 1948 Bullitt endorsed a progressive Republican, Thomas E. Dewey, for president; in all likelihood, he was still counting on a position in the State Department. Truman's unexpected victory destroyed this plan.[28] At the beginning of 1950, he still hoped to return to politics. He felt a mutual respect with Eisenhower, whom he had known since the war in France. Dining with the president at the White House in May 1955, he insisted on a firm policy toward the Soviet Union. He remained committed to European integration, which became the life's work of his friend and former protégé, Jean Monnet.

The fight between the "Russian experts" and the Soviet "fellow travelers"— between the Bullitt-Kennan contingent and the Davies-Welles contingent within the State Department—lasted a long time. In 1960 Dean Acheson, the former secretary of state and adviser to several presidents, wrote that Kennan and Bohlen were dangerous: they peddled "incommunicable" hunches and believed that their advice had to be "accepted by those who have not had the same occult power of divination." Bohlen had told him, "Dean, you came to this field too late to be able to get the feel of it."[29]

The Cold War was in full swing and the Soviet Union was at the center of the public imagination, but many of those experts who worked with Bullitt in Moscow were again being purged from the ranks of the State Department. It seemed that American experts on Russia, with their "occult knowledge," were consistently losing out to their pro-Soviet and allegedly more "liberal" colleagues. But, as Bullitt, Kennan, Bohlen, and Berlin saw it, this was not the point: one could be both liberal *and* anti-Soviet. In fact, confronting the enemies of human dignity in both the United States *and* the Soviet Union was the fundamental liberal challenge.

Over time Bullitt's political essays became bitter. Frustrated about the past, suspicious about the present, and ceaselessly warning about the future, he used increasingly strong language to describe his experience: "While our soldiers, sailors and aviators were fighting with superb skill and courage, our foreign policy was handled with ignorant and reckless disregard of the vital interests of the American people."[30] Stalin in 1947 was employing the same tactics as Hitler in 1936, and America was making the same mistakes as France had made: it did not attack when it should have, letting the enemy grow stronger and awaiting disaster. When he wrote this essay, the Communist Party was the largest political party in the French Parliament. Bullitt warned about a forthcoming national strike in France and the possibility of a Stalinist government in France and later in Italy. His recommendations in 1947 were pretty much the same as they had been in 1918, with one major addition: European integration. "If the remaining European democracies remain separate they will be swallowed one by one by the Soviet dictator." Bullitt applauded President Truman's initiative to provide a massive aid package to Greece and Turkey and suggested that the United States extend this aid to France.[31]

The more he became disillusioned with democratic politics, the more enchanted he became with the military. One of his memos from October 1950 renders the concerns of his old age. Bullitt had attended a luncheon in Washington together with Hoyt Vandenberg (the chief of staff of the US Air Force), Marshal John Slessor (the chief of staff of the Royal Air Force) and Mrs. Alice Longworth (Theodore Roosevelt's daughter). They discussed the strategic balance between the Soviet and American air forces. In the event of a Soviet invasion of Western Europe, it would take the Americans six months to restore its aerial superiority. All the while European and American armies would be fighting against Soviet forces without adequate air support. The conversation became quite emotional: Vandenberg said that he "was lying awake at night thinking of what an American Army might do" in this situation, because in the previous world wars the Americans had fought with complete control of the air.[32] Both commanders agreed that priority should be given to the strategic bombers, and Bullitt was happy with this conclusion.

William Bullitt died in France in February 1967 of chronic lymphatic leukemia, which had progressed steadily in the last decade of his life. He lived to the age of seventy-six, a bitter American and French hero, a lonely man who died with his daughter at his side. Bullitt's body was flown to Philadelphia, and services were held at the Holy Trinity Episcopal Church, with Richard and Pat Nixon in attendance. He started his career trying to mediate between Wilson and Lenin, and he lived long enough to learn that a Soviet-trained assassin killed his old friend John F. Kennedy. One of his last decisions was to quit the Council on Foreign Relations in protest against the politics of this influential body. Another decision was to publish the biography of Woodrow Wilson that he had written with Freud. The publication caused a flurry of criticism; reviewers questioned Freud's authorship, accused Bullitt of forgery, and ridiculed his approach to history. As he prepared his papers shortly before his death, he thought about friends from his youth: Inez Milholland, who sailed with him on Ford's Peace Ship; Chicago journalist Charles Sweeney; Jack Reed; and most painfully, Louise Bryant. He rewrote a poem about them many times:

They are all gone,
Inez, Charlie, Jack,
Louise—the bravest of the brave—
Insane, trailing a dusty cape
In Paris gutters
They are all gone.

We loved each other once
Loved and were sure of life
And of ourselves
Sure we could conquer.
They are all gone.
And I who remain am nothing.

Ten years hence who will remember them?
There will be no one even to remember.
Inez Milholland's voice
Little Charlie Sweeney's smile
And Jack Reed's gaiety.
Or Louise's courage.
They are all gone.

I remain, and hope
Soon to be with them.[33]

CONCLUSION

hus ended the life of man who predicted sharp turns of history and gave
advice to its leaders. He saved Paris and he saved Freud. He did not
save Russia or preserve peace, but nobody could have done so in the twentieth
century. World leaders liked his company but did not heed his advice. Insight-
ful, persistent, and arrogant, a liberal at home and a conservative abroad, a
cosmopolitan who wished that the rest of the world looked like America—
Bullitt presents a respectful, though slightly satirical, portrait of an American
intellectual.

His impact was of a particular kind that could be uneasily summarized by
asking a few "what ifs." If Wilson had not fallen ill in Paris in the spring of
1919 and if he had listened to Bullitt who had returned from Russia with a
sensational offer from the Bolsheviks, the course of world history would have
been different. The Soviet Union would probably not have existed. Perhaps
Bolshevik Russia would have stretched from the Neva to the Urals, America
would have been a member of the League of Nations, Hitler would have been
a famous artist, and Bullitt a great president. Maybe there would have been
no Second World War, no Stalinist Terror, no Holocaust.

But even if Wilson's stroke had not happened, Bullitt had gotten his meeting with the president, and everyone had signed the treaty Lenin drafted with
Bullitt, the Bolsheviks could have abandoned their commitments at any
moment. The Russian Civil War would have resumed, and it is possible that,

confined to European Russia, the Bolsheviks would have been even more radical. A revisionist faction would likely have developed among them, which would have demanded Siberia and the Crimea back, and then Poland or some part of the Balkans. In short, history would not have ended even if Wilson had listened to Bullitt.

If Roosevelt had trusted Bullitt in the mid- and late 1930s, the United States would not have waited for the Molotov-Ribbentrop Pact to be signed, Pearl Harbor to be bombed, or millions of victims to be killed before entering the Second World War. America would have acted in real time, arming France, Poland, Czechoslovakia, and Finland in order to maintain the balance of power in Europe. The war would not have happened, or it would have remained local. The Soviets would not have dominated Eastern Europe, and the Cold War would not have come to be. Without the rest of Eastern Europe, the Soviet Union would have collapsed under its own weight earlier. A united Europe would have developed according to Bullitt's plan, and it might have come to resemble America. The twentieth century would have been different, and probably our world would have been a better place.

But history would not have ended even if Roosevelt had listened to Bullitt. Germany would not have been able to compete in an arms race with the United States—but would the American people have supported such a race in the absence of an attack? Stalin would not have concluded a pact with Hitler before the war—but what would have stopped them from making a separate peace during the war? A possible alliance of Germany, Japan, and Russia terrified Bullitt's mentor, Edward House, back in 1917. The deep and well-founded fear of another pact between Stalin and Hitler motivated Roosevelt's actions, including those that seemed wrong to Bullitt.

The world did not listen to Bullitt, but there were people who did. The ailing Sigmund Freud formulated some of his most bizarre ideas, and had more years of life, because of his friendship with Bullitt. The brilliant George Kennan followed Bullitt when he studied the basics of international diplomacy and the mysteries of Soviet politics. Supported by Bullitt, the unexpected chain of Soviet defectors revealed the sad truth about the Soviet Union to the distrustful world. Materialized by his disciples during the Cold War, Bullitt's futuristic ideas and failed projects gave rise to the Marshall Plan and the subtle art of containing the Soviets. His intrepid French friend Jean Monnet followed Bullitt when he brought the European Union into existence. And his doomed Russian friend Mikhail Bulgakov commemorated Bullitt, merging him with Kant, Christ, and Satan in another bid to end history.

NOTES

INTRODUCTION

1. Walter Isaacson and Evan Thomas, *The Wise Men: Six Friends and the World They Made* (New York: Simon and Schuster, 1986).
2. David Fromkin, *In the Time of the Americans* (New York: Knopf, 1994), xii.
3. John Lukacs, *Philadelphia: Patricians and Philistines, 1900–1950* (New York: Farrar, 1981), 216.
4. Beatrice Farnsworth, *William C. Bullitt and the Soviet Union* (Bloomington: Indiana University Press, 1967); Michael Casella-Blackburn, *The Donkey, the Carrot, and the Club: William C. Bulllitt and Soviet-American Relations, 1917–1948* (Westport, CT: Praeger, 2004); Will Brownell and Richard Billings, *So Close to Greatness: The Biography of William C. Bullitt* (New York: Macmillan, 1988).
5. Office of Oral History of Columbia University, Reminiscences of H. A. Wallace, 2057.
6. Charles Bohlen, *Witness to History, 1929–1969* (New York: Norton, 1973), 20.
7. George F. Kennan, "Introduction," in Franklin D. Roosevelt and William C. Bullitt, *For the President, Personal and Secret: Correspondence between Franklin D. Roosevelt and William C. Bullitt*, ed. Orville Bullitt (Boston: Houghton, 1972), xv.

8. Kennan to Lukacs, December 11, 1976, and August 15, 1978, in *Through the History of the Cold War: The Correspondence of George F. Kennan and John Lukacs* (Philadelphia: University of Pennsylvania Press, 2010), 63, 69.

9. Orville Bullitt, "Biographical Foreword," in Roosevelt and Bullitt, *For the President*, xli.

10. Isaiah Berlin to Joseph Aslop, February 11, 1944, in Isaiah Berlin, *Flourishing: Letters, 1928–1946* (London: Chatto, 2004), 488.

11. William Bullitt, "How We Won the War and Lost the Peace," *Life*, September 6, 1948, 86.

12. Dean Acheson, *Present at the Creation: My Years at the State Department* (New York: Norton, 1969), 47. Bullitt personally attacked Acheson in his Cold War publications, such as William Bullitt, "Can Truman Avoid World War III?" *American Mercury* (June 1947).

13. Orville H. Bullitt, "Biographical Foreword," in Roosevelt and Bullitt, *For the President*, xli.

14. William Bullitt, "A Report to the American People on China," *Life*, October 13, 1935, 35.

15. William Bullitt, *The Great Globe Itself* (New York: Scribner's, 1946), vii.

16. William Bullitt, "The Old Ills of Modern India," *Life*, October 22, 1951.

CHAPTER 1. THE WORLD BEFORE THE WAR

1. William C. Bullitt, "The Shining Adventure," box 112/III/141/103, Bullitt's Archive, at Sterling Memorial Library, Yale University, New Haven, Connecticut (hereafter cited in notes as WCB.SML).

2. Bullitt, "The Shining Adventure."

3. Bullitt, "The Shining Adventure."

4. Steven Watts, *The People's Tycoon: Henry Ford and the American Century* (New York: Knopf, 2005), 228–40.

5. Michael Casella-Blackburn, *The Donkey, the Carrot, and the Club: William C. Bullitt and Soviet-American Relations, 1917–1948* (Westport, CT.: Praeger, 2004), 13.

6. Ernesta Drinker Bullitt, *An Uncensored Diary from the Central Empires* (New York: Doubleday, 1917), 188–89, 163, 26.

7. William C. Bullitt, *It's Not Done* (New York: Harcourt, 1926), 253–54.

CHAPTER 2. COLONEL HOUSE
AND PUBLIC RELATIONS

1. William C. Bullitt, "Freedom of Seas: An American Proposal," *Philadelphia Ledger*, February 22, 1917.

2. [House, Edward,] *Philip Dru, Administrator: A Story of Tomorrow, 1920–1935* (New York: Huebsch, 1912), available at http://www.gutenberg.org /ebooks/6711/.

3. House published his novel anonymously but did not conceal his authorship from his friends, and Woodrow Wilson was one of them. For the history of this publication, see Charles E. Neu, *Colonel House: A Biography of Woodrow Wilson's Silent Partner* (New York: Oxford University Press, 2015), 69–76.

4. House contrasted this situation to the Anglo-Boer war: England gave the defeated Boers a huge grant to help them restore order and prosperity in their country. With British consent a commander of the Boers, Louis Botha, became the prime minister of the new state.

5. Sigmund Freud and William C. Bullitt, *Thomas Woodrow Wilson: A Psychological Study* (Boston: Houghton Mifflin, 1966), 132.

6. George F. Kennan to Bullitt, June 9, 1936, box 112/I/44/1060 (WCB.SML).

7. George F. Kennan, "The Sources of the Soviet Conduct," *Foreign Affairs* 25 (July 1947): 582.

8. William Dodd formulated the thesis that Wilson's anti-imperialist stance and his idea of self-determination had their roots in his southern experience in two works, *Wilson and His Work* and *The Old South*. A southerner and friend of President Wilson, William Dodd later served as Roosevelt's ambassador to Nazi Germany. See William E. Dodd, *Wilson and His Work* (New York: Doubleday, 1920), 60–64.

9. Freud and Bullitt, *Woodrow Wilson*, 191.

10. Susan Schulten, *Mapping the Nation: History and Cartography in Nineteenth-Century America* (Chicago: University of Chicago, 2012), 201.

11. James Srodes, *On Dupont Circle: Franklin and Eleanor Roosevelt and the Progressives Who Shaped Our World* (Berkeley, CA: Counterpoint, 2012), 54.

12. Walter Lippmann and Charles Merz, "A Test of the News," *A Supplement to the New Republic*, August 4, 1920, 3.

13. Ann Douglas, *Terrible Honesty: Mongrel Manhattan in the 1920s* (New York: Farrar, 1995).

14. Charles Seymour, ed., *The Intimate Papers of Colonel House: Into the World War* (Boston: Houghton, 1928), 387.

15. Seymour, *Intimate Papers of Colonel House*, 404.

16. Bullitt, memo, November 18, 1918, box 112/II/107/321 (WCB.SML).

17. Kenneth Durant, memo, December 1936, available at http://www.alexan deryakovlev.org/fond/issues-doc/71027/.

18. Bullitt to Moore, February 22, 1936, box 112/I/58/1430 (WCB.SML).

19. William C. Bullitt, "How We Won the War and Lost the Peace," *Life* 25 (August 30, 1948).

CHAPTER 3. GLOBAL RESPONSIBILITY

1. George F. Kennan, *Soviet-American Relations, 1917–1920*, 2 vols. (Princeton, NJ: Princeton University Press, 1956), 1:14.

2. George F. Kennan, *Russia and the West under Lenin and Stalin* (New York: Little, Brown, 1961), 122.

3. Wilson's Speech in Joint Session, January 8, 1918, is available at http://wwi .lib.byu.edu/index.php/President_Wilson's_Fourteen_Points/.

4. Franklin D. Roosevelt and William C. Bullitt, *For the President, Personal and Secret: Correspondence between Franklin D. Roosevelt and William C. Bullitt*, ed. Orville Bullitt (Boston: Houghton, 1972), xl.

5. Steffens to Reed, February 25, 1918, in Justin Kaplan, *Lincoln Steffens* (New York: Simon and Schuster, 1964), 236.

6. Eastman was married to Elena Krylenko, the sister of Nikolai Krylenko, Trotsky's enemy and the chief prosecutor of the Moscow show trials.

7. Bullitt, memo, November 25, 1918, box 112/II/107/321 (WCB.SML) (all quotations to the end of this chapter are from this memo).

CHAPTER 4. BETWEEN VERSAILLES AND THE KREMLIN

1. John Maynard Keynes, *The Economic Consequences of the Peace* (New York: Skyhorse, 2007), 12, 130.

2. Arthur Meier Schlesinger, *The Coming of the New Deal, 1933–1935* (New York: Houghton Mifflin Harcourt, 2003), 212.

3. William C. Bullitt, "Tragedy of Wilson," manuscript in box 112/III/163/511 (WCB.SML).

4. Bullitt, "Tragedy of Wilson."

5. V. I. Lenin, *Polnoe sobranie sochineniy*, 5th ed. (Moscow: Politizdat, 1970), 42:67.

6. Freud and Bullitt, *Woodrow Wilson*, 151.

7. Freud and Bullitt, *Woodrow Wilson*, 213–14.

8. Bullitt's notes of the meeting, as he published them in William C. Bullitt, *The Bullitt Mission to Russia: Testimony before the Committee on Foreign Relations United States Senate* (New York: Huebsch, 1919), 8.

9. See, for example, John Ure, *Beware the Rugged Russian Bear: British Adventurers Exposing the Bolsheviks* (London: Old Street, 2015).

10. *Bullitt, Mission to Russia,* 20.

11. Bullitt to House, January 30, 1919, box 112/II/110/380 (WCB.SML).

12. Dodd, *Wilson and His Work*, 311–13.

13. Freud and Bullitt, *Woodrow Wilson*, 184.

14. Bullitt, *Mission to Russia*, 27.

15. Bullitt, telegram, box 112/II/107/330 (WCB.SML).

16. The Soviet government published this document in 1934, when Bullitt was the ambassador to the Soviet Union, and Litvinov the commissar for foreign affairs. *Sovetsko-Amerikanskiye otnosheniya*, ed. Maxim Litvinov (Moscow: NKID, 1934), 37–39.

17. Bullitt, telegram, box 112/II/107/330 (WCB.SML).

18. Bullitt, *Mission to Russia*, 39.

19. Freud and Bullitt, *Woodrow Wilson* 220.

20. George F. Kennan, *Memoirs, 1925–1950*, 2 vols. (New York: Pantheon, 1983), 1:80.

CHAPTER 5. RESIGNATION

1. Roland Chambers, *The Last Englishman: The Double Life of Arthur Ransome* (London: Faber, 2009).

2. Lincoln Steffens, *The Autobiography* (New York: Harcourt, 1931), 2:799.

3. Steffens, *The Autobiography*, 2:799.

4. Steffens, *The Autobiography*, 2:799–800.

5. Freud and Bullitt, *Woodrow Wilson*, 213.

6. Bullitt, letter to Wilson, April 6, 1919, box 112/II/107/333 (WCB.SML).

7. Freud and Bullitt, *Woodrow Wilson*.

8. Harold Nicolson, *Peacemaking, 1919: Being Reminiscences of the Paris Peace Conference* (Boston: Houghton Mifflin, 1933), 28, 197, 200.

9. Treadwell, report, May 2, 1919, box 112/II/112/342 (WCB.SML).

10. In contrast, historian William E. Dodd, the future US ambassador to Nazi Germany, blamed Lloyd George. He believed that if the Paris Peace Confer-

ence had accepted Bullitt's proposal, it would have meant the immediate overthrow of Lloyd George. Dodd wrote that Bullitt "resigned in a spirit that revealed a rare mind. Every paper of significance published his vituperative letter," and it signaled the start of the public "war" against Wilson. See Dodd, *Wilson and His Work*, 336.

11. Bullitt, letter to Pettit, April 18, 1919, box 112/II/107/334 (WCB.SML).

12. Wilson quoted in Bullitt, *Mission to Russia*, 11.

13. Freud and Bullitt, *Woodrow Wilson*, 227.

14. Robert Lansing, *The Peace Negotiations* (Boston: Houghton Mifflin, 1921), 112.

15. Freud and Bullitt, *Woodrow Wilson*, 220.

16. Lenin cited in Roosevelt and Bullitt, *For the President*, 9.

17. Bullitt, *Mission to Russia*, 72.

18. Freud and Bullitt, *Woodrow Wilson*, 220, 224.

19. Bullitt, *Mission to Russia*, 74; Bullitt republished this letter in Freud and Bullitt, *Woodrow Wilson*.

20. Bullitt, memo of conversation with Lansing, April 19, 1919, box 112/II/110/376 (WCB.SML).

21. Keynes, *Economic Consequences of Peace*, 3.

22. Keynes, *Economic Consequences of Peace*, 24.

23. Bullitt, "Review of *Economic Consequences of the Peace*," *The Freeman* (1920): 1, in box 112/II/108/345 (WCB.SML).

24. Keynes, *Economic Consequences of Peace*, 24.

25. Bullitt, *Mission to Russia*, 79.

26. This was Philander C. Knox, senator from Pennsylvania and former secretary of state.

27. Bullitt, *Mission to Russia*, 80, 83.

28. Advertisement, box 112/II/107/333 (WCB.SML).

29. Colcord to Bullitt, September 16, 1920, box 112/II/20/438 (WCB.SML).

30. Henry Bernstein, Interview, box 112/II/107/327 (WCB.SML).

CHAPTER 6. *IT'S NOT DONE*

1. George F. Kennan, Introduction to Roosevelt and Bullitt, *For the President*, xv–xvi. Interestingly, Kennan compared Bullitt only to those of his peers whose achievements were high and ends tragic: the musician Cole Porter, the writer Ernest Hemingway, the journalist John Reed, the politician Jim Forrestal, and Jay Gatsby. Bullitt and Fitzgerald took exception to Kennan's

bitter overgeneralization. Their means were very different from Gatsby's, and so were their ends—both died of natural causes.

2. Roosevelt and Bullitt, *For the President*, xvi.

3. Bullitt, *It's Not Done*, 197. Further page references to this work will be given parenthetically in the text.

CHAPTER 7. WIVES

1. Bullitt to Astor, in Roosevelt and Bullitt, *For the President*, 12–13.

2. Orville quoted in Roosevelt and Bullitt, *For the President*, 12.

3. Orville quoted in Roosevelt and Bullitt, *For the President*, xxxviii.

4. Ralph G. Martin, *Cissy: The Extraordinary Life of Eleanor Medill Patterson* (New York: Simon and Schuster, 1979), 283.

5. In fact, these estates were Novoselitsa near Volyn and Yalanets in Podol'e, both in Ukraine.

6. Orville quoted in Roosevelt and Bullitt, *For the President*, 15.

7. Bertram Wolfe, *Strange Communists I Have Known* (New York: Stein, 1965), 23.

8. See Barbara Gelb, *So Short a Time: A Biography of John Reed and Louise Bryant* (New York: Norton, 1973); Mary V. Dearborn, *Queen of Bohemia: The Life of Louise Bryant* (Boston: Houghton, 1996).

9. Reed quoted from Abel I. Startsev, *Russkie bloknoty Dzhona Rida* (Moscow: Nauka, 1968), 265. A survivor of the Gulag, the Soviet historian Abel Startsev read John Reed's archive at Harvard in the 1960s and documented his lively correspondence with Lenin and Lenin's wife, Nadezhda Krupskaia.

10. For a fair account of these last months of Reed's life, see Barbara Gelb, *So Short a Time: A Biography of John Reed and Louise Bryant* (New York: Norton, 1973), 275–83.

11. See Julie Fedor, *Russia and the Cult of State Security: The Chekist Tradition, from Lenin to Putin* (London: Routledge, 2011), 191.

12. Orville, from Roosevelt and Bullitt, *For the President*, xi.

13. Roosevelt and Bullitt, *For the President*, xv.

14. Stearns quoted in Mary V. Dearborn, *Queen of Bohemia: The Life of Louise Bryant* (Boston: Houghton, 1996), 227.

15. Biddle quoted in Virginia Gardner, *Friend and Lover: The Life of Louise Bryant* (New York: Horizon, 1982), 245.

16. Gardner, *Friend and Lover*, 247.

17. "The noted Philadelphia Bill is half kike anyway and so it is really a boon to

humanity." Ernest Hemingway, *The Letters of Ernest Hemingway*, vol. 3, *1926–1929* (New York: Cambridge University Press, 2015), 462.

18. See George L. K. Morris, "A Brief Encounter with Matisse," *Life*, 28 August 1970, 44.

19. Bulllitt, letter, in Dearborn, *Queen of Bohemia*, 241.

20. Max Eastman, *Great Companions* (New York: Farrar, 1942), 174.

21. Bullitt to Bryant, February 19, 1929, box 112/I/11/236 (WCB.SML).

22. Gardner, *Friend and Lover*, 245, 253.

23. Bullitt to Bryant, December 7, 1928, box 112/I/11/237 (WCB.SML).

24. Bullitt to Bryant, March 29, 1929, box 112/I/11/236 (WCB.SML).

25. Gardner, *Friend and Lover*, 257.

26. Bullitt to Bryant, January 30, 1930, box 112/I/11/240 (WCB.SML).

27. Hicks to Bryant, January 30, 1930, box 112/I/11/240 (WCB.SML); Granville Hicks, with John Stuart, *The Making of a Revolutionary* (New York: Macmillan, 1936).

CHAPTER 8. FREUD'S COAUTHOR AND SAVIOR

1. The manuscript is still in the archive: box 112/III/136/1–10 (WCB.SML).

2. Bullitt, "Foreword," in Freud and Bullitt, *Woodrow Wilson*, viii.

3. Freud, Introduction, in Freud and Bullitt, *Woodrow Wilson*, xiii.

4. Freud, Introduction, in Freud and Bullitt, *Woodrow Wilson*, xiii.

5. Mark Solms, "Freud and Bullitt: An Unknown Manuscript," *Journal of the American Psychoanalytic Association* 54 (2006): 1263–98.

6. Freud, Introduction, in Freud and Bullitt, *Woodrow Wilson*, xiii.

7. Solms, "Freud and Bullitt."

8. This and other telegrams cited below were classified documents that Bullitt in Paris, Wiley in Vienna, and Hull in Washington sent each other through the channels of the US State Department. The copies are now in the Sigmund Freud Museum in Vienna, and I am grateful to its curator, Daniela Finzi, for sharing them with me.

9. The Nazi official Anton Sauerwald who was responsible for collecting ransom from Freud and liquidating his publishing house spent so much time with Freud and his books that he became seriously interested in psychoanalysis. He did not know that Wiley in Vienna, Bullitt in Paris, and Hull in Washington, were closely following his moves. See David Cohen, *The Escape of Sigmund Freud* (New York: Overlook Press, 2009).

10. Solms, "Freud and Bullitt."

11. Paul Roazen, "Oedipus in Versailles," *Times Literary Supplement*, April 22, 2005.

12. Freud and Bullitt, *Woodrow Wilson*, 224.

13. Freud and Bullitt, *Woodrow Wilson*, 53.

14. Freud and Bullitt, *Woodrow Wilson*, 37.

15. Bullitt, "Foreword," in Freud and Bullitt, *Woodrow Wilson*, ix.

16. Max Weber, *The Protestant Ethic and the Spirit of Capitalism*, trans. Talcott Parsons (London: Routledge, 1992), 124.

17. Freud and Bullitt, *Woodrow Wilson*, 167.

18. Freud and Bullitt, *Woodrow Wilson*, 62

19. Nicolson, *Peacemaking, 1919*, 52, 197.

20. Keynes, *Economic Consequences of Peace*, 26.

21. Nicolson, *Peacemaking, 1919*, 37, 41–42, 52, 191, 195.

22. For balanced reevaluations of Wilson's role in the Paris talks, see Margaret Macmillan, *Paris 1919: Six Months that Changed the World* (New York: Random House, 2003); Jay Winter, *Dreams of Peace and Freedom: Utopian Moments in the Twentieth Century* (New Haven: Yale University Press, 2008), ch. 2.

23. I am greatly indebted to my discussions of these ideas with Jay Winter.

CHAPTER 9. HONEYMOON WITH STALIN

1. Bullitt's companions on this mournful trip were George Andreychin, a Bulgarian Communist and Trotskyite who was working for the Intourist agency in Moscow, and Eugene Lyons, an American journalist of Jewish Belarusian extraction who recorded the event in Eugene Lyons, *Assignment in Utopia* (New York: Harcourt, 1937), 500.

2. Louis B. Wehle, *Hidden Threats in History* (New York: Macmillan, 1953), 113.

3. LeHand to Bullitt, April 21, 1935 (?), box 112/I/49/1189 (WCB.SML).

4. David Fromkin, *In the Time of the Americans: FDR, Truman, Eisenhower, Marshall, McArthur—The Generation that Changed America's Role in the World* (New York: Knopf, 1994), 130.

5. Wehle, *Hidden Threats*, 115.

6. For example, see Roosevelt, letter from April 21, 1935, in Roosevelt and Bullitt, *For the President*, 113. For rest of this chapter, page references will be given parenthetically in the text.

7. Charles Bohlen, *Witness to History, 1929–1969* (New York: Norton, 1973), 20.

8. Office of Oral History of Columbia University, Reminiscences of J. P. Warburg, 893, 429.

9. Schlesinger, *New Deal*, 212. On the Soviet Union's early dependency on international trade, see Oscar Sanchez-Sibony, *Red Globalization: The Political Economy of the Soviet Cold War from Stalin to Khrushchev* (Cambridge: Cambridge University Press, 2014).

10. See Ephraim Sklyansky's obituary, written by Trotsky, in *Pravda*, 217, September 23, 1925; http://www.revkom.com/index.htm?/biblioteka/marxism/trotckii/politsiluety/279revoluciya.htm/.

11. Cordell Hull, *The Memoirs*, 2 vols. (New York: Macmillan, 1948), 1:303.

12. Stalin, Interview with Walter Duranty, December 25, 1933, published in Stalin, *Sochineniya* (Moscow: Politizdat, 1951), 13:277.

13. Andreychin to Bullitt, December 3, 1933; Bullitt to Andreychin, December 14, 1933, box 112/I/2/41 (WCB.SML).

14. Steffens to Bullitt, November 25, 1933, in Lincoln Steffens, *Letters of Lincoln Steffens*, ed. Ella Winter and Granville Hicks, 2 vols. (New York: Harcourt, 1938), 2:967.

15. Bullitt probably knew about the experiments of the Soviet zoologist Ilia Ivanov, who developed the new methods of insemination in horticulture and tried to apply these methods for the crossing of humans and apes. The American newspapers publicized his experiments. In 1936 the American geneticist and future Noble Prize laureate, Hermann Joseph Muller, visited Moscow. He even wrote a letter to Stalin, in which he proposed the methods of positive eugenics for amelioration of human nature. See Alexander Etkind, "Beyond Eugenics: The Forgotten Scandal of Hybridizing Humans and Apes," *Studies in History and Philosophy of Biological & Biomedical Sciences* 39 (2008): Special Issue "Eugenics, Sex, and the State," 205–10.

16. Office of Oral History of Columbia University, Reminiscences of H. A. Wallace, 2057.

17. Allen Weinstein and Alexander Vassiliev, *The Haunted Wood: Soviet Espionage in America—the Stalin Era* (New York: Random House, 1999), 37.

18. Samuel Harper, *The Russia I Believe In: The Memoirs* (Chicago: University of Chicago Press, 1945), 210.

19. G. N. Savostianov, *Moskva-Vashington: Diplomaticheskie otnosheniia, 1933–1936* (Moscow: Nauka, 2012), 14–16.

20. Savostianov, *Moskva-Vashington*, 16.

21. Grinko quote can be found at http://stalinism.ru/dokumentyi/stenogramma-buharinskogo-protsessa.html?start=43/.

22. Frank Costigliola, *Roosevelt's Lost Alliances: How Personal Politics Helped Start the Cold War* (Princeton, NJ: Princeton University Press, 2012), 268.

23. Peter Rand, *Conspiracy of One: Tyler Kent's Secret Plot against FDR, Churchill, and the Allied War Effort* (New York: Lyons, 2013); Paul Willets, *Rendezvous at the Russian Tea Rooms* (London: Constable, 2015).

24. Reader Bullard, April 15, 1934, in *Inside Stalin's Russia: The Diaries of Reader Bullard, 1930–1934* (Charlbury, Oxfordshire: Day Books, 2000), 256.

25. Kennan, *Memoirs*, 1:79.

26. Kennan, *Memoirs*, 1:81.

27. John Lewis Gaddis, *George F. Kennan: An American Life* (New York: Penguin, 2011), 59.

28. Kennan, *Memoirs*, 1:60.

29. Kennan, *Memoirs*, 1:60.

30. George F. Kennan, *The Kennan Diaries*, ed. Frank Costigliola (New York: Norton, 2014), 93.

31. Kennan, *Diaries*, 93. The term "hoi polloi" refers to the masses, common people.

32. Kennan, *Diaries*, 174.

33. Berlin to Arcadi Nebolsine, February 23, 1959, in Isaiah Berlin, *Enlightening: Letters, 1946–1960* (London: Chatto, 2009), 677.

34. Berlin to Arthur Schlesinger, November 5, 1956, in Berlin, *Enlightening*, 558.

35. Kennan, *Memoirs*, 1:67.

36. Gaddis, *George F. Kennan*, 91.

37. Kennan, *Memoirs*, 1:70.

38. Gaddis, *George F. Kennan*, 201, 211.

39. Gaddis, *George F. Kennan*, 214.

40. Kennan was present at some of these trials, which he interpreted for Ambassador Joseph Davies. While Kennan was writing his memoirs many years after the event, he mixed up his Bolshevik friends Bukharin and Radek; the quote about intellectual friendship actually belongs to Karl Radek, who used these words to characterize his friendship with Bukharin in January 1937 during "the trial of the anti-Soviet Trotskyite Center." Kennan, *Memoirs*, 1:61–62.

CHAPTER 10. BLUFF

1. Roosevelt and Bullitt, *For the President*, 83.

2. Bullitt to Moore, March 29, 1934, box 112/I/58/1419 (WCB.SML).

3. Roosevelt and Bullitt, *For the President*, 83.

4. Bullitt to Moore, June 8, 1935, box 112/I/58/1419 (WCB.SML).

5. Bullitt to Roosevelt, April 1, 1935, in Roosevelt and Bullitt, *For the President*, 121.

6. William Dodd, *Diary* (New York: Harcourt, 1941), 77.

7. Bullitt to Hull, July 23, 1934, box 112/II/135/918 (WCB.SML).

8. Information for this paragraph is from http://irkipedia.ru/content/kitaysko _vostochnaya_zheleznaya_doroga_istoricheskaya_enciklopediya _sibiri_2009/.

9. Troyanovsky to Litvinov, in *Sovetsko-Amerikanskie otnosheniia, 1933–1939*, ed. B. Zhiliaev, G. Savchenko, and G. Sevostianov (Moscow: fond Demokratiia, 2004), 22, 37.

10. Bullitt to Roosevelt, July 23, 1934, box 112/II/135/918 (WCB.SML).

11. M. G. Galkovich to Troyanovsky, May 24, 1935, at http://www.alexan deryakovlev.org/fond/issues-doc/70421/.

12. Savostianov, *Moskva-Vashington*, 45.

13. Litvinov to Troyanovsky, April 10, 1934, *Sovetsko-Amerikanskie otnosheniia* (2004), 110.

14. Divilkovsky, memo, March 7, 1935, in *Sovetsko-Amerikanskie otnosheniia* (2004), 47.

15. Krestinsky, memo, March 13, 1934, in *Sovetsko-Amerikanskie otnosheniia* (2004), 55.

16. Divilkovsky, memo, at http://www.alexanderyakovlev.org/fond/issues-doc/70023/.

17. Litvinov to Troyanovsky, March 14, 1934, in *Sovetsko-Amerikanskie otnosh-eniia* (2004), 57.

18. Sokolnikovva, memo, March 26, 1934, in *Sovetsko-Amerikanskie otnosheniia* (2004), 83.

19. Bullitt to Moore, March 29, 1934, box 112/I/58/1419 (WCB.SML).

20. Divilkovsky, memo, March 11, 1934, at http://www.alexanderyakovlev.org/ fond/issues-doc/70023/.

21. Roosevelt and Bullitt, *For the President*, 60.

22. Roosevelt and Bullitt, *For the President*, 83.

23. Bullitt to Moore, October 6, 1934, in Roosevelt and Bullitt, *For the President,* 99.

24. On February 8, 1934, Troyanovsky said that the Moscow City Council indicated that the contract of rent would be signed for ninety-nine years, for two thousand dollars a year. See http://www.alexanderyakovlev.org/fond/issues-doc/69989/.

25. Bullard, *Inside Stalin's Russia,* 20.

26. For the date of Florinsky's arrest, see the list of victims of the Terror, prepared by the Memorial Society in Moscow, at http://lists.memo.ru/index21.htm/.

27. Rubinin, memo, September 28, 1934, in *Sovetsko-Amerikanskie otnosheniia* (2004), 234.

28. Skvirsky, memo about meeting with Bullitt, September 10, 1934, at http://www.alexanderyakovlev.org/fond/issues-doc/70267/.

29. Boris Skvirsky, memo, January 6, 1935, at http://www.alexanderyakovlev.org/fond/issues-doc/70360/.

30. Troyanovsky to Litvinov, February 7, 1935, *Sovetsko-Amerikanskie otnosheniia* (2004), 298.

31. Rubinin, memo, October 9, 1934, in *Sovetsko-Amerikanskie otnosheniia* (2004), 243.

32. Roosevelt and Bullitt, *For the President,* 93, 99.

33. Bullitt, William C. "A Report to the American People on China." *Life,* October 13, 1947, 36.

34. Litvinov to the Council of People's Commissars, October 7, 1934, at http://www.alexanderyakovlev.org/fond/issues-doc/70300/.

35. "The Project of the Report of the Commissariat of Foreign Affairs about the Development of the Soviet-American Relations in 1935," at http://www.alexanderyakovlev.org/fond/issues-doc/70524/.

36. Bullitt to Hull, telegram, in Roosevelt and Bullitt, *For the President,* 140.

37. Troyanovsky, memo about meeting Bullitt, November 22, 1935, at http://www.alexanderyakovlev.org/fond/issues-doc/70501/.

38. Weinstein and Vassiliev, *The Haunted Wood,* 53.

39. Bullitt to Hull, April 20, 1936, in Roosevelt and Bullitt, *For the President,* 155.

40. Bullitt to Roosevelt, December 7, 1937, in Roosevelt and Bullitt, *For the President,* 243.

41. Bullitt, William C. "How We Won the War and Lost the Peace." Part One, *Life,* August 30, 1948, 83.

42. Sorge received an Iron Cross fighting for the Germans in the First World War

and held a PhD in political science (1919). A convinced Communist, in 1937 he refused to obey Stalin's orders and did not return to the Soviet Union where he would definitely have perished; the Japanese revealed him and executed him in 1941. Despite Sorge's role as the only Soviet spy who correctly informed the Kremlin about the German invasion in 1941, not much is written about him; the fullest biography in Russia still is Mikhail Kolesnikov, *Takim byl Richard Sorge* (Moscow: Voenizdat, 1965).

43. Bullitt to Moore, November 9, 1935, box 112/I/58/1419 (WCB.SML).

44. Kennan, "Introduction," in Roosevelt and Bullitt, *For the President*, xv.

45. Bullitt to Hull, April 20, 1936, in Roosevelt and Bullitt, *For the President*, 156.

46. Troyanovsky to Stalin, January 2, 1936, at http://www.alexanderyakovlev.org/fond/issues-doc/70525/.

47. Umansky to Litvinov, May 20, 1936, at http://www.alexanderyakovlev.org/fond/issues-doc/70945/.

48. Bullitt to Moore, February 22, 1936, box 112/I/58/1430 (WCB.SML).

49. Bullitt, "How We Won the War."

50. Bullitt to Hull, April 20, 1936, in Roosevelt and Bullitt, *For the President*, 157.

CHAPTER 11. THE THEATER OF DIPLOMACY

1. Irene Baruch Wiley, *Around the Globe in Twenty Years* (New York, 1962), 6; at http://www.irenawiley.com/page3/files/page3-1000-full.html/.

2. Wiley, *Around the Globe*.

3. Roosevelt to Bullitt, January 7, 1934, in Roosevelt and Bullitt, *For the President*, 73.

4. Bullard, April 23, 1934, in *Inside Stalin's Russia*, 259.

5. Nakoriakov to Stoliar, March 22, 1934, available at http://www.alexanderyakovlev.org/fond/issues-doc/70042/.

6. Litvinov to Stalin, March 27, 1934, in *Sovetsko-Amerikanskie otnosheniia* (2004), 86.

7. Charles W. Thayer, *Bears in the Caviar* (New York, 1950), 135.

8. Bullard, February 11, 1934, in *Inside Stalin's Russia*, 237.

9. Litvinov to Bulganin, April 1, 1934, in *Sovetsko-Amerikanskie otnosheniia* (2004), 95.

10. Bullitt to Roosevelt, April 13, 1934, in Roosevelt and Bullitt, *For the President*, 82.

11. Bullitt to Roosevelt, March 4, 1936, in Roosevelt and Bullitt, *For the President*,

148. Initially Stalin liked Howard, and their interview was published in the official edition of Stalin's works. But later, Howard published a detailed report about the NKVD terror in the *New York World Telegram* (March 29, 1939). Stalin read the Russian translation of this piece and ordered the NKVD to "kick out" Howard from Moscow; see http://kommari.livejournal.com/2837297.html/.

12. Bullitt to Roosevelt, April 13, 1934, in Roosevelt and Bullitt, *For the President*, 83.

13. Historians still dispute whether there was a sexual relationship between Roosevelt and LeHand; for evidence, see Costigliola, *Roosevelt's Lost Alliances*, 69; Elliott Roosevelt and James Brough, *An Untold Story: The Roosevelts of Hyde Park* (London: Allen, 1974), 145, 187. David Fromkin believes that, in 1932, Bullitt intervened into the old but still lively affair between Roosevelt and LeHand, and the president was jealous. Fromkin, *In the Time of the Americans*, 324. Costigliola does not believe that Roosevelt and LeHand were lovers. Having no position in this controversy, I wish to note that the president certainly knew about LeHand's developing relationship with Bullitt and seemed to support it.

14. Doris Kearns Goodwin, *No Ordinary Time: Franklin and Eleanor Roosevelt: The Home Front in World War II* (New York: Simon and Schuster, 1995), 155.

15. Richard Moe, *Roosevelt's Second Act: The Election of 1940 and the Politics of War* (New York: Oxford University Press, 2013), 173.

16. Bullitt to LeHand, September 21, 1933, box 112/I/49/1181 (WCB.SML).

17. LeHand to Bullitt, July 3, 1934, box 112/I/49/1186 (WCB.SML).

18. LeHand to Bullitt, April 1, 1934, box 112/I/49/1187 (WCB.SML).

19. Bullitt to LeHand, no date, box 112/I/49/1181 (WCB.SML).

20. Roosevelt to Bullitt, April 14, 1934, in Roosevelt and Bullitt, *For the President*, 87; LeHand to Bullitt, May 18, 1934, box 112/I/49/1187 (WCB.SML).

21. Rubinin, memo, May 15, 1934, available at http://www.alexanderyakovlev.org/fond/issues-doc/70184/.

22. Costigliola, *Roosevelt's Lost Alliances*, 75.

23. Roosevelt to Bullitt, January 7, 1934, in Roosevelt and Bullitt, *For the President*, 73.

24. Bullitt to Moore, April 14, 1934, in box 112/I/58/1419 (WCB.SML).

25. Wiley, *Around the Globe*, 95.

26. Kennan, August 20, 1933, in *Diaries*, 86.

27. Costigliola, *Roosevelt's Lost Alliances*, 273.

28. Charles W. Thayer, *Diplomat* (New York: Harper, 1959), 230.

29. Office of Oral History of Columbia University, Reminiscences of H. A. Wallace, 1677.

30. Moore to Bullitt, February 25, 1936, in box 112/I/58/1430 (WCB.SML). With a reference to the Native American usage, Urban Dictionary defines "snag" as a verb: "to go snagging, to go on the prowl, to look for attention from the opposite sex"; http://www.urbandictionary.com/define.php?term=snagging/.

31. Costigliola, *Roosevelt's Lost Alliances*, 270.

32. Costigliola, *Roosevelt's Lost Alliances*, 267.

33. Bohlen, *Witness to History*, 23.

34. Bohlen, *Witness to History*, 20.

35. Costigliola, *Roosevelt's Lost Alliances*, 267.

36. William C. Bullitt, *The Great Globe Itself* (New York: Scribner's, 1946), 64.

37. Costigliola, *Roosevelt's Lost Alliances*, 271.

38. Bullitt to Andreychin, August 19, 1934, Andreychin to Bullitt, no date, both in box 112/I/2/41 (WCB.SML).

39. LeHand to Bullitt, June 4, 1934, in box 112/I/49/1181 (WCB.SML).

40. Roosevelt to Bullitt, June 3, 1935, box 112/I/71/1733 (WCB.SML).

41. Thayer, *Bears in the Caviar*, 154.

42. GPU was the Chief Political Administration, a predecessor of the KGB.

43. LeHand to Bullitt, April 21, 1934, box 112/I/49/1189 (WCB.SML).

44. LeHand to Bullitt, September 24, 1934, box 112/I/49/1190 (WCB.SML).

45. Wiley, *Around the Globe*, 31.

46. Bullitt to Roosevelt, April 1, 1935, Bullitt to Moore, April 26, 1935, in Roosevelt and Bullitt, *For the President*, 116, 121.

47. Wiley, *Around the Globe*, 31.

48. Dodd, *Diary*, 241.

49. Rubinin, memo, February 2, 1935, 297; Krestinsky, memo April 15, 1935, 316.

50. Elena Bulgakova, *Dnevniki* (Moskow: Izd-vo "Knizhnaia palata," 1990), 48–49.

51. Bullitt to Roosevelt, May 1, 1935, in Roosevelt and Bullitt, *For the President*, 117.

52. Bullitt to Roosevelt, May 1, 1935, box 112/I/71/1783 (WCB.SML). Roosevelt and Bullitt, *For the President*, omits some parts of this letter.

53. Thayer, *Bears in the Caviar*, 156.

54. LeHand to Bullitt, April 7, 1935, box 112/I/49/1187 (WCB.SML).

55. Thayer, *Bears in the Caviar*, 162.

56. Wiley, *Around the Globe*, 35.

57. Promoted later in 1935 to the rank of marshal along with Egorov and Buden-nyi, in 1937 Tukhachevsky was accused in conspiracy, tortured, and executed.

58. Bulgakova, *Dnevniki.*, April 24, 1935.

59. Mikhail Bulgakov, *The Master and Margarita*, trans. Michael Glenny (London: Vintage 2004), 299–306.

60. Bulgakov, *Master and Margarita*, 143, 147, 236. *Eyes Wide Shut*, the 1999 film by Stanley Kubrick, is based on the "Dream Story" (1926) by the Austrian writer Arthur Schnitzler, who was well known in Russia; it is quite possible that Bulgakov read his "Dream Story."

61. Bulgakov, *Master and Margarita*, 312.

62. Wiley, *Around the Globe*, 30.

63. Bullitt to Roosevelt, May 28, 1937, in Roosevelt and Bullitt, *For the President*, 215. Orville Bullitt omitted the name of Grace Davidson from the text of this letter when he published it in Roosevelt and Bullitt, *For the President*; it is here reconstructed from the archival document in box 112/I/71/783 (WCB. SML).

64. On February 11, Elena Bulgakova wrote down in her diary that Intourist requested the text of the *Turbins* for Ambassador Bullitt; Bulgakov did not give the text and the courier came again to ask for it on April 13; on May 11 the Yale Theater Association requested the Russian text of the play (Bulgakova, *Dnevniki*, 55, 56, 57). Clearly, Bullitt finally got his text. Since the English translation had already been done and was easily available from its translator, Eugene Lyons, it is clear that Bullitt was specifically interested in the Russian copy. Probably he wanted to use it for his Russian lessons, or he had some other purpose.

65. Bulgakova, *Dnevniki*, 68.

66. Bohlen, *Witness to History*, 21.

67. In the book cowritten with Bullitt, Freud interpreted such a coincidence as meaningful; Freud and Wilson were born in the same year, and Freud brought up this fact as a reason for his interest in Wilson.

68. Bulgakova, *Dnevniki*, 113, 114, 118.

69. For the story of Bulgakov's hypnosis treatment in Moscow, see Alexander Etkind, *Eros of the Impossible: The History of Psychoanalysis in Russia*, trans. Noah Rubens and Maria Rubens (Boulder, CO: Westview, 1996), 296–97.

70. Bulgakova, *Dnevniki*, 92.

71. Bulgakova, *Dnevniki*, 92.

72. Bulgakov, *Master and Margarita*, 290. The novel depicts even such detail as Bullitt's "streptococci infection." As the novel has it, "'My friends maintain

that it's rheumatism,' said Woland, continuing to stare at Margarita, 'but I strongly suspect that the pain is a souvenir of an encounter with a most beautiful witch that I had in 1571.'"

73. Bullitt, Speech in Virginia, July 1935 Press Releases (US Governmental Printing Service, 1936), 15:41.

CHAPTER 12. DISENCHANTMENT

1. Thayer, *Bears in the Caviar*, 95.

2. Thayer, *Bears in the Caviar*, 56.

3. Bullitt to Moore, August 30, 1935, box 112/I/58/1424 (WCB.SML).

4. Bullitt to Roosevelt, June 3, 1935, in Roosevelt and Bullitt, *For the President*, 108.

5. Bullitt to Roosevelt, June 3, 1935, in Roosevelt and Bullitt, *For the President*, 108; Roosevelt to Bullitt, June 21, 1935, box 112/I/71/1783 (WCB.SML); The *Nibelungenlied*, translated as *The Song of the Nibelungs*, is a medieval epic poem with pre-Christian motifs, which served as source materials for Richard Wagner's *Ring Cycle*.

6. Bullitt to Roosevelt, January 1, 1934, in Roosevelt and Bullitt, *For the President*, 62.

7. Report received March 4, 1936, in box 112/II/135/918 (WCB.SML).

8. Thayer, *Bears in the Caviar*, 165.

9. Bullitt to Roosevelt, April 1, 1935, in Roosevelt and Bullitt, *For the President*, 116.

10. Edward Page, memo, December 28, 1941, box 112/I/2/41 (WCB.SML).

11. Andreychin to Bullitt, April 30, September 2, 1942.

12. Bullitt to Hull, April 20, 1936, box 112/II/135/918 (WCB.SML). All the quotations in the next seven paragraphs will be from this letter.

13. Bullitt to Hull, April 20, 1936, box 112/II/135/918 (WCB.SML).

14. For analysis of the role of the Jews in the Soviet bureaucracy, see Yuri Slezkine, *The Jewish Century* (Princeton, NJ: Princeton University Press, 2004).

15. Bullitt to Hull, April 20, 1936, box 112/II/135/918 (WCB.SML).

16. Wiley, *Around the Globe*, 38.

17. Harold L. Ickes, March 26, 1937, *The Secret Diary of Harold L. Ickes* (New York: Simon and Schuster, 1974), 2:103.

18. Bullitt, "How We Won the War."

CHAPTER 13. SAVING PARIS

1. Bullitt to Roosevelt, December 20, 1936, in Roosevelt and Bullitt, *For the President*, 202.

2. Robert Murphy, *Diplomat among Warriors* (New York: Doubleday, 1964), 30–32. See also Roosevelt and Bullitt, *For the President*, 168–69.

3. Ickes, March 26, 1937, *Secret Diary*, 2:103.

4. Ickes, July 3, 1938, *Secret Diary*, 2:415.

5. Martin, *Cissy*, 371.

6. LeHand to Bullitt, September 28, 1939, box 112/I/49/1184 (WCB.SML).

7. Bullitt to Roosevelt, June 13, 1938, in Roosevelt and Bullitt, *For the President*, 267; Roosevelt to Bullitt, August 5, 1937, at https://research.archives.gov/id/16618443/.

8. Ickes, June 26, 1938, *Secret Diary*, 2:408.

9. Ickes, January 22, 1939, *Secret Diary*, 2:562.

10. Bullitt to Roosevelt, October 24, 1936, in Roosevelt and Bullitt, *For the President*, 173–74.

11. Bullitt to Roosevelt, October 24, 1936, in Roosevelt and Bullitt, *For the President*, 186.

12. Bullitt to Hull, May 14, 1940, at http://docs.fdrlibrary.marist.edu/psf/box2/a12aa01.html/.

13. Bullitt to Hull, May 31, 1940, at http://docs.fdrlibrary.marist.edu/psf/box2/t12xx01.html/.

14. Bullitt to Roosevelt, May 16, 1940, available at http://docs.fdrlibrary.marist.edu/psf/box2/t12dd01.html/.

15. Davis to Hull, April 13, 1937, in Irwin F. Gellman, *Secret Affairs: Franklin Roosevelt, Cordell Hull, and Sumner Welles* (Baltimore: Johns Hopkins University Press, 1995), 123.

16. Bullitt to Roosevelt, January 10, 1937, in Roosevelt and Bullitt, *For the President*, 206.

17. Bullitt to Roosevelt, October 8, 1936, in Roosevelt and Bullitt, *For the President*, 180.

18. Bullitt to Roosevelt, November 23, 1937, in Roosevelt and Bullitt, *For the President*, 237.

19. Gaddis, *George F. Kennan*, 133.

20. Bullitt to Roosevelt, April 18, 1940, at https://research.archives.gov/id/16618452?q=bullitt/.

21. Gellman, *Secret Affairs*, 200.

22. Christopher Sullivan, *Sumner Welles, Postwar Planning, and the Quest for a New World Order* (New York: Columbia University Press, 2008), 38.

23. Bullitt to Roosevelt, December 20, 1936, in Roosevelt and Bullitt, *For the President*, 200.

24. Bullitt to Roosevelt, January 10, 1937, in Roosevelt and Bullitt, *For the President*, 205.

25. Bullitt to Moore, November 24, 1936, box 112/I/58/1431 (WCB.SML).

26. Bullitt to Roosevelt, July 23, 1937, in Roosevelt and Bullitt, *For the President*, 225.

27. Bullitt to Roosevelt, January 20, 1938, in Roosevelt and Bullitt, *For the President*, 253.

28. Bullitt to Roosevelt, May 28, 1937, in Roosevelt and Bullitt, *For the President*, 217.

29. Welles to Bullitt, August 24, 1937, in Roosevelt and Bullitt, *For the President*, 240.

30. Bullitt to Roosevelt, October 27, 1938, in Roosevelt and Bullitt, *For the President*, 293.

31. Bullitt to Hull, September 26, 1938, in Roosevelt and Bullitt, *For the President*, 291.

32. Ickes, June 17, 1939, in *Secret Diary*, 2:651.

33. David Reynolds, *From Munich to Pearl Harbor: Roosevelt's America and the Origins of the Second World War* (Chicago: Ivan Dee, 2001), 42.

34. *New Yorker*, December 10, 1938.

35. Albert Connelly, interview with Francois Duchene, at http://archives.eui .eu/ en/files/transcript/15859?d=inline/; also Eric Roussel, *Jean Monnet* (Paris: Fayard, 1996), 156–58.

36. On the role of Monnet's American network in the creation of the European Union, see Pascaline Winand, *Eisenhower, Kennedy, and the United States of Europe* (New York: St. Martin, 1993). Interestingly, this book does not mention Bullitt.

37. Bullitt to Roosevelt, November 24, 1936, in Roosevelt and Bullitt, *For the President*, 186.

38. Kennett S. Davis, *FDR: Into the Storm* (New York: Random House, 1993), 349.

39. Bullitt to Roosevelt, September 28, 1938, in Roosevelt and Bullitt, *For the President*, 299.

40. Davis, *FDR*, 400.

41. Bullitt to Roosevelt, September 16, 1939, at https://research.archives.gov/id/16608708?q=bullitt/.

42. Bullitt to Roosevelt, September 13, 1939, at https://research.archives.gov/id/16608708?q=bullitt/.

43. John R. Gillingham, "The German Problem and the European Integration," in *Origins and the Evolution of the European Union*, ed. Desmond Dinan (New York: Oxford University Press, 2006), 66.

44. Bullitt to Roosevelt, September 16, 1939, at https://research.archives.gov/id/16608708?q=bullitt/.

45. Ickes, March 22, 1939, *Secret Diary*, 2:602.

46. Arthur Schlesinger Jr., "What Made Them Turn Red," *Look*, August 1, 1950; William C. Bullitt, "Ex-Ambassador Bullitt Clarifies His Part in 'What Made Them Turn Red,'" *Look*, October 10, 1950.

47. LeHand to Bullitt, September 5, 1940, box 112/I/49/1193 (WCB.SML).

48. Bullitt to Roosevelt, December 11, 1939, at https://research.archives.gov/id/16608708?q=bullitt/.

49. Bullitt to Roosevelt, June 7, 1940, November 1, 1939, available at https://research.archives.gov/id/16618452?q=bullitt/, 57.

50. Ickes, February 7, 1940, *Secret Diary*, 2:132.

51. Ickes, March 10, 1940, *Secret Diary*, 2:146.

52. Bullitt to Roosevelt, June 11, 1940, in Roosevelt and Bullitt, *For the President*, 464.

53. Telegrams from June 3, 1940, at https://research.archives.gov/id/16618452?q=bullitt/.

54. Bullitt to Roosevelt, October 18, 1939, at https://research.archives.gov/id/16618452?q=bullitt/; Bullitt, telegram to Hull, June 11, 1940, in Roosevelt and Bullitt, *For the President*, 464.

55. Bullitt to Roosevelt, May 30, 1940, in Roosevelt and Bullitt, *For the President*, 440.

56. Bullitt to Roosevelt,, May 30, 1940, in Roosevelt and Bullitt, *For the President*, 441, and at https://research.archives.gov/id/16618452?q=bullitt/.

57. Roosevelt to Bullitt, June 11, Bullitt to Roosevelt, June 12, 1940, in Roosevelt and Bullitt, *For the President*, 465, 468.

58. Davis, *FDR*, 560; Andrea Bosco, *June 1940: Great Britain and the First Attempt to Build a European Union* (Cambridge: Cambridge Scholars Publishing, 2016), 289.

59. Bullitt to Hull, July 1, 1940, in Roosevelt and Bullitt, *For the President*, 481–87.

60. Charles Glass, *Americans in Paris* (London: Harper, 2010), 100.

61. Bullitt to Hull, July 13, 1940, in Roosevelt and Bullitt, *For the President*, 490.

62. Bullitt, draft of speech, August 1940, Roosevelt and Bullitt, *For the President*, 499.

63. Isaiah Berlin to Marie and Mendel Berlin, August 20, 1940, in Isaiah Berlin, *Flourishing: Letters, 1928–1946* (London: Chatto, 2004), 336.

64. Reynolds, *From Munich to Pearl Harbor*, 175.

CHAPTER 14. FRONTS OF WAR

1. Kennan, *Memoirs*, 1:85–86.

2. Bullard, *Inside Stalin's Russia*, 174.

3. Bullitt to Roosevelt, November 3, 1937, box 112/I/58/1440 (WCB.SML).

4. Ickes, June 29, 1940, *Secret Diary*, 2:216.

5. Kennan, *Memoirs*, 1:85, 70.

6. Berlin to Anthony Rumbold, January 24, 1945, in Berlin, *Flourishing*, 521.

7. Bullitt, "How We Won the War and Lost the Peace." *Life*, September 6, 1948, 94.

8. Ickes, October 7, 1940, *Secret Diary*, 2:342.

9. Bullitt, "What Next?" *Life*, April 21, 1941.

10. Bullitt, "How We Won the War," 83.

11. Bullitt to Roosevelt, July 1, 1941, in Roosevelt and Bullitt, *For the President*, 522.

12. Bullitt, draft of the essay "Action, at Last" (1947), box 112/III/150/271 (WCB. SML); Orville Bullitt from Roosevelt and Bullitt, *For the President*, 554.

13. Ickes, June 28, 1941, *Secret Diary*, 3:548.

14. Bullitt, "How We Won the War," 94.

15. Bullitt, memo, November 22, 1941, in Roosevelt and Bullitt, *For the President*, 528.

16. Roosevelt to Bullitt, November 22, 1941, at https://research.archives.gov/ id/16618326/, page 1.

17. Bullitt, "Can Truman Avoid World War III?" *American Mercury* (June 1947): 645.

18. Bullitt to Roosevelt. January 29, 1943, Roosevelt and Bullitt, *For the President*, 580. Further page references to this third letter will be given parenthetically in the text.

19. Bullitt to Roosevelt, January 10, 1937, at https://research.archives.gov/ id/16618443/.

20. James Forrestal, *The Forrestal Diaries* (New York: Viking, 1951), 121.

21. Berlin to Herbert Nicholas, November 26, 1942, in Berlin, *Flourishing*, 421.

22. Bullitt, memo, April 14, 1944, box 112/II/135/920 (WCB.SML).

23. Roosevelt and Bullitt, *For the President*, 604.

24. William Bullitt to Orville Bullitt, October 21, 1944, in Roosevelt and Bullitt, *For the President*, 606.

25. Bullitt's notes, cited in Roosevelt and Bullitt, *For the President*, 605.

26. Charles de Gaulle, *The War Memoirs*, 3 vols. (New York: Viking 1955), 3:160.

27. "Le commandant William Bullitt, / Est le parrain du bataillon, / En Homme il comprit notre fuite, / De grand cœur nous l'en remercions, / En criant, en avant, en avant !"at https://fr.wikipedia.org/wiki/2e_bataillon_de_choc/.

28. Glass, *Americans in Paris*, 413.

29. Bullitt to Orville Bullitt, December 18, 1944, in Roosevelt and Bullitt, *For the President*, 610.

30. Bullitt, "How We Won the War," Part II, *Life*, September 6, 1948, 90.

CHAPTER 15. HOMOSEXUALS

1. Bullitt, memo, April 23, 1941, and memo, May 5, 1943, in Roosevelt and Bullitt, *For the President*, 512–14, 514–16; Dean, *Imperial Brotherhood*, 72–73; Costigliola, *Roosevelt's Lost Alliances*, 74–75.

2. Working for Hopkins, Bohlen made himself indispensable to the diplomacy of Lend-Lease. His job was challenging in many ways; Isaiah Berlin, who befriended him, wrote how Bohlen helped the British delegation in Moscow in the "almost impossible task" of translating Churchill into Russian. The interpreter was proving incapable, and Bohlen "was brought in instead—and then had to translate things like 'the depth of sublime unwisdom' into rapid Russian for Uncle Joe's benefit." Berlin, *Flourishing*, 488.

3. Bullitt, "How We Won the War," Part Two, 90.

4. Bullitt, memo, April 14, 1944, box 112/II/135/920 (WCB.SML).

5. Bullitt, memo, February 1, 1944, Roosevelt and Bullitt, *For the President*, 602.

6. Kennan, who had known Offie over decades, called him "a Renaissance type." George F. Kennan and John Lukacs, *Through the History of the Cold War: The Correspondence of George F. Kennan and John Lukacs*, (Philadelphia: University of Pennsylvania Press, 2010), 63.

7. J. Edgar Hoover to Sherman Adams, Federal Bureau of Investigation, February 11, 1953, U.S. Declassified Documents Online, at tinyurl.galegroup.com/tinyurl/3y6R42/.

8. Freud and Bullitt, *Woodrow Wilson*, 56.

9. R. G. Waldeck, "Homosexual International," *Human Events* 17, no. 39 (September 29, 1960); see also Michael S. Sherry, *Gay Artists in Modern American Culture: An Imagined Conspiracy* (Chapel Hill: University of North Carolina Press, 2007), 69–71.

10. Bullitt to Moore, April 11, 1935, box 112/I/58/1424 (WCB.SML).

11. Dean, *Imperial Brotherhood*, 143.

12. "Details of an in-depth investigation of Charles Eustis Bohlen, a State Department foreign service officer, as requested by Secretary of State John Foster Dulles." Federal Bureau of Investigation, March 16, 1953. US Declassified Documents Online, at tinyurl.galegroup.com/tinyurl/3y8QC0/.

13. Dean, *Imperial Brotherhood*, 137.

14. Dean, *Imperial Brotherhood*, 141.

CHAPTER 16. UNITING EUROPE

1. Gellman, *Secret Affairs*, 350–51.

2. Bullitt to LeHand, November 7, 1943, box 112/I/49/1185 (WCB.SML).

3. Box 112/Oversize/243/15 (WCB.SML).

4. William C. Bullitt, "The Tragedy of Versailles." *Life*, March 27, 1944, 114.

5. William C. Bullitt, "How We Won the War and Lost the Peace." *Life*, Part Two, September 6, 1948, 83.

6. Bullitt, "How We Won the War," 97, 102.

7. Kennan, *Memoirs*, 2:417.

8. Bullitt, "The Tragedy of Versailles," 116.

9. Berlin, *Flourishing*, 622.

10. Kennan, "Long Telegram," February 22, 1946, at http://nsarchive.gwu.edu/coldwar/documents/episode-1/kennan.htm/.

11. Kennan, October 24, 1949, in *Kennan Diaries*, 232.

12. Halford Mackinder, *Democratic Ideals and Reality* (1919; repr. New York: Norton, 1962), 150.

13. Gaddis, *George F. Kennan*, 189.

14. Interestingly, even Isaiah Berlin did not know the source of his friends' inspiration; he believed that the program of the Non-Communist Left was created by Bohlen, Thayer, and himself "in the spirit of a joke which created a movement." See Berlin to Schlesinger, October 21, 1949, in Berlin, *Flourishing*, 134.

15. Kennan to Lukacs, December 11, 1976, in *Through the Cold War*, 68–71.

16. William C. Bullitt, "France in Crisis: To Defeat Communism French Democracy Must Have U.S. Aid," *Life*, June 2, 1947.

17. Forrestal, March 10, 1946, *The Forrestal Diaries*, 46.

18. Bullitt to Moore, March 30, 1936, box 112/I/58/1431 (WCB.SML).

19. Bullitt to Roosevelt, January 29, 1943, in Roosevelt and Bullitt, *For the President*, 585, and similar formulations in Bullitt's 1948 essays in *Life*.

20. Kennan to Leahy, in Gaddis, *George F. Kennan*, 169.

21. Kennan, *Diaries*, 164.

22. Kennan, *Diaries*, 164.

23. Minutes of UK Delegation meeting, August 30, 1947, in Berlin, *Enlightening*, 39.

24. Bullitt, "France in Crisis," 129.

25. Bullitt, "How We Won the War," 83.

26. William C. Bullitt, "A Report to the American People on China," *Life*, October 13, 1947, 143.

27. William C. Bullitt, "How We Won the War and Lost the Peace," Part Two, September 6. *Life*, 1948, 103.

28. Gellman, *Secret Affairs*, 400.

29. Robert L. Beisner, *Dean Acheson: A Life in the Cold War* (New York: Oxford University Press, 2006), 117.

30. William C. Bullitt, "Can Truman Avoid World War III?" *American Mercury* (June 1947): 646.

31. Bullitt, draft of the essay "Action, at Last" (1947), box 112/III/150/271 (WCB. SML).

32. Bullitt, memo, October 1950, box 112/II/135/925 (WCB.SML).

33. Bullitt, draft, box 112/III/163/513 (WCB.SML).

BIBLIOGRAPHY

A NOTE ON SOURCES

This book is based on William Bullitt's personal documents, which are stored in his huge archive in Sterling Memorial Library at Yale University (cited throughout the endnotes as WCB.SML). Louise Bryant's archive is also kept in the Sterling. I have used Bullitt's publications, such as *The Bullitt Mission to Russia*; his novel, *It's Not Done*; the biography of Woodrow Wilson that he cowrote with Freud, *Thomas Woodrow Wilson: A Psychological Study*; the political pamphlet, *The Great Globe Itself*; and a volume of Bullitt's correspondence with Roosevelt. I have used a number of Bullitt's essays; particularly important are his postwar articles in *Life* magazine. Also important were the superb collections of documents published in the Alexander Yakovlev Archive, available at http://www.alexanderyakovlev.org/; the US Declassified Documents of the United States, published by Gale; and the memories about Bullitt recorded by the Office of Oral History of Columbia University.

There are three book-length studies of Bullitt's diplomatic work. Although I often disagree with them, I have used them all in this book. These are Beatrice Farnsworth, *William C. Bullitt and the Soviet Union*; Michael Casella-Blackburn, *The Donkey, the Carrot, and the Club: William C. Bullitt and Soviet-American Relations, 1917–1948*; and the most informative, Will Brownell and Richard Billings, *So Close to Greatness: The Biography of William C. Bullitt*. These books were written by historians of international relations, whereas I was mostly interested in Bullitt as a cultural and intellectual figure. For a better understanding of this aspect of his life, see a chapter on him in John Lukacs, *Philadelphians: Patricians and Philistines*. There is also interesting correspondence between Lukacs and Kennan about this book in *Through the History of the Cold War: The Correspondence of George F. Kennan and John Lukacs*. Bullitt is one of the central, though still underappreciated, figures of American politics after World War I in David Fromkin, *In the Time of the Americans: FDR, Truman, Eisenhower, Marshall, McArthur—The Generation that Changed America's Role in the World*. There is an informative chapter on Bullitt in the Soviet Union in Dennis Dunn, *Caught between Roosevelt and Stalin: America's Ambassadors in Moscow*. For information about Bullitt's intellectual circle, see James Srodes, *On Dupont Circle: Franklin and Eleanor Roosevelt and the Progressives Who Shaped Our World*.

Some members of the staff of the Moscow embassy wrote valuable memoirs. These include Charles W. Thayer, *Bears in the Caviar*; Irene Wiley, *Around the Globe in Twenty Years*; Charles Bohlen, *Witness to History, 1929–1969*; George Kennan, *Memoirs, 1925–1950*. *The Kennan Diaries*, edited by Frank Costigliola, were very helpful. Two recent books by Peter Rand and Paul Willets discuss a curious biography of Tyler Kent, Bullitt's underling in Moscow who became a Soviet or German spy or even a double agent. See also biographies of Bullitt's second wife, *Queen of Bohemia: The Life of Louise Bryant* by Mary Dearborn and *Friends and Lovers* by Virginia Gardner, and a biography of his good friend Cissy Patterson, *Cissy: The Extraordinary Life of Eleanor Medill Patterson* by Ralph G. Martin.

Two remarkable books—Frank Costigliola, *Roosevelt's Lost Alliances: How Personal Politics Helped Start the Cold War*, and Robert Dean, *Imperial Brotherhood: Gender and the Making of Cold War Foreign Policy*—discuss the sexual mores of Bullitt's high-ranking friends and enemies and the "lavender scare," the accusations of homosexuality by Senator McCarthy and his supporters. Rich information on this subject is also contained in M. Stanton Evans, *Blacklisted by History: The Untold Story of Senator Joe McCarthy*.

On Freud and Bullitt, there is substantial but insufficient literature: Paul Roazen, "Oedipus in Versailles"; Mark Solms, "Freud and Bullitt: An Unknown Manuscript"; J. F. Campbell, "To Bury Freud on Wilson."

I first wrote about Bullitt in my book *Eros of the Impossible: The History of Psychoanalysis in Russia*, which was published in Russian in 1993 and then translated by Noah and Maria Rubens and published in English in 1996. In one of the chapters I wrote about the friendship between Bullitt and Freud.

Based on Elena Bulgakova's diary, I wrote that Bullitt was one of the proto-types of Woland, the hero of Mikhail Bulgakov's *The Master and Margarita*. Later, some works referred to this conjecture (Laura D. Weeks, *The Master and Margarita: A Critical Companion*; Boris Sokolov, *Bulgakov: Encyclopedia*; István Rév, *Retroactive Justice: Prehistory of Post-Communism*). Bullitt and Bulgakov's relationship, the Spring Festival, and the Satan Ball, have been mentioned in the Spaso House's official brochure. In October 2010 Ambassador John Beyrle reproduced Bullitt's ball of 1935, calling the event the "Enchanted Ball" and dedicating it to Bullitt and Bulgakov.

SOURCES

Acheson, Dean. *Present at the Creation: My Years at the State Department*. New York: Norton, 1969.

Beisner, Robert L. *Dean Acheson: A Life in the Cold War*. New York: Oxford University Press, 2006.

Berlin, Isaiah. *Enlightening: Letters, 1946–1960*. London: Chatto, 2009.

Berlin, Isaiah. *Flourishing: Letters, 1928–1946*. London: Chatto, 2004.

Bohlen, Charles. *Witness to History, 1929–1969*. New York: Norton, 1973.

Brownell, Will, and Richard Billings. *So Close to Greatness: The Biography of William C. Bullitt*. New York: Macmillan, 1988.

Bulgakov, Mikhail. *The Master and Margarita*. Translated by Michael Glenny. London: Vintage, 2004.

Bulgakova, Elena. *Dnevniki*. Moscow: Izd-vo "Knizhnaia palata," 1990.

Bullard, Reader. *Inside Stalin's Russia: The Diaries of Reader Bullard, 1930–1934*. Charlbury, Oxfordshire: Day Books, 2000.

Bullitt, Ernesta Drinker. *An Uncensored Diary from the Central Empires*. New York: Doubleday, 1917.

Bullitt, William C. *The Bullitt Mission to Russia: Testimony before the Committee on Foreign Relations, United States Senate*. New York: Huebsch, 1919.

Bullitt, William C. "Can Truman Avoid World War III?" *American Mercury*, June 1947.

Bullitt, William C. "Ex-Ambassador Bullitt Clarifies His Part in 'What Made Them Turn Red.'" *Look*, October 10, 1950.

Bullitt, William C. "France in Crisis: To Defeat Communism French Democracy Must Have U.S. Aid." *Life*, June 2, 1947.

Bullitt, William C. "Freedom of Seas: An American Proposal." *Philadelphia Ledger*, February 22, 1917.

Bullitt, William C. *The Great Globe Itself.* New York: Scribner's, 1946.

Bullitt, William C. "How We Won the War and Lost the Peace." Parts 1 and 2. *Life*, August 30, September 6, 1948.

Bullitt, William C. *It's Not Done.* New York: Harcourt Brace, 1926.

Bullitt, William C. "The Old Ills of Modern India." *Life*, October 22, 1951.

Bullitt, William C. "A Report to the American People on China." *Life*, October 13, 1947.

Bullitt, William C. "Speech in Virginia," July 1935, in *Press Releases*, U.S. Governmental Printing Service, 1936, v.15, p.41.

Bullitt, William C. "The Tragedy of Versailles." *Life*, March 27, 1944.

Bullitt, William C. "What Next," *Life*, April 21, 1941.

Campbell, J. F. "To Bury Freud on Wilson." *Modern Austrian Literature* 41, no. 2 (2008).

Casella-Blackburn, Michael. *The Donkey, the Carrot, and the Club: William C. Bullitt and Soviet-American Relations, 1917–1948.* Westport, CT: Praeger, 2004.

Chambers, Roland. *The Last Englishman: The Double Life of Arthur Ransome.* London: Faber, 2009.

Cohen, David, *The Escape of Sigmund Freud.* New York: Overlook Press 2009.

Costigliola, Frank. *Roosevelt's Lost Alliances: How Personal Politics Helped Start the Cold War.* Princeton, NJ: Princeton University Press, 2012.

Davis, Kennett S. *FDR: Into the Storm.* New York: Random House, 1993.

Dean, Robert. *Imperial Brotherhood: Gender and the Making of Cold War Foreign Policy.* Amherst: University of Massachusetts Press, 2001.

Dearborn, Mary V. *Queen of Bohemia: The Life of Louise Bryant.* Boston: Houghton Mifflin, 1996.

De Gaulle, Charles. *The War Memoirs.* 3 vols. New York: Viking, 1955.

Dodd, William. *Diary.* New York: Harcourt, 1941.

Dodd, William E. *Wilson and His Work.* New York: Doubleday, 1920.

Douglas, Ann. *Terrible Honesty: Mongrel Manhattan in the 1920s.* New York: Farrar, 1995.

Dunn, Dennis. *Caught between Roosevelt and Stalin: America's Ambassadors in Moscow.* Lexington: University Press of Kentucky, 1998.

Eastman, Max. *Great Companions.* New York: Farrar, 1942.

Etkind, Alexander. "Beyond Eugenics: The Forgotten Scandal of Hybridizing Humans and Apes." *Studies in History and Philosophy of Biological & Biomedical Sciences* 39 (2008): Special Issue "Eugenics, Sex, and the State," 205–10.

Etkind, Alexander. *Eros of the Impossible: The History of Psychoanalysis in Russia.* Translated by Noah Rubens and Maria Rubens. Boulder, CO: Westview Press, 1996.

Evans, M. Stanton. *Blacklisted by History: The Untold Story of Senator Joe McCarthy.* New York: Three Rivers Press, 2007.

Farnsworth, Beatrice. *William C. Bullitt and the Soviet Union.* Bloomington: Indiana University Press, 1967.

Fedor, Julie. *Russia and the Cult of State Security: The Chekist Tradition, from Lenin to Putin.* London: Routledge, 2011.

Forrestal, James. *The Forrestal Diaries.* Edited by Walter Millis. New York: Viking, 1951.

Freud, Sigmund, and William C. Bullitt. *Thomas Woodrow Wilson: A Psychological Study.* Boston: Houghton Mifflin, 1966.

Fromkin, David. *In the Time of the Americans: FDR, Truman, Eisenhower, Marshall, McArthur—The Generation that Changed America's Role in the World.* New York: Knopf, 1994.

Gaddis, John Lewis. *George F. Kennan: An American Life.* New York: Penguin, 2011.

Gardner, Virginia. *Friend and Lover: The Life of Louise Bryant.* New York: Horizon, 1982.

Gelb, Barbara. *So Short a Time: A Biography of John Reed and Louise Bryant.* New York: Norton, 1973.

Gellman, Irwin F. *Secret Affairs: Franklin Roosevelt, Cordell Hull, and Sumner Welles.* Baltimore: Johns Hopkins University Press, 1995.

Gillingham, John R. "The German Problem and the European Integration." In *Origins and the Evolution of the European Union,* edited by Desmond Dinan. New York: Oxford University Press, 2006.

Glass, Charles. *Americans in Paris.* London: Harper, 2010.

Goodwin, Doris Kearns. *No Ordinary Time: Franklin and Eleanor Roosevelt: The Home Front in World War II.* New York: Simon and Schuster, 1995.

Harper, Samuel. *The Russia I Believe In: The Memoirs.* Chicago: University of Chicago Press, 1945.

Hemingway, Ernest. *The Letters of Ernest Hemingway.* Vol. 3, *1926–1929.* New York: Cambridge University Press, 2015.

Hicks, Granville, with John Stuart. *The Making of a Revolutionary.* New York: Macmillan, 1936.

[House, Edward.] *Philip Dru, Administrator: A Story of Tomorrow, 1920–1935.* New York: Huebsch, 1912.

Hull, Cordell. *The Memoirs.* 2 vols. New York: Macmillan, 1948.

Ickes, Harold L. *The Secret Diary.* 2 vols. New York: Simon and Schuster, 1974.

Isaacson, Walter, and Evan Thomas. *The Wise Men: Six Friends and the World They Made.* New York: Simon and Schuster, 1986.

Kaplan, Justin. *Lincoln Steffens.* New York: Simon, 1964.

Kennan, George F. *The Kennan Diaries.* Edited by Frank Costigliola. New York: Norton, 2014.

Kennan, George F. *Memoirs, 1925–1950.* 2 vols. New York: Pantheon, 1983.

Kennan, George F. *Russia and the West under Lenin and Stalin.* New York: Little, Brown, 1961.

Kennan, George F. *Soviet-American Relations, 1917–1920.* 2 vols. Princeton, NJ: Princeton University Press, 1956.

Kennan, George F., and John Lukacs. *Through the History of the Cold War: The Correspondence of George F. Kennan and John Lukacs.* Philadelphia: University of Pennsylvania Press, 2010.

Keynes, John Maynard. *The Economic Consequences of the Peace.* Cambridge: Macmillan, 1971.

Kolesnikov, Mikhail. *Takim byl Richard Sorge.* Moscow: Voenizdat, 1965.

Lansing, Robert. *The Peace Negotiations.* New York: Houghton Mifflin, 1921.

Lippmann, Walter, and Charles Merz. "A Test of the News." *A Supplement to the New Republic,* August 4, 1920.

Lukacs, John. *Philadelphia: Patricians and Philistines, 1900–1950.* New York: Farrar, 1981.

Lyons, Eugene. *Assignment in Utopia.* New York: Harcourt, 1937.

Mackinder, Halford. *Democratic Ideals and Reality.* 1919. Reprint. New York: W. W. Norton, 1962.

Macmillan, Margaret. *Paris 1919: Six Months that Changed the World.* New York: Random House, 2003.

Martin, Ralph G. *Cissy: The Extraordinary Life of Eleanor Medill Patterson.* New York: Simon and Schuster, 1979.

Moe, Richard. *Roosevelt's Second Act: The Election of 1940 and the Politics of War.* New York: Oxford University Press, 2013.

Murphy, Robert. *Diplomat among Warriors.* New York: Doubleday, 1964.

Neu, Charles E. *Colonel House: A Biography of Woodrow Wilson's Silent Partner.* New York: Oxford University Press, 2015.

Nicolson, Harold. *Peacemaking, 1919: Being Reminiscences of the Paris Peace Conference.* Boston: Houghton Mifflin, 1933.

Rand, Peter. *Conspiracy of One: Tyler Kent's Secret Plot against FDR, Churchill, and the Allied War Effort.* New York: Lyons, 2013.

Rév, István. *Retroactive Justice: Prehistory of Post-Communism.* Palo Alto: Stanford University Press, 2005.

Reynolds, David. *From Munich to Pearl Harbor: Roosevelt's America and the Origins of the Second World War.* Chicago: Ivan Dee, 2001.

Roazen, Paul. "Oedipus in Versailles." *Times Literary Supplement,* April 22, 2005.

Roosevelt, Elliott, and James Brough. *An Untold Story: The Roosevelts of Hyde Park.* London: Allen, 1974.

Roosevelt, Franklin D., and William C. Bullitt. *For the President, Personal and Secret: Correspondence between Franklin D. Roosevelt and William C. Bullitt.* Edited by Orville Bullitt. Boston: Houghton Mifflin, 1972.

Roussel, Eric. *Jean Monnet.* Paris: Fayard, 1996.

Sanchez-Sibony, Oscar. *Red Globalization: The Political Economy of the Soviet Cold War from Stalin to Khrushchev.* Cambridge: Cambridge University Press, 2014.

Savostianov G. N. *Moskva-Vashington: Diplomaticheskie otnosheniia, 1933–1936.* Moscow: Nauka, 2012.

Schlesinger, Arthur, Jr. "What Made Them Turn Red." *Look,* August 1, 1950.

Schlesinger, Arthur Meier. *The Coming of the New Deal, 1933–1935.* New York: Houghton Mifflin Harcourt, 2003.

Schulten, Susan. *Mapping the Nation: History and Cartography in Nineteenth-Century America.* Chicago: University of Chicago, 2012.

Seymour, Charles. *The Intimate Papers of Colonel House: Into the World War.* Boston: Houghton Mifflin, 1928.

Sherry, Michael S. *Gay Artists in Modern American Culture: An Imagined Conspiracy.* Chapel Hill: University of North Carolina Press, 2007.

Slezkine, Yuri. *The Jewish Century.* Princeton, NJ: Princeton University Press, 2004.

Sokolov, Boris. *Bulgakov: Encyclopedia.* Moscow: Algorithm, 2003.

Solms, Mark. "Freud and Bullitt: An Unknown Manuscript." *Journal of the American Psychoanalytic Association* 54 (2006): 1263–98.

Sovetsko-Amerikanskiye otnoshenyia. Edited by Maxim Litvinov. Moscow: NKID, 1934.

Sovetsko-Amerikanskye otnosheniya, 1933–1939. Edited by B. Zhiliaev, G. Savchenko, and G. Sevostianov. Moscow: fond Demokratiia, 2004.

Srodes, James. *On Dupont Circle: Franklin and Eleanor Roosevelt and the Progressives Who Shaped Our World.* Berkeley, CA: Counterpoint, 2012.

Stalin, Joseph. *Sochineniya*, in 13 volumes. Moscow: Politizdat, 1951.

Startsev, Abel. *Russkie bloknoty Dzhona Rida*. Moscow: Sovetskii pisatel, 1968.

Steffens, Lincoln. *The Autobiography*. New York: Harcourt, 1931.

Steffens, Lincoln. *Letters of Lincoln Steffens*. Edited by Ella Winter and Granville Hicks. 2 vols. New York: Harcourt, 1938.

Thayer, Charles W. *Bears in the Caviar*. New York, 1950.

Thayer, Charles W. *Diplomat*. New York: Harper, 1959.

Ure, John. *Beware the Rugged Russian Bear: British Adventurers Exposing the Bolsheviks*. London: Old Street, 2015.

Waldeck, R. G. "Homosexual International." *Human Events* 17, no. 39. September 29, 1960.

Wallace H. A. Reminiscences. Oral History Archives, Columbia University, New York.

Warburg, J. P. Reminiscences. Oral History Archives, Columbia University, New York.

Watts, Steven. *The People's Tycoon: Henry Ford and the American Century*. New York: Knopf, 2005.

Weber, Max. *The Protestant Ethic and the Spirit of Capitalism*. Translated by Talcott Parsons. London: Routledge, 1992.

Weeks, Laura D. *The Master and Margarita: A Critical Companion*. Evanston, IL: Northwestern University Press, 1996.

Wehle, Louise B. *Hidden Threats in History*. New York: Macmillan, 1953.

Weinstein, Allen, and Alexander Vassiliev. *The Haunted Wood: Soviet Espionage in America—The Stalin Era*. New York: Random House, 1999.

Wiley, Irene Baruch. *Around the Globe in Twenty Years*. New York: D. McKay, 1962.

Willets, Paul. *Rendezvous at the Russian Tea Rooms*. London: Constable, 2015.

Winand, Pascaline. *Eisenhower, Kennedy, and the United States of Europe*. New York: St. Martin, 1993.

Winter, Jay. *Dreams of Peace and Freedom: Utopian Moments in the Twentieth Century*. New Haven: Yale University Press, 2008.

Wolfe, Bertram. *Strange Communists I Have Known*. New York: Stein, 1965.

Yakovlev, Alexander. Archive available at http://www.alexanderyakovlev.org/fond/issues-doc/71027/.

INDEX